The Practical Guide to People-Friendly Documentation

Also Available from ASQ Quality Press

ISO 9000:2000 Documentation: Quality Manual and Operational Procedures
Jack Kanholm

ISO 9000:2000 for Small and Medium Businesses
Herb Monnich

Interpreting ISO 9001:2000 with Statistical Methodology
By James L. Lamprecht

ISO 9001:2000 Explained, Second Edition
Joseph J. Tsiakals, Charles A. Cianfrani, and John E. (Jack) West

ISO 9000:2000 Quick Reference
Jeanne Ketola and Kathy Roberts

ISO Lesson Guide 2000: Pocket Guide to Q9001:2000, Second Edition
Dennis Arter and J. P. Russell

ANSI/ISO/ASQ Q9000:2000 Series Quality Standards

The Practical Guide to People-Friendly Documentation

Adrienne Escoe

ASQ Quality Press
Milwaukee, Wisconsin

The Practical Guide to People-Friendly Documentation
Adrienne Escoe

Library of Congress Cataloging-in-Publication Data

Escoe, Adrienne.
   The practical guide to people-friendly documentation / Adrienne Escoe.—2nd ed.
      p. cm.
   Rev. ed. of: Nimble documentation : the practical guide for world-class organizations /
Adrienne Escoe. c1998.
   Includes bibliographical references and index.
   ISBN 0-87389-504-5 (alk. paper)
   1. Quality control—Documentation. I. Escoe, Adrienne. Nimble documentation. II.
Title.
TS156 .E79 2001
658.5'62—dc21   2001040180

© 2001 by ASQ

10 9 8 7 6 5 4 3 2 1

ISBN 0-87389-504-5

Acquisitions Editor: Annemieke Koudstaal
Project Editor: Craig S. Powell
Production Administrator: Gretchen Trautman
Special Marketing Representative: Denise Cawley

ASQ Mission: The American Society for Quality advances individual and organizational performance excellence worldwide by providing opportunities for learning, quality improvement, and knowledge exchange.

Attention Bookstores, Wholesalers, Schools, and Corporations: ASQ Quality Press books, videotapes, audiotapes, and software are available at quantity discounts with bulk purchases for business, educational, or instructional use. For information, please contact ASQ Quality Press at 800-248-1946, or write to ASQ Quality Press, P.O. Box 3005, Milwaukee, WI 53201-3005.

To place orders or to request a free copy of the ASQ Quality Press Publications Catalog, including ASQ membership information, call 800-248-1946. Visit our Web site at www.asq.org or http://qualitypress.asq.org .

Printed in the United States of America

 Printed on acid-free paper

American Society for Quality
ASQ

Quality Press
600 N. Plankinton Avenue
Milwaukee, Wisconsin 53203
Call toll free 800-248-1946
Fax 414-272-1734
www.asq.org
http://qualitypress.asq.org
http://standardsgroup.asq.org
E-mail: authors@asq.org

Dedication

To Anastasia, Annalisa, and Sebastian
and the joy of Grace.

Good keeps on happening.

Contents

Tables, Figures, and Checklists ix
Foreword to the Second Edition xi
Foreword to the First Edition xiii
Preface to the Second Edition xv
Preface to the First Edition xvii
Acknowledgments xix

Part I   Need

Chapter 1   Introduction **3**
  Nimbleness 3
  The Framework 7
  Using This Book 7

Chapter 2   Zero-Based Documentation **9**
  Customers and Other Sources of Need 9
  Litmus Test 14
  Streamlining Success 18

Part II   Implementation

Chapter 3   Hierarchy, Structure, Format, and Style **33**
  Hierarchy and Structure 34
  Format 38
  Style 57

Chapter 4   Usability **63**
  Usability Testing 64
  Readability 65
  Web Design 70
  Internationalization 77
  Presentation Slides 78

Chapter 5   Electronic Options **81**
  Information Management and Knowledge Management 82
  Standardization 83
  Electronic Document Management 85
  System Features 87

E-mail Policy 94
The Case for Imaging 97

Chapter 6   Measured Improvement **99**
Customer Satisfaction 100
Zero Defects 101
Currentness 106
Cycle Time 108
Volume 110
Cost: The Iceberg Model 111

Part III   Application

Chapter 7   Quality Initiatives **117**
ANSI/ISO/ASQ Q9001-2000 118
The Baldrige Award 130
Six Sigma 132
Total Quality Management 134

Chapter 8   Other Applications **137**
Employee Handbooks 138
User Manuals 140
Safety Programs 141
ISO 14001 145
Additional Applications 150

Chapter 9   Documentation Relatives **153**
Records 154
Forms 160
Approval and Digital Signatures 163

Chapter 10   Documentation Center of Excellence **171**
Characteristics of a Documentation COE 172
Outsourcing and Insourcing 175
Skills 179
Self-Directed Teams 180
Roles and Responsibilities 189
Training 190
Accountability 192
Evaluation 193

Part IV   Information Tools

Appendix A   Performance Criteria for Policies and Procedures Writers and Editors **199**

**Appendix B   Performance Criteria for Policies and Procedures Word Processing
and Secretarial Staff** **203**

Appendix C   Resources **207**
Organizations 207
Software 209

References **215**

Index **217**

Tables, Figures, and Checklists

Tables

Table 2.1	Five sources of need	13
Table 2.2	Proposed directives hierarchy, structure, and format	23
Table 3.1	Hierarchy of quality system documentation	34
Table 3.2	Basic hierarchy for corporate documentation	35
Table 3.3	Considerations for selecting procedure formats	49
Table 7.1	ANSI/ISO/ASQ Q9001-2000 clauses that specify or imply data, documentation, and records	122
Table 7.2	Examples of Baldrige Award criteria and documentation requirements and implications	132
Table 8.1	ISO 14001 requirements and implications for documentation and records	147
Table 9.1	Sample legal research index	155
Table 9.2	Sample legal group file	156
Table 9.3	Sample records retention schedule	156
Table 9.4	Sample records listing with retention periods	157

Figures

Figure 1.1	The thud test	4
Figure 1.2	Chronology of *The Practical Guide to People-Friendly Documentation*	8
Figure 2.1	The *any* key	10
Figure 2.2	Customer service feedback	12
Figure 2.3	*I Write for the Reader* bumper sticker	14
Figure 2.4	Producing zero-based documentation	20
Figure 2.5	Announcement to publicize and promote the streamlining initiative	21
Figure 2.6	Self-stick notepad giveaways	21
Figure 2.7	Promotional tent cards	22
Figure 2.8	Preliminary documentation improvement implementation schedule	27
Figure 3.1	Useful policies	36
Figure 3.2	Example of a streamlined company policy	36
Figure 3.3	Sample hard copy procedures table of contents or online menu	37
Figure 3.4	Example A of plain vanilla (or narrative) procedure format	39
Figure 3.5	Example B of plain vanilla (or narrative) procedure format	40
Figure 3.6	Example of play script procedure format	41
Figure 3.7	Example of modular procedure format	42
Figure 3.8	Example of nonstructured and nonmodular plain vanilla format	43
Figure 3.9	Example of structured modular format	44
Figure 3.10	Example of flowchart format	45
Figure 3.11	Process map example	47
Figure 3.12	ABC forms management system operating procedure	54
Figure 3.13	The passive writing path	60

Figure 3.14   Dog puppies   61
Figure 4.1   Example of mixed alignment Web page   71
Figure 4.2   Example of same alignment Web page   71
Figure 4.3   Example of Web page with confusing proximity   71
Figure 4.4   Example of Web page with people-friendly proximity   71
Figure 4.5   Examples of Web pages with confusing contrast and effective contrast   73
Figure 4.6   Example of Web page with complementary graphic and text   76
Figure 4.7   Presentation slides of varying effectiveness   80
Figure 6.1   S&P proofreading defect classifications   104
Figure 6.2   S&P proofreading desk instructions   105
Figure 6.3   S&P proofreading instructions (for online publication)   105
Figure 6.4   Metrics for currentness   107
Figure 6.5   Corporate policies and procedures: coordination and approval   108
Figure 6.6   Sample data: items released, in work, and backlog   109
Figure 6.7   Average monthly cycle time for uploading documents   109
Figure 6.8   Product operations procedures manual volume   110
Figure 6.9   Baseline and target volume metrics   111
Figure 6.10   Hidden costs of documentation systems   112
Figure 6.11   Cost of documentation   113
Figure 7.1   A continuum of quality initiatives   120
Figure 7.2   Common hierarchy for ISO 9001-compliant documentation   121
Figure 7.3   Individual training plan and record   128
Figure 7.4   ISO 9000 in a nutshell   129
Figure 8.1   Group safety training session form   142
Figure 8.2   Hazard evaluation and abatement form   143
Figure 9.1   Determining the scope of legal research   158
Figure 9.2   Example A of chart of approvals   165
Figure 9.3   Example B of chart of approvals   167
Figure 9.4   Private key encryption and public key encryption   169
Figure 10.1   Work team meetings   183
Figure 10.2   Meetings—spawning ground or sewer?   186
Figure 10.3   No Taj Mahal   187
Figure 10.4   Recognition   188

Checklists

Checklist 2.1   Litmus Test   15
Checklist 2.2   Producing Zero-Based Documentation (A Streamlining Effort)   18
Checklist 3.1   Nimble Writing Style   58
Checklist 5.1   Considerations for Standardization   85
Checklist 5.2   Characteristics of an Electronic Document Management System   87
Checklist 5.3   E-mail Etiquette   96
Checklist 5.4   Considerations for Electronic Document Imaging   97
Checklist 7.1   Total Quality Managed Documentation Function   135
Checklist 9.1   Steps for Developing a Zero-Based Records Retention Program   159
Checklist 9.2   Considerations for Nimble Forms   162
Checklist 9.3   Considerations for Charts of Approvals   164
Checklist 10.1   Top 10 Reasons for Outsourcing   176
Checklist 10.2   Considerations for Seeking Outside Assistance—Outsourcing or
                 Insourcing Documentation Function   179
Checklist 10.3   Elements of Self-Directed Teams   181
Checklist 10.4   Guidelines for Conducting a Productive Meeting   185
Checklist 10.5   Ingredients for Team Success   190
Checklist 10.6   One-on-One Training to Write Work Instructions   192
Checklist 10.7   Elements of Team Performance Evaluation   193

Foreword to the Second Edition

Adrienne Escoe's *The Practical Guide to People-Friendly Documentation* takes the best of current communication theory out of the ivory tower and applies it directly to the world of work. The result is a reference designed to help organizations determine the need for documentation and to provide the tools essential to creating documents that reflect users' needs. Other books address principles of technical writing and editing within the context of quality initiatives and standards, but this book approaches these subjects from the perspective of users' needs within various forms of documentation and specialized communities.

Escoe presents useful tests for determining which documents to maintain and which to eliminate. She guides readers to structure a documentation system, format individual documents, and apply writing styles that support users' goals. The book addresses not only such core issues as usability—usability testing, readability, people-friendly Web design, internationalization, and effective presentation slides—but also electronic options for documentation and continuous measured improvement and metrics. The documentation requirements and implications of ANSI/ISO/ASQ Q9001-2000, the Baldrige Award, TQM, and Six Sigma, with illustrative applications, are especially useful for organizations seeking a way to contain their administrative burden. The comprehensive guide for establishing a documentation center of excellence is a bonus. Finally, *The Practical Guide to People-Friendly Documentation* provides sources for additional information and tools—organizations, publications, and software.

This book gladdens my heart as a teacher of writing and as an administrator for programs in technical communication and quality management. I am delighted to see a book that so well represents what it proclaims. This is a usable, accessible text, infused with quality principles, that will bring much needed applications to documentation specialists as well as an informed perspective to those responsible for improving management processes. Even more, I know how much the suggestions in *The Practical Guide to People-Friendly Documentation* are needed in documentation and our organizations. Time is an increasingly precious commodity for employees, companies, and customers. No person and no organization can afford documentation that confuses and frustrates its users. Escoe's book deserves a place on your shelf, or better yet, should remain open on your desk as a guide and ever-friendly resource to quality documentation.

Patricia Hunt, Director
Leadership, Management, and
Communication Programs
UCLA Extension

Foreword to the First Edition

In the swiftly changing realm of global business, every aspect of an organization's operations must be continually evaluated and refocused to ensure alliance with its strategic objectives and an increasingly competitive environment. Frequently neglected, documentation is left to form as it always has, or to be reformed as a byproduct of each unique program or product line.

This book establishes documentation in a proper perspective, helping leaders use it as a resource to reach an organization's goals faster and to stay proactive to the needs of its markets and employees. Following the book's guidelines allows organizations to determine the specific policies and procedures relevant to their objectives and environment, to develop them and maintain them economically, and to take advantage of technology to make documentation readily accessible.

I had the privilege to observe, firsthand, the success of the author's approach to zero-based documentation at a major international company. I saw the positive, measurable impact of a documentation center of excellence, including the development of a team of skilled, responsive employees.

For my business of process reengineering and enablement through technology insertion, Nimble Documentation® provides the practical advice needed on how to facilitate and sustain change in the critical domain of business documentation. I welcome this book to our repository of best practices.

Diane M. Galusky
Director, Systems Delivery
Computer Sciences Corporation

Preface to the Second Edition

Nimble Documentation®: The Practical Guide for World-Class Organizations was well received by readers who sought guidance for trimming, creating, and managing their documentation. In 1997—when *Nimble Documentation®* was written—hard copy policies and procedures were still commonplace in companies of all sizes, although most documents were produced with word processing software. The Internet was catching on, and many companies had their own Web sites or were working on them. But only the largest or the most technologically savvy organizations relied on intranets routinely for managing internal documentation. E-mail was common in many organizations, but sometimes it was restricted to internal communications on a local area network (LAN), and the capability for handling e-mailed attachments was neither universal nor standard.

Back in 1997, off-the-shelf software was available for document control and workflow management, but the choices were limited and many organizations still depended on mainframe computers for storing and retrieving business documents, such as policies and procedures. Back then, platforms mattered. Often, users in the same organization worked on computers with different operating systems, or platforms, that could not talk to each other, such as IBM-compatibles and Macintoshes. Although cross-platform conversion programs were available and some computers could assume the characteristics of a second platform like a change of clothes, standardized equipment and software with seamless connectivity was the exception.

When *Nimble Documentation®* was written, many organizations were still in a downsizing mode or recently recovering from it. Many were short staffed and could hardly afford to maintain voluminous documentation. For them, the concept of zero-based documentation and the litmus test for keeping documentation lean was particularly attractive.

Fast-forward to today. Some organizations are shrinking but some are growing. Intranets abound, and, with some exceptions, personal computers exchange documents and data readily. Word processing software has become nearly standard. Although reliance on hard copy documents endures, most organizations now at least have some provision for electronic document management or are considering or planning conversions. Today, most organizations in the developed world and many in emerging nations have the capability to send and receive e-mail, including attachments, anywhere, although standardization for attachments still is wanting.

The foundation for *The Practical Guide to People-Friendly Documentation* has not changed since *Nimble Documentation®* first was published. It is still documentation need and the concept of zero-based documentation empowered by the litmus test. However, the litmus test now begs a fifth question: Would any harm come to an organization if a document (or document part or feature) were there? With the proliferation of document management software and authoring tools and the resultant ease of creating and managing electronic documentation—particularly Web-based—documentation is sprouting around us like weeds in newly turned soil. Unfortunately, much of what is written confuses and frustrates users and wastes their time.

Especially in this time of fairly low unemployment in many parts of the world, organizations cannot hire qualified people fast enough to fill all job openings. One result? Employee time is more precious than ever, and any means that organizations can find to eliminate counterproductive activity or confusing or frustrating experiences with internal documentation is crucial to their success. Likewise, organizations whose public documentation—such as Web sites, annual reports, and application or registration forms—turns off customers or potential customers will see their business ceded to the competition. That is where the extended concept of Nimble Documentation® can help. It is no longer enough to ensure that every piece of documentation maintained by an organization is truly needed. It is also important to be certain that no piece of documentation burdens users—internal or external.

For all of these reasons, *The Practical Guide to People-Friendly Documentation* adds a chapter on usability, including the basics of usability testing, readability, people-friendly Web design, internationalization, and effective presentation slides. Another new feature of this book is an exploration of information and knowledge management in today's world, with the lines between information, knowledge, and documentation blurring. Practical suggestions for an organization's e-mail are included. Because organizations today transmit so much information and so many documents by e-mail, and few have adequate controls in place for managing e-mail, the book includes considerations for an e-mail policy. In addition, the updated chapter on quality initiatives introduces the documentation requirements and implications of ANSI/ISO/ASQ Q9001-2000, the 2001 performance criteria for the Malcolm Baldrige National Quality Award, and provisions of Six Sigma, an increasingly popular quality initiative. The chapter on other applications now offers information on the documentation requirements of TL 9000, the new quality management system standard for the telecommunications industry. Also, the Resources appendix has been totally updated and now includes software listings for document control, online help, Web page development, and other topics and considerably more entries than Nimble Documentation.® Other helpful revisions in *The Practical Guide to People-Friendly Documentation* reflect valuable reader feedback on *Nimble Documentation®* and recent changes in vocabulary and usage.

Preface to the First Edition

This book is a practical guide for streamlining, producing, and managing documentation, from ISO 9001-compliant policies to work instructions, from process maps to forms, from employee handbooks to user manuals. It is for world-class organizations—companies whose constant and competitive process improvement mirrors their responsiveness to customers and the global marketplace. These are organizations that can afford only trim, current, and accessible documents that add value and are people-friendly. They seek every advantage of technology, such as standardized hardware and software, imaging, and intranets. This book is also for organizations that may be on the cutting edge of their industries, yet have let their documentation systems grow mold. Their cumbersome and obsolete procedures and handbooks can snub customers and suffocate employees—and may be a resource bomb waiting to be detonated by the next legal challenge.

How is *Nimble Documentation*® different from other resources? Traditional systems and procedures (S&P) textbooks, although useful for basic guidance in document hierarchies and structures, typically do not address a wide range of applications, such as quality standards, employee handbooks, and safety programs. They do not deal with human issues, such as self-directed teams, or with continuous measured improvement. How-to books tend to focus on a small slice of the subject, for example, ISO 9000 documentation or records. Other books center on technology issues such as electronic searching, and generally are written for technical users. Many titles are available on format and style, but none highlights the advantages and disadvantages of various ones according to the specific needs of competitive organizations. This volume brings all of these elements together in a single, nontechnical, integrated resource.

This book has many features for a wide range of readers. One major benefit is the concept of zero-based documentation and the litmus test for developing or streamlining documentation. "This test is a clear and compelling analytical framework for rooting out old, useless documents and records and is greatly needed by most, if not all, organizations throughout the world. It is a way of thinning the weeds that have grown in most organizations and turning an overgrown field of organizational activity into a neatly trimmed garden." Another main benefit is the section on format. It gives readers a "valuable set of comparison criteria for developing various types of documentation and serves as a checklist for evaluating current documents and records." The section on style guides readers to recognize the importance of stylistic conventions as a prerequisite to effective communication in today's global organizations. It gives them a tool for meeting the needs of diverse personnel. Also, the chapter on measured improvement helps the many organizations that are struggling to get a grip on their documentation and that often have no idea how to measure the progress of those efforts. The criteria, techniques, and methods described in this chapter assist all types of organizations to develop clear goals and objectives for documentation revision efforts and allow them to determine how well they are documenting and recording organizational learning.

A wide variety of industries and virtually any type of organization can gain much from this book. Information-intensive industries, such as healthcare, software development, publishing, and Internet service providers, can especially profit from it. The book offers much to a broad spectrum of readers, such as quality assurance personnel, S&P staff, operations managers, production personnel, writers, records administrators, librarians and archivists, employee and organizational development facilitators, business and technical writing faculty and students, and process improvement consultants.

Nimble Documentation® is a guidebook, with illustrations pertaining to real business situations drawn primarily from experiences at one of the world's largest companies, but also from many organizations of all sizes across varied industries—manufacturing and service industries as well as public agencies. Simple diagrams, metrics, format examples, and other graphics illustrate key concepts throughout. Checklists provide practical road maps.

The book's foundation is documentation need—including legal requirements, external customers, users, subject matter owners, and certification auditors and examiners—and the concept of zero-based documentation. Although readers can find solutions to many kinds of documentation challenges throughout the book, reading chapters 1 and 2 first provides a useful trail head for exploring any of the other chapters. Chapter 1, Introduction, presents a framework for the book and a useful section, Using This Book; chapter 2, Zero-Based Documentation, describes the litmus test and a case study. The organization of the book supports readers who are seeking to establish a new documentation system or streamline an old one. Subsequent chapters are grouped by *Implementation*, *Application*, and *Information Tools*. To further assist readers, each chapter through chapter 9 begins with examples of solutions presented in that chapter. Appendices are home to performance criteria for S&P personnel.

[Quotations in the preface are from Anton Camarota, a reviewer.]

Acknowledgments

The many kind individuals acknowledged in the first edition, Nimble Documentation,® who generously contributed their knowledge and support also helped to lay a strong foundation for *The Practical Guide to People-Friendly Documentation.*

In addition, I sincerely thank the following family, friends, and associates for sharing their expertise, ideas, materials, and hugs.

Kimberly Allan, John Bacchus, Bob Britton, Denise Cawley, Jim Cery, Stan Cheren, Pamela Coca, Dr. Jack Cole, Jim Dawson, Rey de Leon, Mary Delmege, David Ehlen, Jennifer Escoe, Kristen Escoe, Matthew Escoe, Linda Everett, Linda Field, Linda Fuller, Rita Giebel, Dr. Howard Goldman, JoAnn Hackos, Edna Hetchler, Wayne Howard, Dr. Patricia Hunt, Michelle Jones, Mariette Keshishian, Annemieke Koudstaal, Marty Kress, Judy Lukas, Sharron Manassa, Matt Meinholz, Noreen Norris, Bill O'Connor, Teresa Omar, Joy Osaka-Lu, VeraLouise Pfeiffer, Craig Powell, Ned Racine, Mike Stammer, Dr. Jerry Suitor, Leayn and Paul Tabili, John Tollett, Daria Topousis, Paul Townley-Smith, Gretchen Trautman, my treasured students and colleagues at UCLA Extension, and Troy Vellinga.

Part I

Need

1

Introduction

Solutions presented in this chapter address documentation challenges such as:

- What is the purpose of this book?

- What is Nimble Documentation®?

- Who can this book help?

- How to find information in this book.

NIMBLENESS

Have you heard the *thud test* for evaluating documentation quality? A board member opened a chapter meeting of the Society for Technical Communication with the following story.

> *I asked a technical writer how one of her major clients judged the quality of her work.*
> *"Oh, that's easy," answered the writer confidently. "They rely on the thud test."*
> *"What's that?" I asked.*
> *"After completing each manual, I drop it on the floor," the writer said matter-of-factly. "The louder the thud, the happier the client."*

Although some people measure document quality by weight or volume, many more understand the liabilities of documentation that is too many, too long, and too wordy (see Figure 1.1). These people know that documentation must be clear, concise, current, and accessible. They recognize that world-class companies and public agencies cannot afford inflexible policy manuals, operating procedures that lead to rework, or records that generate liability.

Figure 1.1   The thud test.

The Practical Guide to People-Friendly Documentation is for organizations that want trim, flexible, and accessible documentation, that is, Nimble Documentation.® The approach of this book is to focus on sources of need—external customers, users, subject matter owners, and others—and to address measured, integrated improvement and electronic options, including document control software, intranets, and the Internet. This is a guidebook for organizations that have too much documentation, those that don't have enough, and those that have the wrong kind. It is for organizations that take too long and spend too much money on communicating information. From a zero-based approach to illustrative applications and practical ideas for liberating documentation relatives, such as approval authority systems, this book is an organization's comprehensive resource for responsive written media.

This book is a reference for organizations and individuals responsible for:

- Drafting, coordinating, reviewing, publishing (hard copy and electronically), managing, or purchasing business documentation, including policies, procedures, instructions, records, forms, or approval authority systems

- Leading an organization through a quality initiative, such as ANSI/ISO/ASQ Q9001-2000, or applying for the Malcolm Baldrige National Quality Award

- Improving operating and management processes

- Preparing for or conducting audits

- Purchasing software to develop business documentation

- Training those responsible for business documentation

- Making documentation staffing decisions

- Saving money and time

- Empowering teams

- Designing online documentation systems

- Developing employee handbooks, user manuals, safety programs, and other documentation

Nimble Documentation® flunks thud tests. It is far away from thunder-thud manuals and wearying wordiness. Nimble Documentation® meets minimum requirements for legal, contractual, and business goals. It means information that helps organizations respond quickly to changing market and workplace conditions and doesn't impede business. Nimble Documentation® is easy to access and economical to maintain. It is there when you need it and out of the way when you don't. It can be readily revised, is portable, and suits world-class organizations, which respond quickly to customers and other sources of need, jump operational hurdles, are allergic to waste, stimulate employees, and thrive on continuous constructive change.

Documentation has many meanings, from the broad—anything written in any medium—to the narrow—policies and procedures manuals or perhaps records.

Nimble Documentation® needs to be clear, lean, current, and accessible. First, let's consider some examples of documentation that isn't nimble:

1. An electronics company's policies and procedures manual that includes internal operating procedures for every department whose manager believed a procedure would secure the department's existence

2. A financial software user's guide that buries critical troubleshooting steps in wordy narrative paragraphs

3. A newspaper's Web registration form that rejects subscribers who type dots instead of dashes between numerals in a telephone number

4. A distributor's human resources requisition form that requires eight original signatures, half of which belong to off-site managers and executives

5. A state government's 350-page service guide capped by a one-page index

6. An international defense division's widely distributed e-mail memorandum to communicate signature authority for committing company funds

7. Bulletins and announcements issued in immediate response to various audits, yet in effect for years

8. A table of contents for a school district's employee handbook that requires manual entry of page numbers and headings

All of these examples demonstrate documentation that is unnecessary, hard to access, time-consuming to process, obsolete, incomplete, or resource-gobbling. None of the examples support an organization's responsiveness to rapidly changing conditions—internal or in the marketplace. All can sabotage the best efforts of an agile organization or one aspiring to be.

In all the preceding examples, the perspective is from the document's writer, creator, or sponsor. It is not from that of the user, the reader, or the person who maintains, reviews, or approves it. If a document is created, revised, or maintained according to the writer's or sponsor's needs or goals, the battle for nimbleness will be uphill. If such a document does achieve nimbleness, the accomplishment will be accidental. On the other hand, documents, and the processes surrounding them, designed genuinely from the user's point of view seldom will be cumbersome or slow, assuming skilled implementation of the design and the sponsoring organization's commitment to nimbleness.

Few people read business documentation for recreation. They read it for solutions, which they want quickly.

Take the first example. An employee wants to get something printed by an in-house print shop. She doesn't want to and doesn't have time to search a manual for a company procedure written primarily to secure the print shop's rectangle on an organization chart. The employee's needs would be served better by brief instructions placed at the service counter, where the transaction will take place. That is where the information will be applied.

The software user, in the second example, needs to locate information immediately. Payroll deadlines demand it. What is the solution? Replace the narrative writing with modular instructions that facilitate quick access to information (see chapter 3).

The newspaper subscriber who attempts to register for online access is needlessly confused and frustrated. An example of the acceptable format (that is, a dashed rather than dotted telephone number) alongside the form field would help. Even better would be a field that can accept several common formats for telephone numbers.

Approving the multiple-signature form (the fourth example) takes too long. Anyhow, the last, or last few, signatures represent the only people who actually will read the requisition. Everyone else assumes the next person will. Honesty and capable management dictate that reviewers formally assign authority to the lowest-level employee who has the knowledge and skills to approve the requisition. Another alternative is to use an electronic approval system to speed along the transaction (see chapter 9).

If documentation were created from the user's perspective in examples 5 through 8, it could be transformed in some way to achieve nimbleness. Consider a few other examples, where documentation is created from the user's perspective:

9. A national non-profit's telephone directory that includes fax numbers and e-mail addresses

10. A high-tech machine shop's online procedures that omit related documents and forms, but instead rely on Web links

11. A chemical company's combination safety training needs assessment/training record that eliminates duplicate data entry

12. An automobile aftermarket product manufacturer that uses video clip work instructions, compliant with the QS-9000 standard, for its multilingual workforce

13. A food processor's functional records retention schedule that specifies an easy-to-maintain records inventory

Many examples in this book illustrate how world-class organizations pay attention to document users and other sources of need.

THE FRAMEWORK

Nimble Documentation® is achieved through subjecting it (whether proposed or existing) to a litmus test. Before any piece is added to a documentation system—for example, a new manual, procedure, form, paragraph, phrase, or link—or before a streamlining effort, it is evaluated from a zero base. That means no piece is accepted into the system unless it can be proven to meet clearly defined needs, or its exclusion can be shown to cause possible harm to the organization. In chapter 2, five sources of need are defined: legal requirements, external customers, users, subject matter owners, and certification auditors and examiners. A source of need can be anyone, or any requirement, for whom a service is furnished or to whom a product is delivered. An example is an administrator who follows a user manual developed for a company's new human resources (HR) system. Another source of need is a law requiring a published statement that prohibits workplace harassment. And yet another is to reconstruct a business after a disaster such as a fire, tornado, flood, or earthquake.

Litmus test criteria for Nimble Documentation® can be stated as questions to assess the need for any piece of documentation. In one form or another, the questions focus on legal, contractual, or prudent business requirements (which can originate from several sources), and the harm that might come to an organization if the documentation were never created. The litmus test also addresses usability because documentation that confuses or frustrates users is not nimble. Chapter 2 addresses sources of need and the litmus test for Nimble Documentation.®

USING THIS BOOK

The Practical Guide to People-Friendly Documentation follows a practical chronology for developing a documentation system from scratch or streamlining an existing system. Four major topic groups divide the sequence: *Need, Implementation, Application,* and *Information Tools.* Individual topics, and chapters within each topic group, are developed fully and can be used as stand-alone references to help solve a single or immediate problem; however, readers who consult with only a portion of this book are encouraged to first read at least enough of chapter 2 to understand the advantages and approach of zero-based documentation. This foundation will help readers make sound choices for implementing and applying the concepts. The book suggests solutions for many types of documentation challenges, such as to reduce the size of a policies and procedures manual (chapter 2), format a procedure (chapter 3), ensure usability (chapter 4), determine documentation costs, including hidden resource drains (chapter 6), make a user manual user-friendly (chapter 8), and weigh the advantages and disadvantages of outsourcing a documentation function (chapter 10). Figure 1.2 shows the topic groups and chapters.

The first topic group, *Need*, establishes the rationale for Nimble Documentation® and presents a useful test for deciding which documents, or their parts, to maintain and which to eliminate or avoid including in the first place.

The second, *Implementation*, guides readers to structure a documentation system, including manuals and other document collections; format individual documents; and apply writing styles that support users' goals. This topic group address usability, including usability testing, readability, Web design, internationalization, and presentation slides, and presents a discussion of electronic options for documentation and a chapter on continuous measured improvement and metrics, such as proofreading and defect-free writing, eliminating obsolete documents, and reducing cycle time, volume, and cost.

The third group, *Application*, presents four quality initiatives and their documentation requirements or implications: ANSI/ISO/ASQ Q9001-2001, the Baldrige Award, total quality management (TQM), and Six Sigma. This topic group also illustrates other applications, including employee handbooks, user manuals, safety programs, ISO 14001, QS-9000, TL 9000, and more. Here, too, readers will also find suggestions for creating an easy-to-use records system, efficient forms, and a trim, dynamic approval authority system. The third topic group ends with comprehensive guidance for establishing a documentation center of excellence (COE), either for a large organization that centralizes documentation functions or for a firm that supplies documentation services to other companies, such as writing and editing or desktop publishing.

Finally, *Information Tools* equips readers with sources for additional information, including a list of organizations (and their publications) and software and a generously cross-referenced index to help locate information in *The Practical Guide to People-Friendly Documentation*.

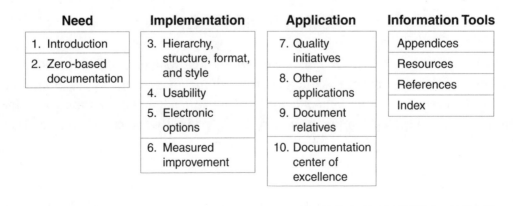

Figure 1.2 Chronology of *The Practical Guide to People-Friendly Documentation*.

2

Zero-Based Documentation

Solutions presented in this chapter address documentation challenges such as:

- How to determine if documentation is really needed

- How to apply the litmus test

- How organizations streamline their policies and procedures

Nimble Documentation® makes life better for organizations. It meets customers' requirements and other sources of need and helps organizations respond quickly to changing market and workplace conditions. It fulfills streamlining initiatives because documentation is published or maintained only when a requirement for it is demonstrated. This chapter presents the source-of-need base for documentation and a litmus test for identifying those needs. Then, the chapter takes us through a few documentation streamlining success stories.

CUSTOMERS AND OTHER SOURCES OF NEED

The saga of the *any* key is a reminder to keep the customer first in documentation. Sometimes the people who develop information systems (IS) are not equally skilled in documenting their systems. Sometimes highly skilled documentation specialists overlook some customers' needs or other requirements. Several years ago, the systems and procedures (S&P) department at a large electronics firm spearheaded the transition to an online storage and retrieval system for management and operating procedures. Near the rollout of the project, the IS department wrote user instructions. After piloting the instructions with novices, S&P decided to simplify and clarify them because many users had trouble following them.

S&P edited the step-by-step instructions so they were easy to follow and piloted them with a new group of users. One day, a pilot user called about the instructions. "I've looked everywhere," she said, "but cannot find the *any* key on my keyboard." Perplexed, an S&P staff member asked the caller to explain. "The instructions say, 'Press any key,' and I can't find the *any* key."

No matter how well we think we are meeting our customers' needs, and other sources of need, assessing success in meeting them is a writer's primary responsibility.

Documentation need originates from at least five sources: legal requirements, external customers, users, subject matter owners, and certification auditors and examiners.

Legal requirements. In the United States, federal and state laws regulate many processes, especially in industries and public service where health and safety are primary concerns, such as foods, pharmaceuticals, nuclear energy, transportation, and law enforcement. In fact, companies in highly regulated industries are some of the biggest consumers of documentation. Organizations in other countries are governed by national and provincial laws and sometimes by requirements

Figure 2.1 The *any* key.

adopted by international consortia, such as the European Union. State laws govern education, banking, environmental management, and many other areas of business. Laws related to employment practices exist at many levels of government. Local zoning regulations affect a company's physical facilities and are just one area of county and municipal legal sources.

External customers. Contracts with paying customers, teaming agreements, purchase orders, specification sheets, and many other written documents dictate the requirements of external customers. Conferences, meetings, and other types of communication often refine external customers' requirements. Unspoken stimuli for meeting external customers' needs, such as competitors' capabilities and benchmarked best practices, also suggest documentation. For example, a software producer packages a quick start instruction booklet with its new, competing product.

In many companies, customers in other functions consult with writers for department procedures, bulletins, memos, and other writing, editing, and document management projects. An S&P department of one company used a feedback sheet to evaluate its customer service and plan corrective action if needed. The department compiled data on department service and on individual writers' and editors' service. Figure 2.2 shows the department's feedback sheet.

Users. A few examples of users include employees who read procedures to obtain management and operating direction, an improvement team that accesses and examines records of equipment output to redesign a part, viewers who communicate with their network provider's technical support through an interactive Web site, job candidates who complete an employment application, and violators who read a statement of their rights in traffic court.

Subject matter owners. Many organizations assign responsibilities for writing, editing, word processing, and publishing to individuals, teams, or departments outside the subject matter functions. Documentation centers of excellence (COEs) (see chapter 10) take advantage of consolidated skills, facilities, and equipment. Traditionally, functional managers have been the subject matter owners, or custodians, but new leadership structures increasingly indicate others, such as teams or process owners, for that role. Subject matter owners typically approve documentation before it is published, revised, or canceled.

Auditors and examiners. Quality, cleanliness, purity, financial practice, and curriculum are just a few domains subject to auditors or examiners, either external or internal. ANSI/ISO/ASQ Q9001-2000 registration requires third-party auditing, although organizations often appoint internal auditors for preregistration evaluation. A few other examples are Baldrige Award examiners, registrar accreditation committees, college accreditation organizations, and scholarship application judges.

Many other sources of need apply to zero-based documentation, but the five just described are common to many industries and public services. They are summarized in Table 2.1.

How do you find out need? Review legal requirements and certification standards. Ask customers what they need in procedures. Would they prefer a "reference document" list, a list of related forms, or a particular format, such as a play script or a flowchart? You can send out questionnaires; but one of the most powerful and efficient vehicles for collecting customer data is well-structured focus groups. Modify the following focus group approach according to the size of your company:

Customer Service Feedback

Writer/Editor _____ Date _____ Customer _____

Systems & Procedures would appreciate your feedback on the recent project we performed with you. Please take a few minutes to complete this survey and mail it to:

Systems & Procedures Dept.
Bldg. XY/MS A100

Thank you for the opportunity to serve you.

Are you a first-time customer of Systems & Procedures?   **Yes   No**

	Strongly Agree	Agree	Somewhat Agree	Disagree	Strongly Disagree
The writer/editor who assisted me was courteous.	_____	_____	_____	_____	_____
The work was performed on time.	_____	_____	_____	_____	_____
My questions regarding policies and procedures were answered to my satisfaction.	_____	_____	_____	_____	_____
The quality of work was excellent.	_____	_____	_____	_____	_____
I use policies and procedures often.	_____	_____	_____	_____	_____
I find policies and procedures understandable and useful.	_____	_____	_____	_____	_____

How can we do a better job for you?

_____

_____

_____

_____

_____

_____

Figure 2.2   Customer service feedback.

Table 2.1 Five sources of need.

Legal requirements	Expressed as laws, regulations, and permits
External customers	Expressed as contracts, purchase orders, or specifications
Users	Personnel who read procedures to obtain management and operating direction
Subject matter owners	Personnel responsible for document content
Auditors and examiners	Examples include ISO 9001 registrars, Baldrige Award examiners, and accreditation judges

- Determine key sources of need (external customers, users, subject matter owners, and so on).

- Request their management's support for participating in the focus group meeting.

- Distribute information about the meeting a couple of weeks *before* the meeting. Include the date, time, location, agenda, and names of participants.

- Describe specific documentation issues to be discussed and ask participants to talk with others in their function or position regarding the issues.

- Appoint a facilitator and scribe to keep the meeting on track and record decisions, respectively.

- Hold a focus group meeting. Gain consensus.

- Publicize decisions to participants and their managers.

- Implement the decisions.

Useful focus group questions relate to the following aspects of documentation:

- Essential parts or sections

- Internal format (for example, logical and comprehensive paragraph numbering and navigation)

- Quality (accuracy, currency, and defect-free copy)

- Access (electronic or hard copy)

- Revision notification system (cover sheets and e-mail)

- Cost (processing, coordination, approval, publication, maintenance, retention, and retrieval)

Because writers rushing to meet a deadline can lose sight of their audience (their readers), a mock bumper sticker was introduced in "Analytical Writing Skills," a course developed for managers at a county probation department (see Figure 2.3). Nimble Documentation®—whether work instructions, Web pages, or memos—accomplishes the writer's goals by meeting readers' needs. An operating procedure that, *to the reader*, is clear, concise, and accessible, saves time and moves the reader closer to the writer's goal. Supervisors who want their staff to review procedures for working with a new machine, for example, should keep work instructions simple and in the employees' primary language. A bank's Web site designer wishing to attract viewers to her

I WRITE FOR THE READER

Figure 2.3   *I Write for the Reader* bumper sticker.

company's online list of CD yields presents Web pages with cutting-edge graphics only if they become visible quickly with common Web browsers. Department managers who want busy staff to know about deletions from a list of approved vendors head memos with short but complete subject lines and limit text to the minimum needed to convey essential information. Although the format and need for these examples vary widely, all are designed to help the reader get the message.

LITMUS TEST

A large electronics firm cut its three-volume procedures manual from about 1000 pages to about 500. Later, the manual was further reduced to a single loose-leaf binder of about 350 pages. A nonprofit aerospace organization slimmed its corporate policies and procedures down by about half. How did they do it?

For as long as anyone could remember at either organization, employees saw their management and operating directive documents as sacred ground. The idea of eliminating any part of the mostly obsolete, cumbersome, and expensive-to-maintain manuals was routinely dismissed as an invitation for government auditors to close down the plant or administrative heresy. In both cases, streamlining the documents was a low priority at best.

Even when executive managers approved projects to slim down the manuals and make them more accessible to users, several internal functions balked at simplifying language, eliminating redundant sections, or making the documents more accessible. In one case, the president announced at his staff meeting that he would look unfavorably upon any division manager who didn't cooperate in the effort. Yet some lower level managers and supervisors insisted customers required the circuitous, confusing, and redundant text and that the directive document improvement team couldn't touch the wording. Auditors, they said, would punish the organization. In the other case, the organization would be violating legal commitments, said a team member.

In both examples, pockets of functional management argued that without great detail in the documents, employees would violate company rules and circumvent established administrative processes.

For all of these reasons, and to establish a consistent standard for achieving nimbleness, the litmus test was introduced—the foundation of a zero-based approach to streamlining documentation.

The litmus test works well in both large and small organizations. It begins by assuming an organization needs no documentation—that's the zero—and adds a document only if it passes a test.

The litmus test is based on the premise that documentation band-aids, for example, procedures or bulletins issued to resolve an audit crisis, are long-term resource drains. Once included in a manual or other medium, documentation band-aids seem to stay there forever. Everyone is afraid to touch them, and their maintenance is costly. There is a better way.

With the zero-based approach, companies typically avoid the justification mode, where departments or individuals argue to keep procedures that support their existence, play into the "that's the way we've always done it" syndrome, or act as document hypochondriacs afflicted with audit band-aids disease. It is far easier to streamline procedures if an organization starts with a clean slate. For organizations that have no procedures (such as start-ups), the zero-based approach is a good way to avoid growing a future document maintenance burden.

A zero-based approach, rather than arguing for *excluding* a given document or portion of one, requires the document's owners to justify its *inclusion*. Request concrete evidence, such as an ANSI/ISO/ASQ Q9001-2000 clause that specifies a procedure on quality records. The not-so-fine distinction is the difference between deleting existing documentation versus starting with nothing and demanding proof to add anything. It is the difference between a lengthy process that may result in minor wording compromises versus a sleek schedule whose major victory is an agile, easy-to-use, world-class manual.

Rather than deciding which existing documents or parts could be sacrificed, streamlining teams for the two organizations assumed no document was needed and added one only if it passed the litmus test.

The litmus test consists of five questions. A positive answer to any one of the first four questions justifies inclusion—or at least further study—of a document or part. Four *no's* and the document, or part of it, is history:

1. Is it required by law?

2. Is it specified by contract?

3. Is it necessary for prudent business operations?

4. Would any harm come to the organization if the document, or part of it, was eliminated?

Even if one of the four questions receives a *yes* doesn't necessarily mean the document, or part, is or will be easy to use. Thus, the reason for the fifth question:

5. Would any harm come to the organization if the document, or part of it, existed?

Checklist 2.1: Litmus Test

❐ Is it required by law?

❐ Is it specified by contract?

❐ Is it necessary for prudent business operations?

❐ Would any harm come to the organization if the document, or part of it, was eliminated?

❐ Would any harm come to the organization if the document, or part of it, existed?

Let's look at some examples for each litmus test question:

1. *Is it required by law?* A city ordinance that prohibits smoking at a company's facility may require employers to state that regulation in an administrative procedure. A state law may specify conspicuously posted notices of its workers' compensation appeals process. U.S. federal law may specify the number of years required to maintain financial records. International legal agreements may outline export documentation requirements.

Teams responsible for streamlining an organization's documentation should ask to see a copy of the applicable law or regulation. Anything less will pile up documentation quickly to pre-improvement levels.

2. *Is it specified by contract?* Many contracts or purchase orders are vague in defining documentation requirements, yet an organization's internal functions often will interpret them narrowly. For example, a contract may read simply, "Seller shall maintain documentation." Yet a quality assurance manager, subscribing to the more-is-better theory of documentation, tells a streamlining team not only what kind of documentation is required by the contract, but also how long the contract states it must be kept! The manager may truly believe there is more to read between the lines. Some people don't realize, or realize later, that unnecessary documentation is a noose by which an organization can hang itself. If the contract doesn't specify more documentation, and no other litmus test question warrants a positive answer, don't add more to your system.

3. *Is it necessary for prudent business operations?* What are prudent business operations? This litmus test component is a bit harder to interpret. What is prudent to an accounts receivable supervisor may be superfluous to a production project manager. What's prudent to a programmer may be inadequate to a buyer. There is no easy answer to all situations, but defining business needs clearly and supporting them with evidence can help.

For example, keeping records specified in ANSI/ISO/ASQ Q9000-2000 is required to maintain certification. For companies registered to ANSI/ISO/ASQ Q9001-2000 and wishing to be recertified to meet marketing objectives, maintaining the records would be justified as a prudent business practice. Other examples of prudent business practices include complying with Baldrige Award criteria, the ISO 14001 standard for environmental management, Food and Drug Administration (FDA) regulations, and any other documentation required for quality, the environment, safety or purity, or other standard to which an organization is certified or at least with which it complies.

In all cases, it is wise to ask to see the business case or the requirements of the standard to apply this litmus test component.

4. *Would any harm come to the organization if the document, or part of it, was eliminated?* The last question is a safety net. Some documentation requirements are less tangible than laws, contracts, or standards. For example, a utility company may target a campaign to sway public opinion toward increasing rates. Without an increase, the company may no longer be fiscally healthy. If reducing the number of mailers sent to customers is seen to hurt the company's

chances for passing an increase, then the answer to question four would have to be *yes*. We rarely think of media mailers when we think of documentation, but don't they share some of the same resource requirements as procedures manuals or records? Doesn't someone in the organization, or a subcontractor, write, edit, and publish each mailer, keep files on each, process returned mailers, and so on?

Harm can come to an organization if it promises documentation to a customer and doesn't deliver. It can be harmful if the absence of expected documentation frustrates employees and reduces productive work time. An organization can be harmed if lack of documentation causes employees to make errors or perform redundant tasks.

How do you test for harm without harming? You do what a jury of peers does. You ask for reasonable evidence. Which brings us to question five of the litmus test.

5. *Would any harm come to the organization if the document, or part of it, existed?* Sometimes a document or part passes the first four questions of the litmus test, so its need is established, but the document or part as it exists or is envisioned could impose a burden on users, customers, or other sources of need. Let's look at a common example: Web pages.

Few of us have surfed the Web without alighting on a page that confuses or frustrates us. Perhaps it's a broken link to a graphic image. Or maybe the fields of a form do not clearly indicate the requested information. What about critical links buried at page edges? Or maybe the problem is a combination of several minor individual annoyances that, together, make visiting a page uncomfortable or deciphering its content unnecessarily time-consuming. For example, pages with low contrast between text and background make us struggle to read the message. Or what about the Internet link that ends in an "Under Construction" page? Navigating to a dead link wastes a reader's time and could be frustrating. It is better to wait to add the link from the source page when the new page is ready for viewing. If you want to generate advance interest in the coming page, post a "Coming Soon" message on the source page. Question five of the litmus test helps us avoid introducing or keeping documentation, or features of it, that harms.

All the best efforts at streamlining an organization's documentation during an improvement initiative may be lost and the situation could worsen if the zero-based approach is abandoned during subsequent documentation reviews or if reviews never happen and documentation is added at will. Every time someone wants to add documentation—whether it is a new policy, link on a Web page, sentence to an existing procedure, copy to a file, mailer, or online form—the originator or another designated party should subject the addition to the litmus test. Otherwise, documentation will put on weight again. This time, people will be less enthusiastic to remedy the problem. They will say, "We've been there, done that." Educate employees, especially leadership, about the costs of cumbersome documentation. Teach them to use the litmus test routinely and build in responsibility for containing documentation. It is that important.

Before using any precious resources to write or revise a document, ask if it is even needed. Ask if it could be a problem for readers or viewers. Whether evaluating existing procedures to eliminate redundancy and improve access or determining whether a new form should be developed, establish decision-making criteria. The litmus test fills that role well.

**Checklist 2.2:
Producing
Zero-Based
Documentation
(A Streamlining
Effort)**

❏ Determine the
   need.

❏ Identify the scope
   of the project.

❏ Gain management
   commitment.

❏ Identify team
   leader.

❏ Identify facilitator.

❏ Identify scribe.

❏ Identify team
   members.

❏ Identify all read-
   ers or viewers,
   including their
   language
   requirements.

❏ Review existing
   documentation.

❏ Review processes.

❏ Perform a
   gap analysis
   between needed
   documentation
   and existing
   documentation.

❏ Determine
   approval.

❏ Identify, select,
   or develop docu-
   ment hierarchy,
   structure,
   and format.

Continued

STREAMLINING SUCCESS

It is one thing to specify the components of Nimble Documentation® and to define a need-oriented, zero-based system and a powerful decision tool, the litmus test, for achieving Nimble Documentation.® It is quite another, however, to redesign, develop, and implement a streamlined system from existing documentation.

Every organization will use different steps and follow a different schedule to streamline its existing documentation system. Organization culture, size, condition of current system, process complexity, number and type of product or service lines, regulatory jurisdiction, industry, employee skills, resources, and many other factors affect a streamlining path. However, successful efforts can guide other organizations to attain their own streamlining objectives. This section presents a composite of success stories of several organizations' achievements in streamlining their documentation. It shows how teams integrated COE characteristics with a zero-based documentation approach (see also chapter 10).

Background

Organizations typically plan and implement streamlining efforts to:

- Meet contractual, legal, and prudent business requirements

- Reduce expenses

- Reduce processing cycle time

- Improve customer satisfaction

- Establish processes and metrics for continuous improvement

- Assume leadership in streamlining documentation and in making information more accessible to users.

A Case Study

Organizations differ in the way they implement a documentation streamlining initiative, depending on many factors, including the organization's culture, industry, size, condition of existing documentation, and many more. We present one organization's implementation activities, following, to give you an idea of the variety of possibilities.

The implementation team's major activities are listed here according to the following headings: project management; hierarchy, structure, and format; data and metrics; and electronic access. This section also presents additional recommendations. Figure 2.4 is a chronology drafted prior to the start of the documentation improvement project. Its usefulness lies in its comprehensiveness.

Project management. A consultant met with the team's leader regularly and participated in weekly, and later, biweekly team meetings and occasional meetings with team sponsors and corporate executives. Project management activities with the consultant, team leader, and facilitator included the following:

- Establish team members' responsibilities

- Assign a monitor from each function

- Schedule project activities

- Communicate with and gain commitment of executive managers

- Publicize and promote the streamlining initiative through company publications and giveaways

- Develop the kickoff presentation

- Prepare metrics of baseline and improved processes

- Research other companies' documentation systems and processes (benchmarking)

- Brief corporate business directors

- Prepare a request for the IS department

- Negotiate the IS department's commitment and resources

- Lead subteam meetings

- Propose archiving and remote storage considerations

- Establish a schedule for revalidating streamlined policies and procedures

❑ Establish document protection.
❑ Establish backup and retention provisions.
❑ Establish metrics for continuous improvement.
❑ Adopt writing style.
❑ Format draft according to processes and responsibilities.
❑ Review draft.
❑ Perform usability testing.
❑ Revise draft.
❑ Proofread revised document.
❑ Submit revised document for approval.
❑ Publish (hard copy or electronic).
❑ Notify users.

The concept of accessing an online system instead of hard copy manuals for corporate policies and procedures was new and not entirely palatable initially to some employees. To assist users in becoming more comfortable with the change, the team developed a publicity and promotion campaign that included articles in the organization's newsletter and announcements in the employee events publication (see Figure 2.5).

The team distributed to each corporate function self-stick notepads (giveaways) printed with an image of a desktop computer, a goals statement, and words promoting clear, concise, and accessible documentation

Once a team (or an individual) determines the need for a document or a group of documents, how do the team members proceed? What are the steps? Although each organization's customers and unique requirements will determine the steps and sequence, the general approach outlined here has worked well for many organizations.

First, the most successful streamlining teams are led by individuals who first gain clear and visible management commitment, including adequate resources for the team to complete its mission. Having a powerful team sponsor helps. A dedicated and skilled team facilitator, preferably a person unaffiliated with the documentation content, helps keep the team on track and doesn't get distracted by content discussions, as a team leader might. The facilitator's role is to assist the team in gaining consensus or making decisions in other ways, staying on topic, respecting starting and ending times, and attending to other important team dynamics and considerations. Some teams use a scribe to record team decisions, but others assign the scribe's responsibilities to the team leader. The strongest teams are represented by individuals from all major functions and alliances affected by the documentation.

Repeat steps in the process as needed, for example, additional revisions after reviews. Also consider document template software. It doesn't replace the hardest part, capturing an organization's own processes in writing (or graphics or video), but it can be a starting point. Be careful, however. The temptation is strong to adopt a template (or borrow another organization's documents) without customizing it thoroughly. You may end up with terminology unfamiliar to employees and a style incompatible with the organization's culture. You may end up with someone else's procedures! And auditors and examiners, rightly, will not accept that. Worse, your organization will miss the benefits that solid documentation affords and may incur liability. The following steps are useful to develop a Nimble Documentation® system from scratch or to improve an existing system.

1. Determine the need (for example, customers' requirements, regulations, laws, business goals, and quality standards or awards).

2. Identify the scope of the project.

3. Gain management commitment.

4. Identify team leader.

5. Identify facilitator.

6. Identify scribe.

7. Identify team members.

8. Identify all readers or viewers, including their language requirements.

9. Review existing documentation.

10. Review processes.

11. Perform a gap analysis between needed documentation and existing documentation.

12. Determine approval.

13. Identify, select, or develop document hierarchy, structure, and format.

14. Establish document protection.

15. Establish backup and retention provisions.

16. Establish metrics for continuous improvement.

17. Adopt writing style.

18. Format draft according to processes and responsibilities.

19. Review draft (for example, by subject matter owners, related functions).

20. Perform usability testing.

21. Revise draft.

22. Proofread revised document.

23. Submit revised document for approval.

24. Publish documents, either as hard copy or electronically.

25. Notify users.

Figure 2.4 Producing zero-based documentation.

NEW! IMPROVED!
POLICIES AND PROCEDURES

Coming to a terminal near you!

Watch for leaner, more accessible corporate policies and procedures debuting on PCs beginning November.

Policies reduced from 89 to 12, procedures about half. Pages skinnied down. Simpler language, too. View the new policies and procedures soon on the Web to find the information you need.

A corporate team has been working in conjunction with CDEFG to transform the policies and procedures into a strong but flexible foundation positioned for a dynamic [organization] future. The new system will save time, dollars, paper, and employee frustration.

Watch for instructions soon, so you too can say "hello" to better working through technology!

Call [   ], team leader, ext. 12345, or [   ], manager, Corporate Directives, ext. 56789, for more information.

Figure 2.5 Announcement to publicize and promote the streamlining initiative.

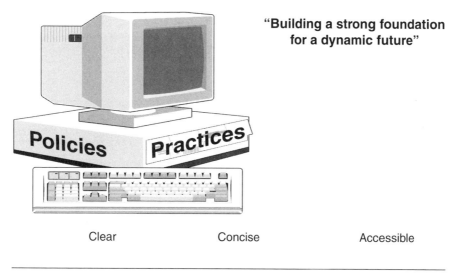

"Building a strong foundation for a dynamic future"

Clear   Concise   Accessible

Figure 2.6 Self-stick notepad giveaways.

(see Figure 2.6). Employees would multiply the value of the giveaways each time they used a self-stick note to send internal correspondence. Also, the team distributed promotional tent cards and placed them on library and cafeteria tables. To maintain readers' interest, two versions of the tent cards were distributed at intervals, each with two different messages (see Figure 2.7). The giveaways and tent cards were printed on the same neon-colored paper of the cover sheets for distributing approval drafts of the newly streamlined policies and procedures. The team's intent was to reinforce each publicity activity by projecting a coordinated image of the streamlining effort.

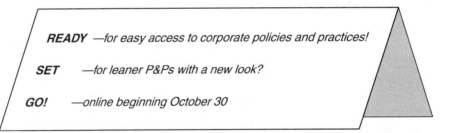

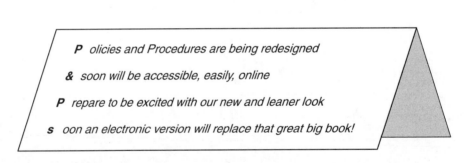

Figure 2.7   Promotional tent cards.

Hierarchy, structure, and format. The team reached consensus on proposing a hierarchy of directive documents and a consistent structure and format for policies and procedures (see Table 2.2). The proposal was modified only slightly during implementation. For example, 12 policies were included instead of 13 policies. The decision process included:

- Define the hierarchy for the organization's directive documents

- Establish a structure for the policies and procedures manual

- Establish the format of policies and procedures

Table 2.2 Proposed directives hierarchy, structure, and format.

	Policies	**Procedures**
Number of Documents	12	TBD
Number of books	1: Policies & procedures combined	1: Policies & procedures combined
Defined	Position of the organization	How-to's: Implement policies (Let people know the established way to do work)
Responsibilities section	Delete	Include if *Responsibilities* format (see **Other sections**, below). Otherwise omit this section and embed responsibilities in *Process* section
Definitions section	Delete	Include only if needed to clarify
References section	Delete	Delete
Other sections	Goal: 1 section without section heading	• *General* • *Process* or • *Responsibilities* (but not *both Process* & *Responsibilities*)
Approval	Executive management	Head of function
Document number system	Maintain basic system	Maintain basic system (flow down from policies)
Paragraph number system	Maintain basic system	Maintain basic system
Approval authority information	Delete	TBD
Date format	Slashes vs. dashes	Slashes vs. dashes

- Design a flow-down document-group numbering system

- Establish a document numbering scheme

- Establish approval authorization levels for directive documents

Prior to the documentation improvement initiative, some of the same information appeared in the separate policies manual and procedures manual. After defining the function of policies and procedures, the streamlining effort yielded one manual housing both the slimmed down dozen or so policies and the procedures reduced by half. Document reviewers deleted the *Responsibilities* section in the policies and also in the procedures when a *Process* section included information about responsibilities. Definitions were pulled out of policies and were made optional for procedures. In other words, they were included only when critical to understanding the procedure, such as for special usage of a term. Because the next track of the improvement initiative was to establish an online system for policies and procedures, where users could search easily across documents on the organization's intranet, the *References* section was deleted from both policies and procedures.

Data and metrics. The corporate directives department began working toward combining its writers' and editors' individual databases for processing documents (including coordinating their review, editing, and publishing) into a standard, departmentwide database, which included document status (for example, *in coordination* or *approved*), number of pages, and other metrics. This activity was completed after the organization accomplished the primary streamlining effort. Major data and metrics for the streamlining initiative included a cost model for processing and maintaining policies and procedures; document volume; currentness; cycle time; zero-defects quality, including standards and measurement; page hits for users of the intranet; zero-based approach to documentation; and editorial guidelines, such as simplified language and reduced verbiage. The team established and maintained volume and currentness metrics during the initiative, and writers and editors became more skilled at editing for clarity and conciseness. Baseline and regular measurement of these data were to be developed. The team largely adopted the zero-based approach to documentation. The intranet page hits metric, which allowed the corporate directives staff and document owners to monitor the frequency with which users view policies and procedures, was developed. Other metrics—cost model data, cycle time, and zero-defects quality—also were developed. The following improvements were accomplished:

- Volume (number of documents and pages). Three-hundred and eight (308) policies and procedures were reduced to 164 streamlined policies and procedures, a reduction of about 47 percent. Individual policies and procedures were streamlined as well; the combined page count was 1094 at the start of the project and 390 at the end—a reduction of at least 64 percent. Further, text clarity and reading ease increased considerably as a result of new editing standards.

- Currentness. Before the initiative, about 62 percent of policies and procedures were from 1–5 years old, 17 percent were published in the last 6–10 years, 9 percent were 11–15 years old, and about 1 percent were older than 15 years. At the end, none of the policies and procedures were older than two years.

With the publication of the in-work 33–36 procedures, none of the documents would be older than two years. This accomplishment was particularly significant because of the organization's substantial changes; an accelerating rate of change both within the organization and specific to the industry; and rapidly changing HR, environmental, and other regulations affecting all organizations in the region and in the industry. Reviewing policies and procedures regularly and revising them accordingly were never more important. Streamlining the documentation system and individual policies and procedures allowed the organization to do that faster.

Electronic access. The streamlining team's leadership and the organization's IS department collaborated with the consultant to design, develop, and implement the online document system. Except for closed areas, nearly all of the organization's employees became able to access and easily search the policies and procedures and other corporate information on the organization's intranet. The pages (screens) were designed in HTML format and the streamlined policies and procedures were published on the intranet. "What a relief to not have to hoist multipound volumes about and search for some elusive detail in a policy!" said an executive vice president, in a congratulatory e-mail message to the team.

During the first few months of the new system, both old and new policies and procedures were available in separate online databases. A special screen allowed users to identify at a glance the documents that had been added, revised, or canceled during a moving window of 12 weeks. That way, users who hadn't accessed the system because of vacation, travel, or other reasons, could learn of the changes that had been made during their absence.

The team secured internal training for users, for example, Netscape Navigator training.

Hard copy distribution was virtually phased out, but the corporate directives department maintained signed, hard copy masters and history files of all policies and procedures.

The team planned to install a terminal in the library to allow employees to access the online documentation. It also was working on alternatives for closed areas and electronic coordination (reviews) of draft policies and procedures.

The online system was designed, developed, and implemented through the following activities:

- Define attributes of a people-friendly, easy-to-search online system

- Eliminate hard copy manuals (retaining masters and a handful of hard copies for critical areas that had limited or no access to the online system)

- Present the proposed online system to the organization's user group

- Define the schedule for conversion to the online system

- Draft the initial design of intranet Web pages

- Pilot test the initial design and revise

- Provide central area access to the system

- Coordinate document format troubleshooting (some applications needed initial modification)

- Coordinate development of user instructions

- Coordinate uploader training

- Develop alternatives for closed areas (for example, distribute CDs)

- Establish hotline support

- Propose passive e-mail notification of document additions, revisions, and cancellations

- Develop training alternatives

Additional recommendations. The organization implemented additional recommendations for continuing to grow a documentation COE. Primarily, suggestions fell into five areas: database, metrics, cost, proactive role in electronic access, and writing standards.

1. *Database.* Established a single database of policies and procedures, including key process dates, page numbers, coordination status, and disposition. Off-the-shelf software automatically generates data, saving writers' and editors' time and increasing data accuracy.

2. *Metrics.* Provided charts regularly (for example, monthly or quarterly) of key metrics such as volume, proofreading, processing cycle time, customer satisfaction, intranet page hits, and other data that helped COE staff continue to improve processes. Mapped activities and identified value-added and non-value-added tasks. Eliminated or reengineered non-value-added tasks.

3. *Cost.* Knowing the cost of each major process helped the COE make the best decisions about its processes. For example, if a requester submitted a new draft procedure, the COE estimated the cost

of producing and maintaining the document and persuaded the organization to reconsider a request, especially if the document was only marginally useful. It was hard to run a business well without knowing how much it costs to do business. It was worth spending some time initially to gather cost data. See the cost model in chapter 6 for a way to measure documentation processing costs.

4. *Proactive role in electronic access.* COE personnel, in addition to the organization's IS department, were proactive in helping employees use the new online system for policies and procedures. COE staff participated in cascade training. That is, the staff were trained in locating and searching documents on the intranet and then, in turn, trained other employees.

The COE staff members maintained a database of help requests directed to them to pinpoint areas where more publicity or training was needed and where the system might need some adjustment to make it easier for employees to use.

5. *Writing standards.* To achieve consistency in writing and editing (which aids readers) and save time resolving editorial issues, the COE adopted a writing style guide and a departmental writing convention guide that was specific to the organization and its documentation.

Figure 2.8 shows the schedule for implementing documentation improvement at the organization. It is a useful model for others.

Model Schedule for Implementing Documentation Improvement:
Where Do We Go From Here

Notes: Assume team members are responsible for all activities unless otherwise noted. Assume team modifies the chronology according to its own information and expectations.

Track 1: Revise, Rework, Improve Policies and Procedures

1A: Foundation—Facts and Data (weeks 1–4)

1. Develop cost model for gathering data.

2. Determine basic metrics for existing policies and procedures including:

   • Cost

   • Processing cycle time (number of days)

   • Currentness (percent last reviewed within team's standard of 36 months)

   • Volume (number of documents)

3. Corporate Directives graphs baseline basic metrics and maintains the information monthly.

4. Pilot one section of the manual to determine an estimate of basic metrics for reengineered policies and procedures. Use the criteria of legal, contractual, and prudent business practice. Assume zero-based documentation.

5. Estimate target basic metrics for reengineered policies and procedures and implementation costs.

6. Refine team goals to include estimated variances in metrics.

1B: Commitment (weeks 5–8)

7. Present the data and goals (see 1A: Foundation) to the organization's executives and directors one-on-one and to their staff meetings. Request their commitment for zero-based documentation and resources.

8. Consult with executive managers regarding minimum requirements for regional offices.

9. Meet with function heads and approvers for each section of the manual. Request their commitment to zero-based documentation and resources.

10. Present the data and goals to the customer. Request the customer's support.

11. Present the data and goals to bargaining unit leaders. Request their support.

12. Publicize commitments and support. Use quotations wherever possible (for example, in the organization newsletter).

1C: Manual and Document Structure (weeks 2–10)

13. Review, then decide on a hierarchy of directives. Define each type of directive to be maintained in the system.

14. Decide on the basic content and target number of policies. (Include satellite office members in all policies decisions.)

Figure 2.8   Preliminary documentation improvement implementation schedule.

15. Determine format for the policies.

16. Identify the disposition for each existing policy (whether it will remain, become a procedure, be consolidated with other policies, or be canceled).

17. Ask the managers to identify representatives from each function to participate in one or two highly structured focus group meetings to determine a procedures format. The representatives also lead the work team group for actual streamlining of procedures. Consider eliminating facsimile forms from procedures.

18. Propose a structure for satellite office procedures (for example, policies only, policies with matrix flow down). Consult with satellite office heads to plan implementation of the satellite office manual where it is different from headquarters.

19. Personally and by memo invite each identified functional area representative. Send a copy to their immediate supervisor. Include the agenda in the memo, especially the original team's recommendations for any elements to eliminate or revise (such as Purpose or References).

20. Convene the focus group. Reach a consensus on format.

21. Consult with each functional area, and determine which (if any) portion and extent of procedures to decentralize (such as analysis, coordination, text processing, or the entire process). Review Team 1 (earlier team) survey data to identify procedures where employees might desire more detailed information (such as HR).

22. Corporate Directives recommends a writing style guide and standard text processing software, considering compatibility with candidates for electronic text retrieval system. It presents its recommendations to the team and receives the team's approval.

1D: Content (weeks 7–25)

23. Determine the participants for each functional area's work team, in conjunction with the identified work team leader. Assign a Corporate Directives writer and editor as a consultant to each work team (on call).

24. Supply the work teams with the procedure format, writing style guide, and text processing standards. Work teams adopt zero-based documentation criteria. Negotiate target dates for submitting drafts of procedures or other disposition decisions to Corporate Directives (consolidating, moving to lower-level directive, canceling, or streamlining). Require monthly status reports from each work team to be submitted to Corporate Directives, Directives Team to include metrics on the number and percent of procedures accomplished and remaining to be reviewed, dispositioned, redrafted, and so forth. Present monthly status (metrics) to function heads. Work teams complete and submit drafts.

25. Corporate Directives edits drafts and prepares them for approvals.

26. Corporate Directives publishes the new manual and provides an audit trail.

Track 2: Improve Electronic Access (sketch of a few proposed activities—weeks 2–?)

27. Consult with IS specialists and Team 1 survey results to develop criteria for rating off-the-shelf client-server document management packages. Be sure to include purchase, licensing, and maintenance costs. A small sample of other features includes:

Figure 2.8 Preliminary documentation improvement implementation schedule *(continued)*.

- Adequate number of possible simultaneous users

- Balancing sophisticated searching with extensive training requirements; generally, the more precise the search capabilities, the more training needed

- Response capabilities, such as the ability to request org charts from on-line screens

28. Research off-the-shelf packages according to identified criteria. Review literature and benchmark or benchtrend with other large companies (what works for 30 users won't necessarily work well for 3000).

29. Participate in demonstrations of off-the-shelf packages.

30. Tentatively identify the package that best meets the organization's criteria.

31. Pilot the package with a portion of the revised policies and procedures.

32. Estimate the time to reach a break-even point for implementing the electronic document management system. Plan to maintain two systems simultaneously during the toddler months of the electronic system.

33. Gain commitment for budget and HR for conversion investment (see methods in Track 1). Seek applications for the system outside of Corporate Directives (such as cafeteria menus, rideshare information, credit union rates, internal job opportunities, and clubs). Plan to upload approved organizational announcements and urgent information bulletins immediately, even during the phase of redundant systems (hard copy and electronic). These applications will help speed acceptance of the conversion and will help employees become familiar with the system.

34. Sponsor a conversion implementation team.

35. The conversion implementation team determines elements and timeline. Examples of critical elements include:

- Standard naming and menu conventions

- Screen identification, such as manual name and document name

- Closed area considerations and alternatives

- Just-in-time printing

- E-mail notification

- Centralized versus decentralized uploading

- Conversion date and notification schedule for canceling all but emergency hard copy manuals (Recommend four to six months notification with regular notification updates)

- Publicity campaign for conversion

- User and information provider training schedule

- Central access to system, such as the library or cafeteria terminals

- History files, off-site storage (disaster recovery considerations)

- Electronic coordination

- Accommodate lower-level (how-to) directives

36. Establish and implement information provider maintenance, such as menu revision.

Figure 2.8 Preliminary documentation improvement implementation schedule *(continued).*

37. Publicize the electronic document management system.

38. Train users and information providers.

39. Develop hot line support during and following the conversion. The hot line function maintains user metrics to identify problems and consider modifications, publicity, and training.

40. Develop or apply a system feature to measure use, such as the number and type of directives hits.

Track 3: Achieve Other Process Improvements (weeks tbd)

41. Streamline coordination process. Consider electronic coordination.

42. The team or Corporate Directives establishes a revalidation process requiring approval, revision, or cancellation of procedures (*x*-year cycle). Establish revalidation metrics, maintain, and publicize monthly.

Figure 2.8   Preliminary documentation improvement implementation schedule *(continued)*.

Part II

Implementation

3

Hierarchy, Structure, Format, and Style

Solutions presented in this chapter address documentation challenges such as:

- A useful hierarchy for company documentation

- When to use a plain vanilla text format for procedures

- When to use alternative formats such as play script, process map, or video

- The advantages and disadvantages of Web-based documents

- The critical elements of a procedure

- When to use passive and when to use active sentences

- How to avoid "dog puppies" for concise writing

This chapter introduces the *Implementation* topic group of this book. Once an organization commits to streamlining its existing documentation or creating a nimble system from scratch, it must define the vehicles for fulfilling the need. The way the system and its parts are organized and presented (that is, its hierarchy and structure, and the format and style of documents) should facilitate access to and comprehension of needed information.

For the purposes of this book, *hierarchy* is the relationship of manuals, or other groups of documents, to each other. For example, quality policies may be the broadest or highest level of direction on processes and responsibilities that affect the quality of an organization's products or services. These policies may be implemented by standard operating procedures—the how-to's—which are the next level. Finally, work instructions, detailed direction for each job, flow down from the procedures. *Structure* is the way documents are organized to form a manual or other group of individual documents, such as procedures. The internal organization of an individual document is its *format*, for example, what sections of a procedure are included, such as Purpose, Process, and References, and how they are presented, such as plain vanilla text, play script, process map, or on the Web. Finally, *style* is at the level of paragraphs, sentences, phrases, words, and mechanics.

From a practical hierarchy compliant with ANSI/ISO/ASQ Q9001-2000 to a compact structure for corporate policies and procedures to a format for a multilingual workforce to a Web page style that speeds forms processing, this chapter provides practical guidance for implementing a world-class documentation system.

HIERARCHY AND STRUCTURE

Defining a common hierarchy of management and operating documentation is especially important in large companies, but it is needed by organizations of every size. Most often, we see policies, procedures, work or desk instructions, and specifications. Good information access and traceability dictates that higher level documents flow down clearly and logically to lower level ones.

Draft an enabling directive document (such as a procedure) that defines your organization's document management program, including the purpose and format of each type of document. This may be the first procedure in the series. The hierarchy of quality system documentation shown in Table 3.1 is useful, but is only one structure among many adopted by organizations.

It would be hard to imagine a nimble quality system policies manual longer than 30 pages. No more than 20 is better. However, a quality system manual containing both policies and procedures likely will be longer. Three examples of procedures are internal auditing, nonconforming product and corrective action, and training. Work instruction topics could include data entry and recording results of corrective action. Job descriptions could include quality assurance manager, HR coordinator, and receptionist. Results of design reviews and unique identification of product are records. Forms, both electronic and hard copy, could include a purchase requisition and customer satisfaction questionnaire. An example of data is results of monitoring and measuring the effectiveness of the quality management system.

Table 3.1 Hierarchy of quality system documentation.

Component	Description
Policies	Highest level directive documentation
Procedures	What processes shall be performed by what function
Work instructions	Step-by-step direction on how to perform processes
Job descriptions	Responsibilities for assignments or positions
Records	Evidence of events and results
Forms	Information templates
Data	Facts, information, and statistics

It is prudent, and required by law, to maintain internal controls for transactions, for example, to commit company funds. However, the less bureaucratic the approval authority system, the better it is for everyone. Rather than specifying in a procedure who has authority to sign for what, maintain a separate chart of approvals. That way, when individuals change positions, the procedures that mention the individual's authority will not have to be revised—and writers won't have to search through all the procedures for the employee's name. To further reduce maintenance, list approval authority by function or process rather than by employee name and provide links to approvals in online procedures. See chapter 9 for more on approval authority systems.

Bulletins, memos, or announcements convey urgent or temporary information. They can be holding places for a procedure being written. Establishing expiration dates for bulletins is a good idea. Otherwise, they have a way of piling up and are challenging to maintain or access. Seasonal information or reminders lend themselves well to temporary bulletins, such as company policy on holiday activities and accepting gifts from vendors.

Table 3.2 shows a basic hierarchy that is useful for a management and operating directive document system.

Using the Nimble Documentation® approach, many large organizations have streamlined their top-level policies to about a dozen one-page documents from 75 or more policies originally—without losing essential information. For companies with more than 500 employees, policies covering the functions shown in Figure 3.1 and perhaps a couple of additional ones to meet an organization's special needs are useful. A single policy statement may be adequate for smaller organizations.

Figure 3.2 is an example of a streamlined policy. It communicates the company position on business operations. Note its broad terms and brevity.

Not every level is needed for every organization. The fewer levels, the better. A company with a single product line and simple processes may be able to assemble a single-volume quality manual, or group of Web pages, that includes the firm's quality policy and procedures relating to the quality of its product. Work instructions may be posted in transparent sleeves above corresponding machinery or be available online at an employee's desk. Cross-functional work and flexible positions may nullify the usefulness of static job descriptions. Posted work instructions may capture needed direction adequately.

Table 3.2 Basic hierarchy for corporate documentation.

Component	Description
Policy	Position of the company
Procedure	Detail of process and responsibility Implements policy
Desk or work instruction	Step-by-step performance of a job
Form	Information template
Approval system	Authorization to commit funds or other resources Implements forms transactions
Bulletin	Temporary or urgent direction for any level of specificity

1. Human Resources

2. General Management (or Administration)

3. Property or Material (or Purchasing)

4. Legal (or Contracts)

5. Finance

6. Facilities

7. Information Resources (including public information, IS, and e-mail)

8. Ethics

9. Safety and Health

10. Security

11. Quality Assurance

Figure 3.1 Useful policies.

THE GHI

COMPANY   **POLICY**

SUBJECT: Business Operations

NUMBER: BUO-1
DATE: May 13, 2002
PAGE: 1 OF 1

The Company conducts business prudently. It exercises and effectively communicates adequate controls to manage its operations and commitment to promote and safeguard its assets.

The President and Chief Executive is authorized to approve and delegate all internal actions and external commitments required for business operations according to (1) the chart of approvals and (2) management directives disseminated by policies, bulletins, procedures, organization charts, and organizational announcements.

Management communicates complete and timely information regarding federal, state, and local government action that could affect the Company and informs government authorities of the characteristics, needs, and interests of the Company.

As a good citizen of the community, the Company informs the public of its activities and participates in community affairs to promote a better understanding of the Company and its mission. To protect its assets, including its positive public image, the Company registers original and distinctive names, logos, marks, publications, and other items with agencies of the federal government and establishes guidelines for their use.

We C. Policy, Sr.
President and CEO

Figure 3.2 Example of a streamlined company policy.

A consistent, integrated document numbering scheme supporting broad to narrow information helps users place documents within an overall hierarchy and facilitates access to other documents with broader and narrower scopes. For example, a company's HR policy is numbered HR-4. A procedure covering the company's career development system is identified as HR-4-2. A work instruction for processing a job transfer application is HR-4-2-3, and the application is company form 4-2-3A. The approval authority system indicates employees authorized to approve transfers via form 4-2-3A. Such a numbering scheme helps users find all of the information they need to handle the transfer process and can help intranet Web browsers order search results for easier information access.

Tables of Contents, Online Menus, and Indexes

A table of contents section in a hard copy manual or an online link list or menu is important for maintaining change notices and revisions. The most useful hard copy tables have space to write in document revisions and additions and their issue dates, and online menus are organized by category. Documents are alphabetized by title and include issue dates. Cover sheets for distributing hard copy documents explicitly instruct users to update their table of contents when filing new or revised documents or deleting obsolete or canceled ones. An updated table should be distributed at intervals corresponding to the frequency of revisions, additions, and cancellations. Semiannual and quarterly distribution schedules for hard copies are common. The revision date is printed on the table itself, along with information identifying the manual. Figure 3.3 shows a brief table of

[XYZ LOGO]	**Contents**	**Operating Procedures** Number: XYZP TOC Date Issued: December 20, 2001 Page: 1 of 1

XYZP Number	**Title**	**Date Issued**
4-2	Directive Document System	8/20/2001
4-2-3	Chart of Approvals	8/7/2001
4-2-4	Forms Management System	8/21/2001
6-2-2	Training	9/10/2001
7-3	Design Control and Configuration Management System	8/7/2001
7-3-1	New Product Brief Development	8/20/2001
7-4-1	Vendor Qualification	8/23/2001
8-5-1	Continuous Measured Improvement (CMI) Plan	8/7/2001
8-5-2	Corrective Action	9/10/2001
8-5-3	Employee Suggestion Program	8/7/2001

Figure 3.3 Sample hard copy procedures table of contents or online menu.

contents for a new company just beginning to develop its documentation system; the document numbers correspond to major clauses of ANSI/ISO/ASQ Q9001-2000.

The key to locating information in hard copy manuals is a comprehensive index with generous cross-references. Not all employees look up information using the same words that writers think they will. Prepare an index with many synonyms. (See chapter 8 for more on indexes in user manuals.) Take advantage of the index feature of major word processing programs. But keep in mind that an index is a maintenance-intensive part of documentation. Every time a document is revised, it spawns an obligation to review all index entries related to the document. Publish a revised hard copy index according to the frequency and extent of document revisions. Semiannual or quarterly indexes are common.

However, more and more organizations are moving to online document management systems to facilitate information access. Part of the appeal (and savings) of cutting-edge online systems is their automated indexing capabilities and powerful search engines. Some systems can search not only for synonyms but also for more general and also narrower terms. Many can be used for context-dependent searches. For example, users interested in documents related to software engineering might not want to retrieve documents associated with an organization's Software Engineering Division. The most powerful systems will have both automated index and context-dependent search capabilities.

FORMAT

Documents are vehicles for communicating information. They are successful to the extent they do that according to customers' requirements. In chapter 2, five sources of need are identified (and probably there are many more), which include users as internal customers and external customers. How do you format a document to meet a customer's requirements?

To illustrate format alternatives, their relative advantages and disadvantages, and their elements, let us look at standard operating procedures, a common vehicle for communication and the common denominator of most organizations' documentation systems. Considerations for formatting procedures, however, work well for other documents. Individual format elements, such as scope or responsibilities paragraphs, differ for policies, user guides, forms, bulletins, organization charts, and so on. And because companies vary in their culture, history, and receptivity to new approaches, several alternatives are illustrated. Selecting an option should be based on the organization's and its customers' needs and readiness.

Variations within each format include indentations, if any; heading style and contents; graphic emphasis, such as lines and boxes; and many others. The possibilities are nearly endless. Following this section, important elements of a procedure are discussed, across many formats and variations.

Advantages and Disadvantages of Several Document Formats

Formats for standard operating procedures include variations of:

- Plain vanilla text (or narrative)
- Play script
- Modular
- Flowchart
- Process map
- Video
- Audio
- Web

Headers in the following examples vary but are not necessarily tied to the particular format illustrated. Headers can include the company logo, document type (procedure), title, document number, revision letter and date issued, approval, page of total number of pages, and a separation bar.

Plain vanilla text (or narrative). Essentially, the plain vanilla text format presents paragraphs with a few headings (see Figure 3.4). Paragraphs may be indented or not, headings may be numerous or few, and numbering can be applied to major sections only or every paragraph (or something in between). More or less, this is the traditional format seen often in manufacturing and design firms. To demonstrate this format's versatility, a second version of the plain vanilla text format is shown in Figure 3.5; this one has a spare numbering scheme.

[XYZ LOGO]	**Operating Procedure**

Receiving Inspection

Number:	XYZP 7-4-3
Date Issued:	Rev. A
	May 5, 2001
Page:	1 of 1

1.0   SCOPE
Applies only to shipments received at the Buffalo plant from outside suppliers.

2.0   PROCEDURE

2.1   Field Installation (Site)

2.1.1 Inventories and marks up the shipper within 24 hours of arrival.

2.1.2 Dispositions any discrepancies between shipping's copy of the shipper and installation's copy of the shipper as follows:

   A. Site supervisor contacts shipping lead.

   B. Lead determines availability of the discrepant material.

   C. If discrepancy remains unresolved, site supervisor calls Installation (Buffalo) and issues a field request for missing items.

   D. If site has parts not identified on the shipper, field installation office calls shipping and resolves discrepancy.

2.1.3 Faxes the marked-up shipper to Buffalo field installation office c/o the installation coordinator.

2.2   Installation (Support Coordinator)

2.2.1 Forwards faxed copy of shipper to planning.

2.3   Planning (Clerk)

2.3.1 Clerk matches and attaches the faxed copy of the shipper to the planning copy of the shipper and files them together.

   Note: Planning's copy should be filed only with field installation's copy.

Figure 3.4   Example A of plain vanilla (or narrative) procedure format.

Advantages

The plain vanilla text format conserves paper by fitting many words on each page. It meets traditional expectations and looks like what many people think a procedure should look like. Typically, auditors are familiar with this format. Numbering sections to the third digit (Figure 3.4) helps users communicate, for example, when a user calls out a paragraph. Numbering to this extent also helps viewers if conversion is made to an online system. The numbering scheme of the second version of this format (Figure 3.5) is aesthetically more pleasing. Also, for many writers, plain vanilla text is easier to write than other formats.

[XYZ LOGO]	**Operating Procedure**
Receiving Inspection	Number: XYZP 7-4-3 Date Issued: Rev. A May 5, 2001 Page: 1 of 1

1.0   SCOPE

Applies only to shipments received at the Buffalo plant from outside suppliers.

2.0   PROCEDURE

Field Installation (Site)

    A. Inventories and marks up the shipper within 24 hours of arrival.

    B. Dispositions any discrepancies between shipping's copy of the shipper and installation's copy of the shipper as follows:

        1. Site supervisor contacts shipping lead.

        2. Lead determines availability of the discrepant material.

        3. If discrepancy remains unresolved, site supervisor calls Installation (Buffalo) and issues a field request for missing items.

        4. If site has parts not identified on the shipper, field installation office calls shipping and resolves discrepancy.

    C. Faxes the marked-up shipper to Buffalo field installation office c/o the installation coordinator.

Installation (Support Coordinator)

Forwards faxed copy of shipper to planning.

Planning (Clerk)

Clerk matches and attaches the faxed copy of the shipper to the planning copy of the shipper and files them together.

    Note: Planning's copy should be filed only with field installation's copy.

Figure 3.5 Example B of plain vanilla (or narrative) procedure format.

Disadvantages

The narrative format takes longer than others to locate information. It does not reflect energy or project a dynamic image. Numbering to the third digit (Figure 3.4) is cumbersome to read.

Play script. The play script format is action oriented. A popular version of this format includes two sections: scope and procedure. The procedure section is divided into responsibilities and actions. Responsibilities, which are listed on the left, are numberless. Action paragraphs typically are numbered simply with uppercase letters and Arabic numerals. Numbering schemes for the play script format vary. Figure 3.6 is the XYZ engineering company's procedure in a play script format.

[XYZ LOGO]   **Operating Procedure**

Receiving Inspection

Number:	XYZP 7-4-3
Date Issued:	Rev. A
	May 5, 2001
Page:	1 of 1

1.0 SCOPE

Applies only to shipments received at the Buffalo plant from outside suppliers.

2.0 PROCEDURE

Responsibility	Action
Field Installation (Site)	A. Inventories and marks up the shipper within 24 hours of arrival.
	B. Dispositions any discrepancies between shipping's copy of the shipper and installation's copy of the shipper as follows:
	1. Site supervisor contacts shipping lead.
	2. Lead determines availability of the discrepant material.
	3. If discrepancy remains unresolved, site supervisor calls Installation (Buffalo) and issues a field request for missing items.
	4. If site has parts not identified on the shipper, field installation office calls shipping and resolves discrepancy.
	C. Faxes the marked-up shipper to Buffalo field installation office c/o the installation coordinator.
Installation (Support Coordinator)	Forwards faxed copy of shipper to planning.
Planning (Clerk)	Clerk matches and attaches the faxed copy of the shipper to the planning copy of the shipper and files them together.

Note: Planning's copy should be filed only with field installation's copy.

Figure 3.6 Example of play script procedure format.

Advantages

The play script format facilitates finding information for which each function is responsible. White space is friendly to readers. This format reflects more energy than the plain vanilla text and projects a more dynamic image.

[XYZ LOGO]		**Operating Procedure**
Title: RECEIVING INSPECTION		Page 1 of 1
Number: XYZP 7-4-3		Approved By: Quality Manager
Revision: A		Date Issued: May 5, 2001

Reason   Consistent quality of purchased material

Scope   Applies only to shipments received at the Buffalo plant from outside suppliers.

Responsibility   Field Installation

Procedure

1. **INVENTORY and MARK UP the shipper within 24 hours of arrival.**

2. **RESOLVE discrepancies between shipping's copy of the shipper and installation's copy of the shipper as follows:**

If shipping's copy of the shipper **agrees** with installation's copy of the shipper—	—MOVE material to staging platform
If shipping's copy of the shipper **disagrees** with installation's copy of the shipper—	—Site supervisor: • CONTACT shipping lead and describe discrepancy. —Lead: • DETERMINE availability of discrepant material.
If discrepancy is **resolved**—	—MOVE material to staging platform.
If discrepancy is **unresolved**—	—Site supervisor: • CALL installation's office (Buffalo). • ISSUE field request for missing items.
If parts **identified** on the shipper—	—MOVE material to staging platform.
If parts **not identified** on the shipper—	—Site supervisor: • CALL shipping and resolve discrepancy.

3. **Fax marked-up shipper to Buffalo field installation office c/o installation coordinator.**

Figure 3.7 Example of modular procedure format.

Disadvantages

The play script format consumes more paper—if hard copy—or more screens—if electronic—than other formats. Its numbering scheme can be confusing because several paragraphs are assigned the same number. This format is nontraditional, therefore some employees may need training and time to adjust to it. Also, writing in the play script format is more difficult for many writers than other formats.

Modular. The modular format works well with fairly straightforward, step-by-step procedures and especially with those that have *if–then* decision points. Parts of the procedure, or modules, are self-contained. Usually, a separate modular procedure is required for each function or process. The first modular format example for the XYZ engineering company applies to the field installation function only (see Figure 3.7). Module numbers are kept to a minimum. Then, for contrast, Figure 3.8 shows a nonstructured text procedure (plain vanilla text format minus the section headings and indentations) and Figure 3.9 shows Raymond Urgo's structured/modular format for backing up information on a PC.

Advantages

Modular formats facilitate finding information. Their partitioned, graphic layout is easy to follow. If–then decision points are set off; they do not interfere with the procedure's flow. Minimum numbering is unlikely to distract readers. Modular formats project a contemporary image often associated with software user manuals and other high-tech products.

BACKING UP YOUR FILES ON A PERSONAL COMPUTER

It is imperative to make frequent backups of your files to safeguard and preserve your data. If a file is deleted for some reason, the only way to recover its data is from a backup copy. You should back up your files on a scheduled basis. Also, back up the files when they are new or when the information is highly critical.

The number of diskettes you will need for the backup depends on how much data are in a file. (A 3.5-inch diskette holds 1.44 megabytes.) Backup diskettes must be formatted ahead of time because formatting does not occur during the backup process.

From the File Menu of the word processing program, highlight the name of the file to be backed up. From the Edit Menu, select the option BACK UP. A pop-up window will inform you to insert a diskette. At this point, insert a diskette into the drive and press ENTER to continue. If a pop-up window says the backup is completed, exit the Edit Menu. If the window says the backup is incomplete because there is insufficient space, replace the diskette with another formatted diskette then press ENTER to continue the backup.

Always remember to remove the diskette. It may be helpful to place a label on the diskette and write the name of the file on the label.

There are two sources of information in the event that you need more information on backing up your file. One is the user guide for the word processing software. The other is the PC Workstation Support Group.

Source: Raymond E. Urgo, handout at presentation to Orange Empire section of American Society for Quality Control, 1995. Used with permission.

Figure 3.8 Example of nonstructured and nonmodular plain vanilla format.

Disadvantages

Modular formats consume more paper—if hard copy—or more screens—if electronic—than structured (divided into sections, paragraphs numbered) plain vanilla text. Procedures designed to this format usually take longer to develop. Like the play script, modular formats are nontraditional. Some employees may need training and time to adjust to them. For many writers, the modular format is the most difficult text format.

How to Back Up Files on the Personal Computer

Importance	It is important to back up files to safeguard and preserve your data. If a file is deleted or the hard drive fails, the backup copy is the only way that you can recover the lost information.
When to back up files	It is best to back up your files on a scheduled basis, especially when a file is new or the information is highly critical.
Before you begin	Before you begin a backup, you must have a sufficient number of formatted diskettes. (One 3.5-inch diskette holds 1.44 megabytes.)
Procedure	From your word processing program, follow these steps to back up your file.

Step	Action
1	Open the File Menu.
2	Highlight the name of the file to be backed up.
3	Open the Edit Menu.
4	Select the option BACK UP.
5	Insert a formatted diskette into the drive.
6	Press the ENTER key for the backup to occur.
7	Wait until a message appears. <table><tr><th>IF this message appears . . .</th><th>THEN . . .</th></tr><tr><td>Backup completed</td><td>• Go to Step 8.</td></tr><tr><td>Backup not completed—insufficient space</td><td>• Remove the diskette. • Insert another formatted diskette. • Repeat Steps 6 and 7.</td></tr></table>
8	Exit the Edit Menu.
9	Remove the diskette.

For further information	For further information, either • Refer to the word processing software user guide, or • Contact your PC Workstation Support Group.

Source: Raymond E. Urgo, handout at presentation to Orange Empire section of American Society for Quality Control, 1995. Used with permission.

Figure 3.9   Example of structured modular format.

Flowchart. A procedure structured as a flowchart relies largely on graphics to convey information. This format also is often used as a step between the process interview for generating a procedure and a written draft. Documentation teams use flowcharts routinely to see a process without text distraction. Flowcharts help individuals spot non-value-added activities and needlessly cumbersome processes. For some employees, flowcharts are foreign and intimidating, but most see them as helpful tools.

Flowchart steps are depicted by standard geometric shapes. The flowchart format shows processes and direction at a glance, including easy-to-spot decision points. It is often used as a preliminary step in drafting a procedure in a more traditional, written format. Many organizations tape a huge sheet of paper to the wall and draw a master flowchart of their functions in preparation for writing traditional procedures. Others use flowcharting software and project draft flowcharts as they are developed.

Figure 3.10 shows the receiving inspection procedure rendered in a flowchart format.

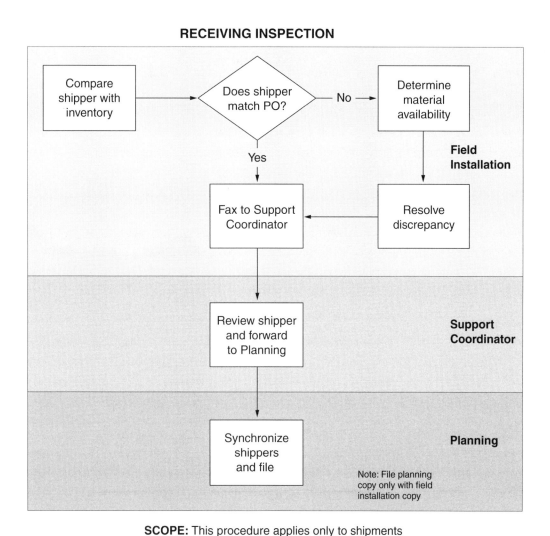

RECEIVING INSPECTION

SCOPE: This procedure applies only to shipments received at the Buffalo plant from outside suppliers.

Figure 3.10   Example of flowchart format.

Advantages

A flowchart's graphic representation, for most people, is easy to follow. If–then decision points draw the reader in quickly because of their distinctive shape. The flowchart format, because it contains few words, usually is easier to understand by users who may be less than proficient in the language of the procedure. This format projects a contemporary image often associated with software development and other high-tech processes. Flowcharting software is readily available, becoming more standard in companies, and is likely to be compatible with standard word processing software.

Disadvantages

The flowchart format takes longer to develop with conventional office suite software or requires specialized software, which may not be standard in a company. Procedures written in the flowchart format may be nontraditional for many companies (but are becoming more popular, especially with quality assurance organizations and process improvement teams). Some employees may need training and time to adjust to it depending upon the software used. Procedures written in flowchart format may not lend themselves well to text-based importing and exporting activities.

Process map. The flowchart format modified to include additional dimensions, such as multiple functions and decision points, becomes a process map. If a process is cross-functional, maps are an especially useful tool for improving it. Process maps accomplish two major objectives: They document primary steps in a process, and they show the relationship between functions involved in a process. In improvement efforts, teams use process maps to analyze the way a process currently is being accomplished, develop a better way, and then implement the changes. As a procedure format, the process map documents primary steps in a process and shows the relationship between responsibilities or functions involved in the steps. Process maps graph movement and direction. Teams use the process map format as a preliminary step in writing a traditional procedure, especially if more than one function is involved. An example of a process map is presented in Figure 3.11. Groups involved in the process are listed on the left. On the right are rectangles that show process activities and ovals depicting measurement points.

Advantages

The process map graphic format, like the flowchart's, is easier for many people to follow than written procedures, especially if proficiency is limited in the primary language of the documentation. Process mapping software is becoming more available and may be standard in a company. Process maps can show cross-functional responsibilities at a glance. Procedures represented in process map format show activities occurring simultaneously.

Disadvantages

Like the flowchart format, the process map's takes longer to develop with conventional office suite software. Process mapping software may not be standard in a company. Procedures written in the process map format are nontraditional (but, like the flowchart format, are becoming popular with quality assurance organizations and process improvement teams). Most employees need training and time to adjust to the process map format. Procedures written as process maps may be difficult to import and export with text-based software.

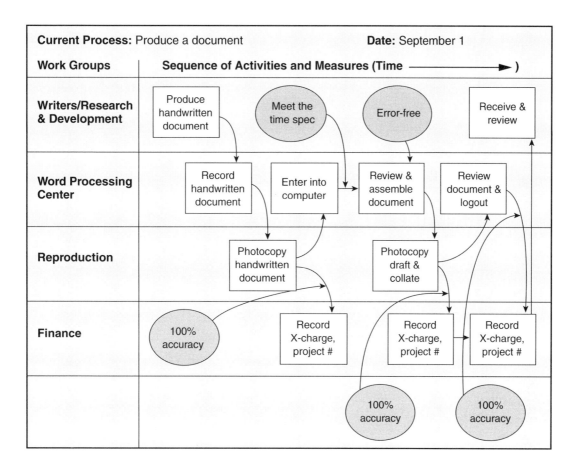

Source: The Rummler-Brache Group. *Cross-Functional Process Flow*, 1987. Adapted and used with permission.

Figure 3.11   Process map example.

Video. Organizations are beginning to use video formats for their procedures. Video clips are getting easier to include in computer-delivered documentation. Video is an acceptable alternative to written procedures for meeting quality and industry standards, such as ANSI/ISO/ASQ Q9001-2000.

Advantages

Video is useful for showing a technical process in detail and for a multilingual workforce. Sophisticated videos can illustrate several processes or functions simultaneously. Employees are used to viewing monitors, like televisions, and generally find videos more appealing than written or graphic documents.

Disadvantages

Videos are costly to produce, compared with other procedure formats, and are costly to update as processes change. Equipment for showing videos may not be readily available at all sites where procedures are needed in an organization. It may be time-consuming to access just a small piece of information at a time. Not all auditors accept videos yet in lieu of more traditional procedure formats.

Audio. A few organizations take advantage of the benefits of spoken procedures, either on tape, compact disk (CD), or from a computer.

Advantages

An audio format makes sense for visually impaired employees. It is also useful for sighted employees who have limited reading skills or for those who wish to learn a process while driving or in other alternative settings.

Disadvantages

Formats other than audio generally are more useful for locating small segments of information quickly. However, segmented audio clips in computer software are becoming more commonplace. Audio recorded procedures may be costly to update.

Web. All of the formats described in this chapter may be used on a Web site—Internet or intranet—particularly for procedures rendered as a PDF (Portable Document Format) file, which essentially provides a picture of the document. The Web presents some unique alternatives to hard copy, video, or audio publication. Instead of separate procedures to guide users through a traditional manual, Web help software, such as ForeHelp, RoboHelp, and True Help, assists viewers at the point of use (see Appendix C, Resources, Software, Online Help). For example, hovering a mouse over a field on an online form can display an instruction for completing the field. A hyperlink embedded in an online procedure can supply a definition for unusual vocabulary, precluding the need for a definitions section in each procedure. Viewers who are familiar with the vocabulary can skip the link and continue reading without interruption. Online authoring software can serve as a one-stop shop for writing and editing procedures.

Advantages

A procedure available on an intranet or Internet can take on many of the format characteristics of its hard copy siblings. It can be easy to maintain and search for information, and can save paper. A Web-based procedure can include video and audio clips to illustrate processes. Web links can eliminate the need for some sections of procedures, for example, definitions or glossaries and reference lists. Web procedures can accommodate graphics. Web procedures rendered in HTML (hypertext markup language) can cross platforms, thereby affording access by both PC and Macintosh computers. Online authoring tools can assist writers and editors in developing procedures. Many users, especially the younger or more technologically savvy, are apt to perceive Web-based procedures as more contemporary and less bureaucratic.

Disadvantages

Online procedures can present the same disadvantages as similarly formatted hard copy procedures. Graphics or other elements may not appear as intended on some monitors. Some employees, for example in the field or at security posts, may not have ready access to the Web. Other locations, such as destructive environments, may preclude computer access. Online documents are not as portable for many users unless the documents are printed out first, which can negate many of their advantages. Online procedures may be temporarily unavailable because of system maintenance, power outages or other emergencies, or disasters, or unavailability of qualified personnel to maintain the system. Employees may need special training to create or access Web-based documentation. With

Table 3.3 Considerations for selecting procedure formats.

Considerations	Procedure Formats							
	Plain vanilla text	**Play script**	**Modular**	**Flowchart**	**Process map**	**Video**	**Audio**	**Web**
Time-consuming or costly to produce			X	X	X	X	X	X
Graphic				X	X	X		X
Written language reliant	X	X	X					
Special training needed			X	X	X			X
Dynamic				X	X	X		X
Shows multiple functions at glance					X	X		X
High-tech look		X	X	X	X	X		X
Paper and screen thrifty	X							X
Good prelim to written				X	X			
Easy to find info		X	X		X			X
Shows decision points			X	X	X			X
Good for text-based import and export	X	X	X					
Good for visually impaired							X	
Good for hearing impaired	X	X	X	X	X	X		X

some applications, users may have difficulty seeing the big picture at a glance, for example, with organization charts that have no readily available zoom feature. Wide availability of online authoring tools may promote publication of poorly written procedures.

Table 3.3 summarizes major considerations for selecting the procedure formats just described.

Format Elements

Few topics related to documentation attract as much controversy as the elements to include in a document. Some insist that all procedures should have a purpose or rationale statement. Others see this element as redundant.

Going back to the basics of Nimble Documentation,® the zero-based approach is extended to format elements. In chapter 2, the litmus test was presented for deciding whether to include a document. This customer-based test asks if the document is required by law, contract, or prudent business practice, including quality and industry standards, and whether the organization will be harmed if the document were not there. The litmus test also asks if any harm would come to an organization if the document were included. Applying the test to format elements, ask: Is the element required by law, contract, or prudent business? Will the organization be harmed if the element were omitted? Will the organization be harmed if the element were there?

Try the litmus test with one of the most controversial elements, the purpose statement, which is found at the top of plain vanilla text, play script, and other formats for policies, procedures, work instructions, and other documents. Does any law require a purpose statement? Does a contract require it? What about prudent business? Can you think of any standard that specifies a statement of purpose? Is there anyone who can prove his or her organization will be hurt if a procedure goes without a purpose statement? What about harm if a purposeless purpose statement remained in the document? Few purpose statements pass the litmus test. An alternative is to strengthen the title so the document's purpose is clear. Banish statements like:

> **PURPOSE:**   The purpose of this procedure is to establish a procedure to . . .

Review other documentation for similar statements. Instead of beginning a memorandum with, "The purpose of this memo is to . . . ," write a clear and concise subject line. Tell the purpose of a letter directly, without telling your readers, "The purpose of this letter is to . . ." If the purpose of your document is unclear on its own, rewrite it so it is clear.

When an organization establishes a system for the first time or embarks upon a major documentation overhaul, a fine opportunity emerges to assemble document owners, usually representatives of functional areas, and ask them what elements they need. Hold a focus group meeting and challenge participants to show why they need a purpose statement or any other element. Many organizations have done that and, along with other streamlining actions, cut the page count of written procedures by about one-third to one-half, or more. Keeping out unneeded document elements allows readers to locate information faster, reduces processing and maintenance time, and lowers expenses.

Other document elements that are candidates for the litmus test follow, along with considerations for their inclusion. Be sure to see chapter 4, too, for document elements, such as navigation tools, that apply most often to Web-based documentation, for example, links, frames, graphics, and help functions.

- Organization name
- Logo
- Document-group title
- Document title
- Sections

- Document number
- Date
- Revision letter or number
- Page number
- Approval

- Related documents
- Numbering scheme
- Forms
- Definitions
- Records

- Font or typeface
- Justification
- Readability
- Headings
- Styles

Organization name. Readers expect the company or division name to be at the top of a document. That is where readers are likely to look first. Headers that include the organization name on every page help readers distinguish a document source, which is especially useful with suppliers, customers, or partners; or parent, sibling, or offspring organizations, for example, corporations, divisions, and subsidiaries. The most nimble online systems are capable of heading printouts with the company or division name. Printed pages have a way of getting separated; an organization name on each page aids in their identification. Web pages likewise should identify the organization.

Logo. The decision to include a logo—preferably in the header, where people usually expect it to be—is based upon several factors. One is the importance of quick identification. Is a hard copy document likely to be mixed with others from other organizations, for example, a purchase order or letter? Another is the organization image. Will a logo-graced newsletter help market a school district department's services? Will a logo-topped quality policy help corporate divisions blend after a consolidation or merger? Consider omitting the logo or using a simpler one if it slows Web site viewing or becomes scrambled on systems that lack more sophisticated software.

Document-group title. A corporate policies and procedures manual is a document group. Naming the manual, again preferably in the header, helps distinguish the document's source in the same way as the organization name. Although this element becomes less important as organizations use electronic document management systems, which can search across manuals, world-class systems name document groups on every printed or online printable page.

Document title. The same considerations apply to memoranda and e-mail subject lines as to directive document titles. Include a title that covers the scope of the document, yet is concise. Save readers' time thumbing or scrolling through the wrong documents. Preclude the need for a purpose statement. A memo inviting employees to a meeting that will address vacation policies should be introduced by a subject line something like:

> **SUBJECT: Meeting to Address Vacation Policies**

In very busy offices, including the meeting date in the subject line might be even better for catching the attention of readers so they will put the meeting on their schedules, for example:

> **SUBJECT: Meeting 9/15/2001 to Address Vacation Policies**

A too-general subject line is likely to fall to the bottom of a paper pile or e-mail in-box, such as:

SUBJECT: Administrative Meeting

Document number. Many document number schemes are serviceable. The handiest correspond to quality or industry standards. For example, a distributor adopts a document number scheme for its work instructions according to ANSI/ISO/ASQ Q9001-2000. The work instruction for "Buyer" is numbered 7.4, akin to ISO 9001's section *7.4, Purchasing.* A credit reporting service uses Form 8.5.2 for its "Corrective Action Report," which corresponds to ANSI/ISO/ASQ Q9001-2000 section *8.5.2, Corrective Action.* The best document number system defines a clear flow down from higher level or broader documents. The same number stems are assigned to a policy, for example, and related procedures, forms, and records (such as financial policy number FL-3 and procedure FLP-3.4). An integrated number scheme for an organization's entire documentation system facilitates information access and includes documents from policies to desk or work instructions to forms and records.

A minor consideration for document number is the number format. Before a documentation improvement initiative, one company division numbered its procedures the same way it formatted the date on those procedures: 09-04-03 and 09-04-96, respectively. The fact that these two numbers were immediately above one another in the header sometimes confused readers, if only for a moment. Fortunately, the division redesigned the date format to include slash rather than dash separators: 09/04/96. It was easier for readers than renumbering procedures. Another option would have been to spell out the date: September 4, 1996, which also avoids confusions based on the century.

Date. See the *Document number* section regarding possible confusion between a document number and the day it was issued. In many organizations, the date a document is published is not the same date it is signed. Does date mean the day the document appears online or the day copies are distributed? Or does it represent the day the document owner approved it? Legal challenges have been raised regarding the date that an HR policy was in effect and conflicting interpretations of the document's date. Avoid diverting your organization's resources needlessly. If an element is likely to be interpreted in more than one way, either revise the element (for example, change this one to *date published* or *effective date*), or define format elements in the system's enabling document.

Also, consider that traditional formats for dates vary among nations. For example, in the United States, MMDDYY (Month Day Year) is common, although DDMMYY is used sometimes. In Europe and Asia, however, DDMMYY is the traditional date format. Organizations doing business internationally should know that 3-12-03, for example, may mean March 12, 2003 in one country, but December 3, 2003 in another. A four-digit year also helps prevent misunderstandings.

Revision letter or number. Revision letters or numbers on procedures, forms, and records may be a quick way to determine a document's version. Some standards auditors insist on including revision letters or numbers. However, if the date is clear and there is no need to identify the document's original issue, a revision letter or number is redundant. It is an additional element to process and maintain.

Page number. To prevent separating document parts unintentionally or having recipients read just one side of a document that is printed back-to-back, include the statement *page X of Y*. If another element clearly indicates the end of a one-pager, for example a closing or signature line, a page number is unnecessary.

Lengthy hard copy manuals that are revised frequently should be paginated by sections. That way, users can add or replace pages without reissuing the entire manual. One common numbering scheme is I-1, I-2, I-3 (for the first section), II-1, II-2, II-3 (for the second), and so on. Use a loose-leaf binder or another binding method that permits easy page insertion and removal.

Sections. What sections should be in a procedure? The answer depends on several factors. Include a *Scope* section only if some documents apply to only some employees, processes, sites, or divisions. Some organizations use the term *Applicability* or *Applies To* instead of *Scope*. Use a *General* section, and then another section below it, if some information in the document applies to all processes or functions under the title's umbrella (goes in the *General* section), but some information applies only to portions of it (goes in a subsequent section, for example, *Sampling Separation*). Include *Policy* (or *Procedure*) and *Responsibilities* sections if they need to be distinguished from each other. Whatever you do, don't repeat information in both places. If the process is more important than who or what function performs it, use only a *Policy* (or *Procedure*) section. If the opposite is true, format the document according to *Responsibilities*, referring to processes in the context of the performing position or function. It is acceptable to have some documents in a manual follow a *Policy* format and others a *Responsibilities* format. Figure 3.12 shows an operating procedure formatted according to *Responsibilities*. Note a *Scope* section is included because the company has branches in other states where different procedures are followed.

Related documents. Documents accessible through an online document management system that has a powerful search engine may not need this section. It is a remnant of hard copy manual days. It is expensive to maintain and prone to audit problems. Every time a referenced document is added or deleted, all documents that refer to the addition or deletion need to be located and then updated. Viewers can search for a term online and locate all related documents. However, where it is necessary to consult documents that may not be online, for example, manufacturers' specifications, a *Related Documents* section could be essential. An organization may be able to delete this section even in a hard copy documentation system if the system's structure is especially clear and information overlap across documents is rare. Other terms for this section are *Applicable Documents* and *Relevant Documents*.

Numbering scheme. Numbering schemes for document groups were discussed in the Hierarchy and Structure section of this chapter. Internal numbering, especially for directive documents, applies to document sections and paragraphs. Several factors contribute to the choice of numbering scheme, including communication ease, online versus hard copy system, and aesthetics. Documents that change frequently or are reviewed often by outside organizations may benefit from a scheme where every paragraph, subparagraph, and point is numbered. That makes it easier for employees, auditors, vendors, and others to communicate about individual paragraphs. In such situations and for the same reasons, bullets are discouraged. In a complex document, however, subparagraphs could push numbers to the fifth place or further, for example paragraph 6.1.2.2.3. The

[LOGO] ABC Company

Operating Procedure

Forms Management System

Number:	ABCP 4-2-4b
Date Issued:	August 7, 2003
Page:	1 of 1

1.0 SCOPE

Applies to business transactions between ABC Company (ABC) employees in Santa Ana and with ABC customers, co-marketers, vendors, and visitors.

2.0 RESPONSIBILITIES

2.1 Administration or Designee

A. Maintains a consistent forms management system to authorize, communicate, clarify, simplify, and control business transactions.

B. Assigns form numbers that correspond to ABC's quality system requirements.

C. Maintains and periodically distributes an index of ABC's current forms.

D. Reviews and coordinates new or revised forms to meet ABC's business goals, including improving the efficiency of information handling.

E. Reviews and coordinates requests to cancel obsolete forms or forms that no longer meet ABC's business goals.

F. Submits requests to Purchasing to print ABC forms used in large quantities.

G. Maintains stock of frequently used forms to meet user demand.

H. Maintains on ABC's server a master copy of each infrequently used form for employees to print as needed.

I. Maintains master copies and history files of ABC's forms.

J. Coordinates periodic reviews of forms for currentness and continuing need, and maintains records of the reviews.

2.2 Managers, Supervisors, or Designees

A. Originate new forms, or revisions, pertaining to business transactions involving functions under their responsibility.

B. Approve cancellation of obsolete forms or forms that no longer meet ABC's business goals.

2.3 Purchasing

Arranges printing of ABC forms used in large quantities.

Wee R. Nimble, Chief Operations Officer

Figure 3.12 ABC forms management system operating procedure.

document then is cluttered with numbers and consumes a lot of paper or screens. It also looks uninviting. A compromise is to number to the second or third place, and then use letters, or to mix numbers and letters, including Roman numerals.

As already mentioned, numbers rather than bullets aid in communicating about particular document segments. For immediate impact, however, such as in marketing pieces or critical memos, bullets are preferred instead of numerals because bullets minimize the amount of discrete information presented to the reader. They "hit" the reader more quickly. Every numeral in a sequence is a new bit of information that readers have to process. It takes readers slightly longer to comprehend numbered items versus bulleted ones:

1. Plastic pouches are stored above the bench.

2. Metal ties are stored below the bench.

3. The Traveler is fastened to the front of the batch.

On the other hand, every bulleted item, beginning the same, does not need the additional processing:

- Plastic pouches are stored above the bench.

- Metal ties are stored below the bench.

- The Traveler is fastened to the front of the batch.

Online systems may pose a special challenge to document numbering schemes. Scrolling lengthy documents without plentiful paragraph numbers as guideposts can disorient a user. For example, in the middle of a screen, a user sees paragraphs C and D. There is no indication what section or major paragraph the user is viewing. If the document were in hard copy, on the other hand, the reader could easily see several pages of it at the same time. Aesthetics may need to take a secondary role to users' convenience, and all paragraphs, subparagraphs, and points may need to be numbered.

However, to convey a breezier image, aesthetics may be placed above other considerations. For example, only major headings and paragraphs could be numbered in a work instruction that serves as a marketing piece for a desktop publishing firm. Leaving many headings and paragraphs unnumbered can present a less "procedurish" image.

Forms. Don't include copies of forms in policies, procedures, work instructions, or any other directive document—period. And don't even consider generating a separate procedure for filling out a form. When a form changes, which happens often in growing, merging, or reengineered organizations, if a copy of the form is incorporated in a document, the document becomes obsolete and must be updated. Refer to a form by name or number, not revision or date, in the body of the document. There is no need to list forms again in a *Forms* section. Users—people who fill out forms—should not have to open an online procedure or locate a hard copy manual to complete a form. Make the form clear so instructions are unnecessary; try a new form draft on people unfamiliar with the form's processes. Revise any unclear parts. If a hard copy form is necessarily complex, place instructions on the back of it. If it is computer-generated on demand and prints only on one side, include instructions on the face, but only for the potentially confusing parts. Or insert a link to the online form.

Definitions. Some standards and regulations require that documents segregate definitions at the beginning or end of them for specified terms or words with special interpretations. More often, terms are consigned to a *Definitions* section by tradition. The best place to define a special term is in the body of a document, where the term is used, unless the term is used in many places in the document. That way, the reader does not have to flip pages or scroll to understand a process. The best way to define terms is with documents on an intranet. In each document that requires a definition for a specific term, embed a link to the term's definition. That way, a reader who already understands the term won't be distracted, and a reader who doesn't can get the information quickly. A common online database for definitions, with links to it, can prevent multiple interpretations of a term and reduce the burden of maintaining definitions in many spots.

Records. A section that lists related records, such as forms, may be useful to include in a hard copy procedure. However, inclusion imposes additional maintenance activity and may introduce opportunity for error: If a record changes, then the procedure needs to be revised. Listing records without revision dates can help minimize maintenance requirements. For online documents, links to the records themselves conveniently replace records lists.

Approval. Many specifications and standards, such as ANSI/ISO/ASQ Q9001-2000, require approval of initial documentation and revisions. Approval can be identified by a hard copy signature or by an online printed name (approval line) backed up by a signature or password-approved master. Organizations automating their documentation systems often fail to adopt a different set of considerations for their online systems. For example, a signature line at the bottom of a hard copy document may be appropriate. Readers can see at a glance the authority for the document. Online, however, the approval should be indicated at the top of a document. Readers should not have to scroll to the end, or press a quick key, to find out who authorized the document. To facilitate updating some documents without reissuing a manual, approval for each document is recommended over a single one for an entire manual. Also consider the many electronic document control software packages that sport built-in online approval. (See chapters 5 and 9 for more on electronic and digital signatures.)

Font or Typeface. Technically speaking, *typefaces* are the source of *fonts*, such as computer screen fonts (generally jagged-looking bitmapped characters) and printer fonts (smooth, ink-printed characters). Commonly, however, font and typeface are used interchangeably. Typefaces generally fall into two categories: (1) serif and (2) sans serif (without serifs). In simple terms, letters in a serif typeface, such as Times New Roman or Times, have curvy ends and those in a sans serif typeface, such as Arial or Helvetica, have straight or unadorned ends. For many people, serif typefaces are easier to read and more comfortable for extended or continuous text, primarily because the curliness helps readers distinguish individual letters and provides visual continuity across words. Also, for many, sans serif typefaces look cleaner and are more legible on computer screens. However, the research is inconclusive. Many writers use sans serif headings and serif body text in the same document for the best of both worlds. (See Schriver 1997 for a more detailed discussion of typeface.)

Justification. For years, writers have understood that right-justified text is hard to read. Some of the research that addresses the way the eyes move when people read finds that readers have more difficulty (take longer) sweeping back to the next line of text when text is right justified, partly because right-justified text is nearly always also left-justified, except for captions and form fields. It's a bit like trying to find a house in a row of matching houses. The eye flits back and forth and the reader sometimes loses his or her place in split seconds. Although newspapers tend to right-justify text, newspaper columns generally are much narrower than policies or procedures. For user-friendly business documentation, you would be wise, generally, to use ragged-right and not right-justified text.

Readability. *Readability* refers to how easy it is to read extended lengths of text, as opposed to *legibility*, which refers to how easy it is to recognize short bursts of text. Popular word processing software, and spelling and grammar checkers, often include estimates of readability. However, the estimates usually are from one readability formula, which can be misleading for some kinds of documents. Some readability formulas are based on the number of syllables, others on sentence length, and still others on word novelty. Formulas also include more than one element. Rely on factors other than the formulas alone when estimating the readability of a document. For example, first graders rarely have difficulty recognizing the word *dinosaur* because of their recreational experiences, such as movies, games, and coloring books. Yet, according to some readability indexes, *dinosaur* is higher than a 1.0 level word. Also, organizations often use polysyllabic technical words that are common either within the organization or its industry. Use readability estimates as one way to determine if the estimated reading level of a document matches the range of reading abilities of intended users. Consider adjusting sentence length, vocabulary, and other features to modify readability, if the estimated level and range differ significantly. (See chapter 4 for more guidance on readability.)

Headings. To help readers locate information readily, emphasize headings and subheadings by bold type or other means, make levels of headings consistent throughout each document, and use headings generously to break up long stretches of text. Take advantage of the styles feature built into popular word processing software, to reduce word processing time and so heading consistency can be maintained automatically when headings are revised (see more on styles, below).

Styles. Skilled writers and word processing professionals know that using styles in word processing software reduces processing time and inconsistencies. Using styles is more important today than ever because styles are the handle that allows documents to transport information into other applications nearly seamlessly. For example, styles defined in Microsoft Word become the basis for formatting documents in most Web-based help software, like RoboHelp or ForeHelp. Styles also enable automatic generation of tables of contents and other document features.

STYLE

This book includes a discussion on writing style because style can make a huge difference in how well documentation achieves its goals. Few people look forward to reading wordy, circuitous procedures. Few enjoy shoveling to dig out important information in a bulletin.

**Checklist 3.1:
Nimble
Writing Style**

❑ Write
   conversationally.

❑ Choose active
   versus passive
   voice according
   to goals.

❑ Emphasize.

❑ Be concise.

Nimble Documentation® is not only more pleasant to read, it is also more effective. It saves time. It is more likely to be read, so people will be less likely to make mistakes, displease customers, or incur liability. Comprehensive guidance on helpful, rather than hurtful, writing style is beyond the scope of this book; however, a few tips are offered in this section that can significantly improve the quality (read usefulness) of your documentation. The four areas are (1) conversational rather than musty style, (2) active versus passive voice, (3) emphasis, and (4) conciseness. Also addressed is a way to standardize your documentation to reduce time spent over resolving writing convention controversy.

Use a conversational style. Avoid rubber-stamped phrases. This is a problem especially with bulletins, reports, and forms, but also with employee policies. Here are some examples of rubber-stamped phrases:

- Attached you will find, as per your request, two copies of the form.

- Regarding the matter and due to the fact that the plant closes . . .

- This is to advise you that submitted herewith is your notification of our compliance with subject standards.

- We deem it a great pleasure to approve your request as per memo of the 12th of August.

Rubber-stamped phrases are called that because little thought is given to what value they add to writing. Habit dictates their use. Take them out. Write instead:

- We have attached two copies of the form.

- Attached are two copies of the form.

For the next ones, just state your message. Leave out the rubber stamps. For example:

- The plant closes on . . . .

- We comply with subject standards. See attached . . . .

- We approve your request of August 12.

Write active. Nothing tightens up a document faster than converting passive sentences to active ones. Long, passive constructions wear out readers. Here are examples:

- Passive example: Corrective action is escalated by supervisors.

- Active example: Supervisors escalate corrective action.

Write active sentences when the information must be clear and direct and when it is important to identify responsibility. The active voice may be inappropriate if you wish to de-emphasize the actor or emphasize the action. Switch to the passive voice when you want to hide the actor of your message, when the news is bad, when you want to be more tactful or soften the message, or when the action is more important than the actor. The subject of the sentence *performs* the action in the active voice. The subject *receives* the action in the passive voice. Here are a few examples:

Passive voice	**Active voice**
• A written evaluation will be made after six months of employment, which will be presented to the employee before a raise is recommended.	• The supervisor evaluates the employee's work in writing after six months of employment, then may recommend a raise.
• Initial figures for the bid are to be submitted before the June 1 deadline.	• Submit initial figures for the bid by May 30.
• When the quality plan is complete, it is to be rerouted for final approval.	• Reroute the completed quality plan for final approval.
• The raw data are submitted to Data Processing by the department rep every week on Friday.	• The department rep submits the raw data to Data Processing each Friday.

With passive writing you can reach your destination, but the path won't be as smooth, will take longer, could cost more, and may get you hurt or lost (see Figure 3.13).

Emphasize. Use space (sometimes called *white space*)—generous margins, and space above, between, and below—to call attention to critical information, such as steps that readers historically overlook, and processes that, if not followed, result in waste or confusion.

Use indentations, graphics, boxes, underscoring, **boldface type**, or *italics* to emphasize information. Too many kinds of emphasis in the document, however, confuse readers. Get over the novelty of nearly unlimited colors or typefaces. Too much variety is distracting. Construct sentences and paragraphs to call attention to segments of writing. Position the most important piece of information either first or last. Use very short sentences to invite reading. But vary sentence length or the emphasis-intended sentences will lose their power to attract.

Be concise. Get out that hoe and weed your documentation. Use one or two simple words instead of a phrase and avoid *dog puppies* (redundancies), like the ones in Figure 3.14.

To avoid wasting time repeatedly on editorial conventions, such as whether to capitalize a recurring term, a documentation team should adopt a writing style guide and perhaps issue a brief guide

Figure 3.13 The passive writing path.

tailored to any special editorial needs of the organization. *The Chicago Manual of Style* (University of Chicago Press 1993) is one style guide. Another is *The Microsoft Manual of Style for Technical Publications* (Microsoft Press 1998). There are many others. Choose one that is comfortable and abide by it. Most organizations have a few writing conventions that, when violated, upset a few staff, such as spelling out executive titles or capitalizing the word *company*. Include known preferences to smooth the writing process.

```
a bolt of lightning . . . . . . . . . . . . . . . . . . . . lightning
absolutely sure . . . . . . . . . . . . . . . . . . . . sure
advance warning . . . . . . . . . . . . . . . . . . . warning
bad disaster. . . . . . . . . . . . . . . . . . . . . . disaster
basic fundamentals . . . . . . . . . . . . . . . . . fundamentals
blend together . . . . . . . . . . . . . . . . . . . . . blend
blue in color. . . . . . . . . . . . . . . . . . . . . . blue
consensus of opinion . . . . . . . . . . . . . . . . consensus
continue on . . . . . . . . . . . . . . . . . . . . . . continue
cooperate together. . . . . . . . . . . . . . . . . . cooperate
during the course of. . . . . . . . . . . . . . . . . during
each and every . . . . . . . . . . . . . . . . . . . . each OR every
end result . . . . . . . . . . . . . . . . . . . . . . . result
final conclusion . . . . . . . . . . . . . . . . . . . . conclusion
first and foremost. . . . . . . . . . . . . . . . . . . first OR foremost
forever and ever. . . . . . . . . . . . . . . . . . . . forever
glance quickly . . . . . . . . . . . . . . . . . . . . . glance
kneel down . . . . . . . . . . . . . . . . . . . . . . kneel
large in size. . . . . . . . . . . . . . . . . . . . . . large
major breakthrough . . . . . . . . . . . . . . . . . breakthrough
mix together. . . . . . . . . . . . . . . . . . . . . . mix
new beginning . . . . . . . . . . . . . . . . . . . . beginning
new innovations. . . . . . . . . . . . . . . . . . . . innovations
passing fad . . . . . . . . . . . . . . . . . . . . . . fad
past history . . . . . . . . . . . . . . . . . . . . . . history
personal opinion . . . . . . . . . . . . . . . . . . . opinion
qualified expert . . . . . . . . . . . . . . . . . . . . expert
refer back . . . . . . . . . . . . . . . . . . . . . . . refer
```

Source: Adapted from Yvonne Lewis Day.

Figure 3.14   Dog puppies.

4

Usability

Solutions presented in this chapter address documentation challenges such as:

- Why take the time to perform usability testing?

- How useful are readability formulas?

- What are the basics of people-friendly Web design?

- Isn't *internationalization* a synonym for *translation*?

- What are the features of effective presentation slides?

The quality of documentation (whether instructions for assembling a wheelbarrow or policies for subcontracting quality assurance consulting) in many—some would argue, most—organizations is, at best, an afterthought. Ironically, some of the poorest-quality documentation we have seen is intended to fulfill the requirements of quality programs, such as corrective action or internal auditing procedures.

Consider that every document, or part of a document, written for an organization consumes at least some of the following resources: writer's salary and benefits; paper and pen, or hardware, software, and electronic media; facilities; utilities; review and approval; retention and retrieval provisions; and more—or contractor fees that bundle the other resources. Organizations pay a lot for documentation. What sense does it make not to ensure its quality?

Writing for the customer or user (see the bumper sticker proposed in chapter 2) and the cost of documentation demand that we determine how well we meet the customer or user's requirements and that we continuously monitor that determination. How do we do that? The same way as for any product or service routinely safeguarded by a quality assurance system—that is, by measuring or testing. In fact, a mantra for usable, responsive documentation could be: *Treat every document as you would your product or service.*

This chapter begins with an exploration of usability testing and its role in Nimble Documentation.® Then, the chapter explores readability and its impact on document quality, and the benefits and limitations of readability formulas. Another section presents the basics of people-friendly Web design, most of which apply as well to hard copy documentation. The section on internationalization addresses documentation for global markets. Finally, the chapter offers pointers on creating viewer-friendly, effective presentation slides.

USABILITY TESTING

Karen Schriver, in *Dynamics of Document Design* (1997), champions usability testing to ensure that documentation meets customer (reader or viewer) requirements. It is not enough to evaluate documentation by traditional standards such as grammar, usage, or the attractiveness of layout or graphics. A pretty document that doesn't help a customer or user accomplish the intended goal of the document is a bundle of resources misspent. A document that frustrates or angers a user is even worse.

Schriver outlines activities to test the usability of a document, the most important being to observe and query representatives of the customer or user population while they are reading or viewing the document. In one of Schriver's studies on usability testing, the tested document was a VCR instruction guide. A critical part of the testing was performing several tasks according to the guide. However, virtually any document could be tested for usability. For example, a corrective action procedure and corrective action request (CAR) could be tested with participants attempting to follow the procedure to enter information on the CAR. Representative customers could test a Web page for ordering products online. Usability testing can disclose important problems that even experienced writers, editors, and document design experts might fail to detect.

Surveys, questionnaires, and focus groups are other ways to determine a document's usability. Software developers and manufacturers, in particular, create special environments, such as usability laboratories, to observe users unobtrusively as they work with products prior to release or during improvement trials.

Several reasons justify the time and expense of conducting usability testing on documentation. One is to improve the comprehensibility of documentation. Sometimes writers are so close to the content that subconsciously they "fill in the gaps" when writing, leaving out information that readers need. Or writers may not know the correct information. Readers may be confused by the holey or erroneous document and (1) have to reread portions of it, which can be annoying and wastes time; (2) "fill the gaps" with inaccurate information, which often leads to frustration, or worse, if they are attempting to follow the document to perform an activity; or (3) give up reading and use another means to obtain information, which can mean phone number hunting, interrupting a colleague, or other burdensome action. None of the alternatives is attractive.

Another justification for usability testing is to help writers know their readers. Observing readers as they follow written procedures or hearing them think aloud about what they are reading releases important information about the documented process or product. Readers might reveal information about related processes or products, previously unreported problems, marketability, feasibility, or any other number of issues.

Finally, usability testing reveals how readers feel about themselves. Confused readers often blame themselves when documentation is difficult to read, which might be the last thing an organization wants. Assembly instructions, user manuals, or procedures that make readers feel stupid aren't likely to generate enthusiasm for a product or commitment to a process.

Although huge product rollouts might clearly justify extensive usability testing for user manuals or online help, how much and what kind of usability testing is right for a safety manual, quality procedure, or an intranet form?

Pinpointing the effort and expense that is reasonable for a given document is difficult. However, the litmus test can help. Assuming that the document passes the first four steps of the test—that is, the document is required by law, contract, or prudent business, and omitting it could be harmful—ask what harm could come to the organization if this document, or a part of it, existed? A safety manual for a nuclear power generator, obviously, warrants redundant usability testing to ensure that operators can follow the manual to the letter.

The amount of usability testing needed for a quality procedure is less clear, but, at the least, a group of employees or subcontractors or other business partners should read the procedure and use it to perform the process described. The best situation is to assign testers who are unfamiliar with the process described. If any problems surface, revise the procedure and test it again.

Test an intranet form by asking folks to complete it before the form is available to all intranet users. Posting the form to a dummy or non-production Web site often is a wise choice.

Measuring or observing the following characteristics, although not exhaustive, can help build a starter list for usability testing:

- Comfort/discomfort

- Speed

- Action/inactivity

- Meaning/confusion

- Perception

- Feelings, such as confidence or anxiety

- Abandoning the document

Observers can record users' comments by classification, measure and record speed by parts of the document or specific activities, or tally difficulties by classification or activity.

READABILITY

Readability refers to how easy it is to read a *lot* of text, extended text, pages and pages of text. *Legibility*, by contrast, refers to how easy it is to recognize short pieces of text, such as headlines, buttons, signs, and banners.

Although readability formulas largely have fallen out of favor (probably in part because of their limitations), they can be useful and generally are integrated into major word processing software.

Readability formulas can be used to evaluate the approximate difficulty level of reading material. Writers can use the formulas to help determine (don't overlook the word *help*) whether a piece of writing is suitable for its intended readership. Writers can apply the formulas after a rewrite to see if they've lowered the readability level sufficiently. (Presumably, readability formulas can be used to raise readability levels, but it is hard to think of a valid reason to do that.) Documents written at the sixth through eighth level of difficulty, commonly, are appropriate for the general population. Lower levels would be helpful for populations that have limited education or literacy or a primary language other than the one in which the document is written. Clear and generous graphics may help an otherwise higher level document be easier to understand even though readability formulas usually ignore graphics. Documents intended for highly educated readers or those with specialized technical vocabulary may be written at or may test at higher levels of readability.

George Spache, originator of the Spache Readability Formula, said that much of what constitutes a good story or those elements that produce highly readable factual material is elusive. Responsibly, Spache uses the term *estimation* to discuss readability. He notes four methods for estimating readability, only one of which is readability formulas:

1. Professional judgment

2. Grading by publishers

3. Book lists and indexes

4. Readability formulas

Professional judgment. Writers, editors, teachers, and librarians often depend upon their experiences and knowledge to judge the reading difficulty level of a document. Sometimes they are good at estimating, other times, not so good. Spache refers to children's books that don't sell and textbooks that are hard to read at their published grade levels because professional judgment has missed the mark. He admits that this method can be useful but lacks a point of reference and fine discriminations, as between successive age groups of readers.

Grading by publishers. Inexperienced professionals and textbook committees and commissions often rely on publishers' grade-level designations. But teachers often complain that publishers misgrade books.

Book lists and indexes. At least hundreds, maybe thousands, of book lists and indexes have been published that estimate readability. Earlier lists differ greatly from each other, placing the same books at widely varying levels. Later lists represent pools of opinions and so reduce the severity of the estimate error. But, according to Spache, group opinion does not guarantee accuracy.

Readability formulas. This method estimates the comparative difficulty of reading selections according to sentence length, word novelty, number of syllables, and other factors. The resulting levels are a practical way to express the material's reading difficulty.

Extensive research on readability shows that professional opinion and readability formulas tend to result in fairly close approximations of reading difficulty (or reading ease). So why bother with the formulas? The more data points of readability estimation, the better the determination of reading difficulty or ease. But don't rely on reading formulas alone.

Depending on the formula, readability formulas, according to critics, may overlook word context or syntax, paragraph structure, content organization, or subject matter difficulty (like the word *giraffe*—usually an easy word to understand if you are reading about animals or zoos). Others claim some readability formulas do consider those elements.

It is best to understand readability formulas, including their strengths and limitations, and learn how to apply them along with other methods for estimating reading difficulty or ease. Just add them to a writing and editing tool kit and pull them out when you think they can help.

Common word processing software has provisions for estimating readability, generally found within spelling and grammar checking tools. For example, at the end of the spell checking process, depending on the software settings, a number will be displayed for the *Flesch Reading Ease* and one for *Flesch-Kincaid Grade Level*. Consider these numbers estimates of readability. Because of the limitations of readability formulas, it might be best to use more than one formula to estimate the reading difficulty of a particular document or part.

A few of the readability formulas besides the Flesch (level 5 through college) are:

- Spache—used for reading material intended for grade levels 1, 2, or 3 and relies in part on a published word list.

- SMOG—used for levels 4 through 18, below.

- FOG—below.

- Fry—from Edward Fry, Rutgers University, for levels 1 through college—uses a published graph.

Several of the formulas and procedures for computing them are presented following.

Flesch Readability Formula

Use *sampling* for documents over about 500 words or *entire document* if the document is about 500 words or less, or if you want a closer estimate.

Sampling

1. Count at least three 100-word samples from the document.

2. Count the number of sentences in each sample.

3. Count the number of syllables in each sample.

4. Find the *average sentence length* by dividing the total number of words in all samples by the total number of sentences in all samples.

5. Find the *average number of syllables per 100 words* by dividing the total number of syllables in all samples by the number of samples.

6. Apply the steps in the Flesch Readability Formula, following.

Entire Document

1. Count the number of words in the entire document.

2. Count the number of sentences.

3. Find the *average sentence length* by dividing the number of words by the number of sentences.

4. Count the syllables.

5. Find the *average number of syllables per 100 words* by dividing the number of syllables by the number of words and multiplying the result by 100.

6. Apply the Flesch Readability Formula, following.

Flesch Readability Formula

1. Multiply the *average sentence length* by 1.015.

2. Multiply the *average number of syllables per 100 words* by .846.

3. Add the result of #1 and #2.

4. Subtract the result of #3 from 206.385.

5. Refer to the Flesch Scale.

Flesch Scale	
Result	**Level**
90–100	5
80–90	6
70–80	7
60–70	8 and 9
50–60	10–12
30–50	13–16 (college)
0–30	College graduate

SMOG Readability Formula

Sampling

Count 10 consecutive sentences near the beginning, 10 near the middle, and 10 near the end of a document. (The SMOG readability formula, apparently, is not intended for documents with fewer than 30 sentences.) Use the computation method immediately following or the word count table below the computation method.

1. From a total sample of 30 sentences, count words of three or more syllables, including repetitions.

2. Take the square root of the nearest perfect square (example below, so don't worry).

3. Add three (constant).

4. The result is the grade level.

Example of SMOG.
First sample = 21
Second sample = 14
Third sample = 32
Word count = 67
Square root of 64 = 8
SMOG = 8 + 3 = 11 grade

Or use the SMOG Conversion Table, below.

Total Word Count	Approximate Grade Level
0–2	4
3–6	5
7–12	6
13–20	7
21–30	8
31–42	9
43–56	10
57–72	11
73–90	12
91–110	13
111–132	14
133–156	15
157–182	16
183–210	17
211–240	18

FOG Readability Formula

Each element, that is, a word with one or two syllables, is assigned a point value of 1.

1. If a word has more than two syllables, assign it a value of 3.

2. Names, cities, states are each considered one element.

3. Add the total count. The sum is the FOG Count of the sentences.

4. Divide the FOG Count by the number of sentences. A semi-colon is considered a period for this purpose.

5. To find the grade level of difficulty:

If the FOG Count is 20 or more, divide by 2 to get the grade level of the sample.
If the FOG Count is under 20, subtract 2 and then divide by 2 to get the grade level.

According to literature about the FOG Readability Formula, to write within the comfortable reading level of the average person, keep the average FOG Count under 20.

WEB DESIGN

First, a caveat: Entire volumes are devoted to Web design. This section is not designed to explore Web design in depth, but to offer a few possibilities within the context of creating highly usable documents in the most general terms for both the Internet and an organization's intranet.

Robin Williams and John Tollett's *The Non-Designer's Web Book* (1998) presents several basics of Web design, seven of which we discuss in this chapter:

1. Alignment

2. Proximity

3. Repetition

4. Contrast

5. Navigation

6. Frames

7. Graphics

This chapter also addresses online help, which can be a channel to nimble policies, procedures, user manuals, and other business documentation.

Alignment

Many people confuse *alignment* with *justification* (as in *left justification*). *Aligned* text (and graphics) are lined up against an imaginary ruler. The ruler can be placed anywhere, not only along a screen edge. Visualize the ruler about two inches in from the left edge of the screen. Picture lines of text all starting along this ruler. Now place another ruler about two inches from the first. Line up some text along this line too (like in the second of two columns). Now move the imaginary ruler horizontally across the center of the screen. See the tops of the words lined up with each other against the ruler across the page. So alignment can be vertical or horizontal. Perhaps even diagonal? *Justified* text, however, usually means that lines of text are lined up against the left screen edge, the right edge, against both edges (which sometimes creates rivers of white space in the text), or centered. (See Figures 4.1 and 4.2 for examples of Web pages with mixed alignment and same alignment, respectively.)

Text aligned variously flush left, flush right, and centered—all on one screen—looks amateurish and information can be more difficult or slower to find. The rule of thumb here is to stick with one kind of alignment on a Web page, or maybe on the entire Web site. Web editing software generally provides for aligning text. Look first for the feature in the software's table tools.

Proximity

Proximity means the relationship of items, for example, text and graphics, to each other. Close proximity refers to items fairly close to each other. They seem to relate to one another. Items that are spaced too far apart make it harder for readers to relate the items together. If the space between all items is the same, it is difficult for readers to know which item belongs with which. Many forms, for instance, have field names positioned the same distance between two fields. The reader has to stop and decide to which field the field name belongs. A caption far from its graphic or a subhead far from its text produces the same result. (See Figures 4.3 and 4.4 for examples of Web pages with confusing and people-friendly proximity, respectively.)

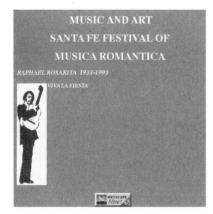

Source: Robin Williams and John Tollett. *The Non-Designer's Web Book*. Berkeley, CA: Peachpit Press, 1998. Used with permission.

Figure 4.1 Example of mixed alignment Web page.

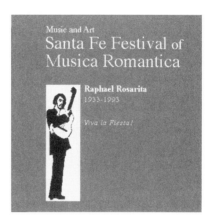

Source: Robin Williams and John Tollett. *The Non-Designer's Web Book*. Berkeley, CA: Peachpit Press, 1998. Used with permission.

Figure 4.2 Example of same alignment Web page.

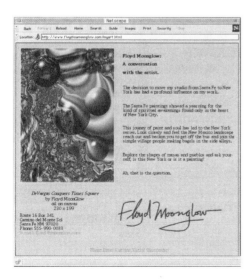

Source: Robin Williams and John Tollett. *The Non-Designer's Web Book*. Berkeley, CA: Peachpit Press, 1998. Used with permission.

Figure 4.3 Example of Web page with confusing proximity.

Source: Robin Williams and John Tollett. *The Non-Designer's Web Book*. Berkeley, CA: Peachpit Press, 1998. Used with permission.

Figure 4.4 Example of Web page with people-friendly proximity.

Repetition

The principle of *repetition* is repeating some elements throughout a Web site to tie all the pages together so the site looks like a family instead of unrelated people. It brings some of the same benefits of well-functioning family life: comfort, familiarity, and consistency. Repetition helps readers find their way back when links carry them to other sites. Web designers create repetition by placing a recognizable element at the same location on every page within a Web site, or by using the same color, same typeface, and same format for headings, links, bullets, and other elements. That way, readers quickly recognize a heading or other element for what it is. By seeing identical bullets, readers know that a given item belongs on a bulleted list, and so on. Readers don't have to learn the lay of the land, so to speak, for each new page they visit on the site.

Contrast

Contrast can grab attention on Web pages. The trick is to make the contrast strong. If the contrast is weak—for example, colors that differ just slightly from each other—then the message will be weak. If the goal is to draw an item out, then the goal in that case will be missed.

To achieve the greatest impact, choose one element, for example, color, and make it contrast strongly with nearly everything else on the page. A red word stands out from black words that surround it all over the page. A navy word doesn't stand out as much. If you don't want to interrupt readers' thoughts, however, limit contrast.

A contrast focal point is an element that dominates a page, by size, color, graphic, or other means. Use focal points to call attention to your organization, say via a logo, or to an important point, for example, with a bold graphic element:

See Figure 4.5 for examples of Web pages designed with confusing and effective contrast.

Navigation

The primary objective of navigation is to help viewers find their way to and from elements or pages of a Web site, both Internet and intranet. It is not novelty, creativity, or mastery of the latest design technology, although those objectives might be useful for other reasons. Although not its principal role, navigation tools that help make viewers' little journeys enjoyable can also help strengthen the goal of the Web page, as any document that is used to persuade, inform, or entertain. Standard navigation tools are text links, buttons, bars, and graphics, with or without animation.

Source: Robin Williams and John Tollett. *The Non-Designer's Web Book.* Berkeley, CA: Peachpit Press, 1998. Used with permission.

Figure 4.5   Examples of Web pages with confusing contrast (left) and effective contrast (right).

Navigation tools that deliver information to viewers quickly generally have the following characteristics:

- Recognizable as a navigation tool

- Grouped at one part of a page

- Available at several places on pages that require scrolling

- *You-are-here* signs

- Visible and useable with:

  - Common browsers, including recent older versions

  - Standard size monitors

  - Standard resolution

- Reasonably fast loading with common modems

Recognizable as a navigation tool. Few Web experiences are as frustrating as circling a page looking for the little hand (☝) or other symbol that indicates an active link. Sometimes parts of graphics intended to be links are inactive, coming alive only when the user clicks on exactly the right place. Other links are broken or too far from their text labels. Thoughtful designers place text links or descriptive labels that substitute for missing graphics.

Grouped at one part of a page. Grouping links at the top, side, or bottom of a Web page helps viewers locate them.

Available at several places on pages that require scrolling. Many Web visitors have short attention spans. Don't be stingy with links, especially on long pages. Repeat links so that they are visible wherever the viewer might be on a page. That might mean a graphic version of a link in a prominent place with its text twin somewhere else on the page.

You-are-here *signs.* Like on the directories in shopping malls, *you-are-here* signs help viewers find their way. Designs for *you-are-here* signs include links that change color during a visit to that page, lose their underscore, fade, open a small window, or become inactive.

Visible and useable with common browsers, including recent older versions, and standard size monitors at standard resolutions. As we go to press, Netscape Navigator and Microsoft Internet Explorer are the two most common browsers. Web pages that look wonderful with one may be misaligned or missing parts, graphics, links, or other elements with the other. Test the usability of each page with both browsers, including a few older versions, and revise the page if problems appear. Do the same with small, medium, and large monitors set at a couple of common screen resolutions. Not every user has the latest screen size or views with the same resolution.

Reasonably fast loading with common modems. As DSL, cable modems, and other telecommunications options replace dial-ups, more and more users enjoy faster and faster access to Web sites. Although for most situations, accommodating every type of vintage technology is unreasonable, consider users and present alternatives wherever feasible. Test pages to ensure fairly speedy loading with common access. Then, offer assistance for aged technology. For example, establish text placeholders for graphics that may take extra time to load on slower dial-up modems.

Additional characteristics may define desirable navigation tools, but when you consider navigation tools for the Internet or an intranet, go back to the last couple of questions of the litmus test for Nimble Documentation®: Ask if omitting the proposed tool would cause harm or if including it would.

Frames

Areas of a Web page that are separated from the rest of the page by a rule, color, pattern, graphic, or other visible means and that act apart from the rest of the page are called *frames*. Elements of frames can link with other page elements or other pages. Frames can be useful for keeping navigation tools visible in the same place on every Web page. However, frames can also pose problems with accessing a Web site or printing Web pages. Multiple frames, each with its own scroll bar, especially, can be distracting and annoying to users. Online menus embedded in frames can disappear when printing or can be the only portion of a page that prints. Common browsers may not readily find Web pages if the meta data (hidden information coded into a Web page) about the frame is placed in the wrong spot. Skillful and judicious use of frames is best left to experienced Web designers.

Graphics

Each of us has seen documents—both boring ones and jazzy ones—that are confusing because the graphics don't seem to go with the text or are useless. Either the graphics are too far away from the text (proximity) or they seem to be "saying" something different than the text. Or the graphic adds nothing of value to the document, but consumes memory and viewer time and attention.

This book does not attempt to explore Web graphics in depth, but offers a few basic pointers on the effective use of graphics, including placement, content, and color.

Placement. It seems an obvious mistake, but Web pages abound that place a picture or other graphic element far from the text that relates to it. And very large, especially colorful or dramatic, or high contrast graphics draw the viewer's attention, though sometimes *away* from the information that the writer wants the user to view. Also, consider the prime position for visibility. In most Western cultures, it is at the top right of the page. That is why newspapers typically feature important stories or photographs at the top right of the first page. The size and format of some newspapers were designed specifically to allow readers who fold them to comfortably read articles and view photographs in the upper right quadrant in their entirety, especially in tight places such as crowded subway cars. Similarly, the most coveted placement for display advertisements is at the upper right.

For most effective placement, put graphics very close to related text; use large, colorful, dramatic, or high contrast graphics only where you intend the viewer's eyes to go first; and place graphics on the upper right part of the page only when you want viewers to see the graphics first.

Content. Substantially identical content of graphics and text reinforce each other and generally strengthen viewers' comprehension. However, complementary content—that is graphics and text that have different content—may be effective if both are needed to help the viewer understand the information. For example, an image of a burning structure may be presented along with text that cautions the viewer to use safety procedures (see Figure 4.6). Graphics that are unrelated or only weakly related to text can confuse readers and slow information retrieval.

Never place heater near curtains, bed linens, furniture, or other objects that can catch fire.

Figure 4.6   Example of Web page with complementary graphic and text.

Color. Unlimited color schemes are tricky to use. Without special care, they can create visual clutter and obscure the intended message of the site. A limited color scheme used consistently can help to distinguish the site and strengthen the message. For example, a predominately green and gold scheme on the Web site of an organization involved in finance, such as a CPA firm or a bank or an accounting department, can communicate stability and prosperity. Similarly, the Web site for a medical device firm might use a clean white background with blue or black contrast elements to convey purity. Chocolate brown and tan might work nicely for a candy company.

Another consideration of color is technology. Although a technical discussion on color technology is outside the scope of this book, a couple of basic principles are presented here. Many graphic software applications have features for selecting RGB color (that is, the red, green, and blue light from monitor screens). RGB color differs from hard copy printing color, which is designated by CMYK (or cyan, magenta, yellow, and black [*k* is the last letter of *black*]). Browser-safe colors—that is, colors that appear true or nearly true on most monitors—can be designed with RGB color values. Or you can forget this whole discussion and rely on the colors presented by popular Web authoring software, such as Netscape Composer, Microsoft FrontPage, and Macromedia Dreamweaver. Monitor screen resolution is another important consideration. The resolution can affect the number of colors that can be displayed. The number of colors that a monitor can display makes a difference in the way a page looks. But only 216 colors are common to popular browsers and computer operating systems, or platforms. A greater number of colors can result in the browser mixing colors to approximate the desired color, which may not look good onscreen. Test your colors to see how they look on monitors at several common resolution settings, with different-sized monitors, and with a variety of popular browsers and common operating systems.

Online Help

A wonderful feature of electronic documentation is the capability of assisting users without disturbing those who need no assistance and without adding to the length of a given document. Online help can be as close as the click of a button at the point of use. For example, a user manual accessible on an intranet might have a challenging sequence of steps, each requiring complex processes. Online help can present links to detailed information or answers to questions about individual steps.

Well-designed online help can allow a user to click on the point of information and receive assistance in a separate window without needing to leave the page to look in another document, which can be a particular advantage for software documentation writers. Online help can include sound or video clips or other aids to understanding. (See Appendix C, Resources, Software, Online Help.)

INTERNATIONALIZATION

Global readership no longer is *becoming* a critical issue for documentation. It already is. Partly because the Internet has placed products and services in front of users all over the world and also because many nations have lowered their traditional trade barriers, international sales are rising. From employee recruiting brochures to ANSI/ISO/ASQ Q9001-2000-compliant procedures, and from operating instructions to online help, document creation and production have to meet many international requirements. Although language is the most obvious element of global documentation, it is not the only consideration. Internationalization "is a matter of designing your wares with the world in mind." (International Communications, 1999, p. 51). Documents that work well across international boundaries exclude references to individual culture and feature jargon-free content and stretchable layout, support for automated formatting, and standard conventions for graphics.

Humor—always a potential source of misunderstanding in communication—presents a special challenge for translating documents that lack non-verbal signals such as facial expressions. An e-mail message meant to be funny, for example, can be interpreted by a foreign reader literally or as sarcasm. Slang and idioms can confuse readers. For example, a literal translation of the English idiom "raining cats and dogs" might mean animals falling from the sky instead of a downpour of water. Cultural references, such as religious symbols and ethnic stereotypes, may offend. Metaphors that work in one region may confuse readers in another, such as those about cooking, money, or sports. Think of "dough," "clams," and "bucks" in English. Acronyms and abbreviations, unexplained, may defeat a document's goal, especially in languages that have no provision for them.

Because languages vary in the number and length of words needed to convey the same message, layouts that enable ready expansion or contraction minimize the production burden. For example, content that takes two pages in one language might take three in another.

Automated formatting maintains document consistency, speeds production, and contains costs. Use software-defined styles, rather than formatting individual characters or paragraphs, to keep accurate page numbering against tables of contents and figures, despite expanded or contracted translated content. Other candidates for automated formatting, depending on software, include headers and footers, index markers, and cross-references.

Another area of consideration is software capability for graphics. International Communications (1999) presents several guidelines for internationalizing graphics. Among them are industry-standard file formats and anchoring graphics to text. For example, software manuals that use cross-platform compatible screen captures such as TIFF or EPS formats are easier to convert. Similarly, anchoring graphics maintains the relationship between graphics and corresponding text, when expanded or contracted text repaginates.

Many other features that help preserve document accuracy and economy, particularly software capabilities, are outside this birds-eye view. Visit the Society for Technical Communication (STC) at www.stc.org for more information on internationalization.

PRESENTATION SLIDES

Let's look at the features of effective presentations. However, this section is not intended to address all the aspects of an effective presentation. For example, this section doesn't discuss issues such as managing stress, voice modulation, handling challenging participants, and contingency planning.

Presentation slides can be a form of documentation that meets the requirements and implications of quality initiatives, such as team reviews for Six Sigma (see chapter 7).

Effective presentations typically are built upon seven considerations: (1) objectives; (2) viewing audience; (3) repetition; (4) detail; (5) type; (6) graphics; and (7) suspense, surprise, and novelty.

Objectives

Like other documents, presentation slides (depending on the industry, sometimes known as *transparencies*, *viewgraphs*, or *vugraphs*) have or should have one or more objectives: (1) inform, (2) persuade, and (3) entertain. Identify the objectives early for efficiency and effectiveness in designing a presentation. For example, if one of the document's objectives is to entertain, consider funny graphics or surprises. If it is to persuade, consider building up a convincing argument by addressing and eliminating potential objections.

Viewing Audience

Who is the viewing audience? Why are they watching the presentation? How receptive are they? Are their minds open or already made up? If made up, are they for the presenter's approach or against it? Do they think well of your organization or is there an image problem? If you develop your presentation without identifying the audience, a fair chance exists of having the presentation fail, despite riveting graphics, legible type, and sexy technology like a state-of-the-art projection setup. If your audience is expected not to be receptive, consider beginning your presentation with telling them you know that. Be courageous and candid with your slides and the audience more likely will help you meet your objectives.

Repetition

You've heard it before: *Tell them what you are going to tell them. Tell them. Then tell them what you told them.* In other words, use an early slide to present an overview, contents list, syllabus, or agenda and repeat the slide at the end of the presentation. Superimposed on the graphic, list each major topic in the presentation. Some professional presenters say that people do not remember what they hear as well as they remember what they read or see. So in an oral presentation, repetition must make up the difference. State three times any idea you want your audience to retain.

Detail

A slide is not the place to present masses of detail. Any time that people spend straining to read the screen is time they are not listening to you or concentrating on your message. If your audience truly needs the detail to meet your objectives, put the details in a handout and tell them the details are there. Use as few slides as possible to convey your message. A 20-minute presentation shouldn't have 100 slides. Because it takes about 20 to 30 seconds just to focus on a chart if it is complex or in an unfamiliar style, be generous in allowing time not just to present slides, but to allow your audience to digest the thoughts behind them. If the idea or information is important enough to be in your presentation, it probably merits at least two minutes of discussion. So a 20-minute presentation should have no more than about eight or nine slides.

Type

Don't try to squeeze the entire presentation on one slide. Consider limiting your presentation to no more than 30 words per slide. Use simplified charts. Avoid detailed timelines. They can make some viewers seasick! Use only key words or phrases, not full sentences. If meaning isn't compromised, eliminate punctuation such as ending periods. Initial-capped, left justified, ragged right type is easier to read on a slide than right justified type set in full capitals. A general rule, depending on the typeface, color, and other factors, is to use at least 36-point type for body text, and larger type for headings and titles. For very small rooms and audiences, you can try smaller type, but don't get too used to it. Then, proofread, proofread, proofread your slides. Some people in your audience are compulsive editors and get distracted by typos. And they stop paying attention to the speaker or the message.

Graphics

Experiment with graphics to replace all or part of your words. But watch out for overused clip art, such as the bunch of people from Microsoft Office or the cartoon character looking through a magnifying glass.

Keep the background simple to help viewers focus on your message. Black or dark blue type on white or bright yellow gives high contrast. White or yellow type on black or dark blue background is even more effective for slides. However, if you must print out slides on slow inkjet printers, don't use a solid color background. Slides will use up too much ink and take a long time to print. Solid color backgrounds are best used with computer projection equipment.

Suspense, Surprise, Novelty

Microsoft PowerPoint and other popular presentation software are capable of introducing suspense, surprise, and novelty. In PowerPoint, click on the *Slide Show* menu to find many ways to enhance a presentation. You can add sound effects like a camera snapping a shot, have bullet points fly in from several directions, and have words and even letters appear in formation. Too much novelty, however, causes weariness and can confuse and distract people. Try inserting a couple of blank lines instead of text and have your audience suggest points to fill them in. The interaction keeps viewers attentive. For a challenging topic, consider listing a few points first and then a blank line or two. That helps viewers orient themselves to your content.

See Figure 4.7 to compare several ways of presenting the same content with varying degrees of effectiveness.

Slide 1: Too much text, no graphics.

Barriers to Learning

There are many barriers to effective learning. One of the worst things a presenter can do is to read notes verbatim. Another problem is when the organization is unclear. Especially if the presentation is given in a monotonous voice. And nobody wants to view one slide after another after another. Also, the content must be interesting to maintain viewers' interest.

Slide 2: Bullet text is effective, but graphics would help.

Barriers to Learning

- Reading notes verbatim
- Unclear organization
- Boring content
- Never-ending slides
- Monotone voice

Slide 3: Bullet text and graphics are effective. An option is to have individual bullets fly in as presenter addresses each.

Barriers to Learning

- Reading notes verbatim
- Unclear organization
- Boring content
- Never-ending slides
- Monotone voice

Slide 4: Presenter speaks content to maintain audience focus.

Barriers to Learning

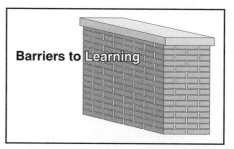

Slide 5: Structure enables audience interaction. Audience supplies bullet content.

Barriers to Learning

- _____
- _____
- _____
- _____
- _____

Figure 4.7 Presentation slides of varying effectiveness.

5

Electronic Options

Solutions presented in this chapter address documentation challenges such as:

- What is information management and knowledge management?

- What are the benefits of standardization?

- Why use an intranet for document management?

- What features should be considered when establishing an online documentation system?

- Who needs an e-mail policy?

- How can electronic imaging help and how can it hurt?

By far, the greatest gains in meeting customers' and other sources of needs and in reducing cycle time and costs of directive documents are in adopting an effective electronic document management system. Preparing documents with word processing or desktop publishing programs and placing them on computers, even providing access to them through a LAN, is not the same thing.

Nimble Documentation® demands consistent, streamlined processes to ensure reliable results, reduce processing time, and contain costs. When personnel performing the same function use the same processes (for example, tracking coordination of document reviews and uploading), they minimize opportunity for miscommunication and error. The rhythm of work continues uninterrupted if one person is absent. Further, as workload peaks and dips, standardization allows staff to perform understaffed functions temporarily. Automating processing facilitates standardization, and an electronic system can contribute to consistent, trim, and cost-effective documentation. However, processes should be automated only *after* zero-basing the documentation (see chapter 2) and improving the processes to eliminate defects and rework; automating inefficient processes *first* would only increase the rate at which mistakes are made.

This chapter begins with a discussion of information and knowledge management and the roles they are winning from document management. Then, the chapter addresses standardization, including references to a corporate documentation function that standardized its hardware and software. Next, the chapter presents major considerations for an automated document management system, including input, access, viewing, searching, printing, storage, logistics, and systems support. The chapter concludes with discussions of e-mail and electronic imaging.

INFORMATION MANAGEMENT AND KNOWLEDGE MANAGEMENT

Information management, until fairly recently, largely referred to handling, processing, storing, and retrieving *documents*—those tangible, recognizable information "containers," such as policies, procedures, memos, and handbooks. With the blistering speed with which electronic communications have transformed business processes, including the Web—the Internet, intranets, and extranets—information management and now knowledge management assumes a whole new meaning. A company policy is likely to be embedded in a Web page along with other company information. Technical specifications for a product manufactured by a company are written into the same database that holds the company's accounting procedures, although perhaps with a different degree of protection from unauthorized use. The lines separating documents and information or knowledge are blurring.

Authors tag chunks of information with often hidden *meta data*, that is, information about the information, such as category of information (for example, text or graphics); revision history; and information owner or custodian. Technical writers, editors, information owners, and others use the same chunks in e-mailed correspondence with suppliers, annual reports to stockholders, Internet order sheets for customers, and extranet lists for business partners.

Electronic portals accept user inquiries and deliver information seamlessly and transparently from multiple repositories and information systems, including legacy libraries, new databases, and diverse software applications. Data output from numerous sources and locations all over the world compiles neatly for many purposes, for example, reports, management and team reviews, and training curricula.

Although far from the only kind of information management or knowledge management, *single sourcing* promises one of the most nimble and economic approaches and is getting lots of attention. Essentially, single sourcing works like this. First, writers, editors, and information owners or managers profile target or user communities and identify required output. They skillfully write, or reuse what others have written, and tag the information electronically according to highly standardized rules. Then they deliver the information in all sorts of formats and information products, including hard copy and electronic media. In its most advanced use, the information is reassembled according to the needs of individual recipients based on attributes such as geography, language, job function, income, and many others.

JoAnn Hackos and Ann Rockley (1999) identify company department sources that typically feed information into the single sourcing process, as follows.

Technical Documentation departments:

- User guides

- Online help

- Reference documents

- Reports

- Technical specifications and design documents

- Policies and procedures for internal staff and customers

- Intranets and extranets

Marketing and Public Affairs departments:

- Newsletters

- Brochures

- Product information sheets

- Proposals

- Press releases

- Speeches

- Presentations

- Web sites

- Responses to customer inquiries

Human Resources:

- Training materials

- Policies and procedures

Think of the applications in the quality assurance community: quality manuals, calibration reports, customer satisfaction surveys, cost-of-quality data, job descriptions, inspection records, vendor qualifications, and training assessments. Although implementing single sourcing requires investment—such as revising materials and retraining staff—especially at its initiation, consider the benefits. Just a few are: eliminated redundant or repetitive information, error reduction, increased productivity, shorter cycle time, and cost savings.

STANDARDIZATION

A documentation function typically realizes a fast return on investment when it standardizes computer hardware. The installation of new, standardized computers and peripherals, selected by a center of excellence (COE), is credited with maintaining one S&P department's productivity despite the retirement of several staff members. In the following case, standardization was so instrumental in process improvement that the positions left open by the retirees were withdrawn.

Under a reorganization plan, an S&P department had consolidated several groups that handled documentation at the same facility. Several employees came from a manufacturing division, where they coordinated, edited, and published product operations procedures. Others came from one of the company's IS departments, where they maintained the procedures manual. A property documentation function transferred in and so did the function that had handled configuration management procedures and engineering procedures. The department also included writers and editors who were responsible for a wide spectrum of procedures and bulletins, organizational announcements, organization charts and statements of responsibility, forms, and an approval authority system.

Employees from some of the functions came with their PCs. Others brought their Macintoshes. Some of the staff were trained to use, and happy with, obsolete word processing software. Others knew WordPerfect best. Most used Microsoft Word. Even the communications software varied. Existing documentation that required revision was embedded with fonts that were compatible with some of the printers but made other ones freeze. Some of the printers could be used only with some of the computers.

Staffing reductions compelled the department to find a more consistent way of doing business. A team investigated the feasibility and costs of standardizing the department's hardware and software. The team members interviewed each department staff member, found out his or her needs and experience, consulted with the IS department, and issued recommendations. They considered their customers' software because other functions frequently sent rough drafts on disk to the department. The team weighed the anticipated learning curve for new equipment and software. They looked at the department's graphics needs. But more than anything, the team members saw the labor expense of continuing to work with incompatible equipment and mismatched software. Their findings justified replacing nonstandard hardware and software and obtaining staff training.

To avoid disrupting service to customers, the department planned a step-by-step conversion, enlisting the aid of IS consultants when department expertise excluded some conversion steps. All department staff were trained before the switch was complete.

At another company, employees who handled the company's policies and procedures maintained two different databases for coordinating new documents and revisions. Each employee took responsibility for different sections of the manual and kept track of the process independently. One kept a computerized database; the other kept handwritten notes. When either person was unavailable, work in their sections halted. If a customer called, it was difficult to report document status.

Another way organizations can benefit from standardized documentation processes is to share macros and style sheets for word processing and other software. Experienced text processing specialists can establish shortcuts to formatting documents and post them on a networked server or intranet site so anyone assisting can maintain the processes. Having several procedure writers adjust individual paragraph formats is a big time waster. Also, the auto text feature of popular word processing packages can be used to standardize frequently used terms, saving time and reducing error potential. Consistent use of macros and style sheets can result in cycle time savings and fewer errors and is essential for managing information across delivery applications. The benefits of automating repetitive tasks are considerable—well worth the initial time and cost investment of advanced training.

Also, standard writing guides for documentation functions work wonders to maintain consistency and prevent needless controversy. Two guides are best: a published style manual and a list of organization-specific writing conventions.

Standardized processes and products have the greatest impact when:

- They meet customers' requirements

- The processes are used often

- They return quality, cost, or cycle time benefits over their expense

- Their intended users reach consensus

- Staff are trained in their use

- The standards are documented, accessible, and reviewed regularly for continued improvement

ELECTRONIC DOCUMENT MANAGEMENT

Just a few years ago, an exciting electronic document management system allowed key word searches across manuals and up and down tiers. Today, electronic networks, including intranets, speed document processing and access.

In the 1980s, Videotex by DEC could be customized to suit large documentation systems. Content owners specified keywords for each document, up to a limit that increased with each software upgrade. Staff trained on mainframes uploaded documents. Users could access the system on many kinds of terminals and by modem from remote locations: dumb terminals, workstations, and desktop computers. Menus listed documents, but they could be selected only by commands. Soon, the command legends appearing at the bottom of the screen that once were seen as helpful became annoying to users, who now were becoming familiar with graphical user interface (GUI) computers, such as the point-and-click Macintoshes and then Windows and other operating systems.

The mainframe-hosted document storage and retrieval systems were a tremendous improvement over hard copy manuals. Documentation functions of many large companies were transformed. Users, reluctant at first to part with paper, began to feel comfortable with online searching. Both management and audit personnel were happier because nearly every employee had access to up-to-date manuals. Revised hard copy keyword indexes, which consumed extensive resources to update, publish, and

Checklist 5.1: Considerations for Standardization

❏ Meets needs

❏ Frequently used

❏ Saves time

❏ Reduces or eliminates errors or rework

❏ Designated by consensus

❏ Cost reasonable for results

❏ Training available

❏ Documented

❏ Accessible

❏ Reviewed regularly

distribute, were obsolete even before they were delivered. With the online system, an updated index was accessible the same day a document was revised. Change notices no longer were necessary to publish and file. With minor programming, special menus could display all documents that were added, revised, or canceled over a recent, selected period of time, for example, 12 weeks—a boon for employees returning from travel or leave.

Today's online electronic document management systems have many additional features. Web-based systems have powerful search engines that allow sophisticated searching. Personnel who upload documents no longer need to enter keywords individually. Browsers now support context-specific searches and searches by synonyms, broader terms, narrower terms, and other options. Commands are no longer required; users can access documents by pointing and clicking.

Intranets are now one of the most versatile vehicles for online systems. Users typically access information via Netscape Navigator or Microsoft Internet Explorer, two standard browsers. Documentation staff upload new or revised documents and archive canceled ones. Scripts automate menu changes. Specially designed menus help users find information. Documents are listed several ways, including by document number and alphabetically by title. Users can find documents also on 12-week screens (new, revised, and canceled documents). They can also search for information by entering a document number, title, or topic. The Webmaster's e-mail link, posted at the bottom of each screen, gives users access to technical support.

An online system is an excellent medium for hosting quality system documentation, for example to comply with ANSI/ISO/ASQ Q9001-2000 or QS-9000 requirements. For both, a series of intranet pages or menus can be designed to link higher tier documents to lower tier ones. For example, clicking on a link embedded with the purchasing section in a quality system manual brings up a standard operating procedure on purchase orders and also work instructions for a buyer position. A world-class online system also includes links to related forms and data, such as vendor qualification forms and records of contract reviews, and both current and archived records are readily accessible. The benefits of such a system are: accessible, current document versions; no paper manuals for users to maintain (except a few for emergencies); printing on demand; reduced costs; reduced time from document approval to publication; and faster and less frustrating searching.

Increasingly, document management software designed specifically for quality systems is built for use on intranets. The software often integrates several document management functions in one package, for example, review and approval, corrective action coordination, "tickler" functions (reminders of actions due), forms development, data entry and compilation, procedure and flow chart development, and e-mail notification and distribution.

Other electronic document management systems feature Web-based authoring, which allows document owners to create or revise documents online, including meta data (information about the document, such as ownership, revision history, and identification). One of the challenges, however, of direct online authoring is ensuring that authors are skilled in producing highly readable documents. Often, unfortunately, directly authored documents reflect deficits in writing and editing skills, to the user's detriment. Rocket scientists, quality engineers, and accountants don't always produce clear and concise documents.

Writing and editing skills, already important for producing user-friendly documents, are becoming even more critical as document management moves toward information management and knowledge management and its emphasis on single sourcing (see the first section of this chapter).

SYSTEM FEATURES

Before organizations invest in hardware and software to convert their hard copy documentation, they would be wise to compare a list of world-class system features with their customers' requirements and their own current ability to meet those needs. Note that many of the listed features also apply well to CD distribution, an aid to organizations with security-restricted or otherwise limited telecommunications. In this alternative implementation, updated CDs are delivered regularly to replace obsolete ones, which are collected and reused. The following list includes features recommended for information input, access, viewing, searching, printing, storage, logistics, and systems support.

Input

Input features for standardized electronic document management systems focus on protecting information from unauthorized revision, two-way communication with users, timely review, and specialized training and skills.

"Locking" information through software and restricting input access to a few individuals, but including at least one backup, is essential to maintaining document integrity. Documents on the system are read-only to everyone else. The system should also allow distributed input, which means that authorized personnel at multiple locations can add, revise, or delete information. For example, a revision to the quality system manual may come from the quality assurance department or documentation function, or a job description may be uploaded in HR. In a distributed input system, entering information for each document is restricted specifically to that document.

Another input feature is the capacity for interaction, for example, to allow viewers to transmit questions and comments and to allow providers to respond. Often, response boxes are integrated into the system. This feature is used frequently to request items, such as preprinted forms, that may be unavailable online.

Compatibility with tickler software is an important input feature where providers are responsible for notifying personnel of document review dates at regular intervals. For example, if operating procedures specify that a document needs to be reviewed at least once every two years, the system should be able to integrate information accessed in advance with tickler software so staff will not have to reenter the same document information, such as document title, number, and review due date.

Systems that include or have options for training provide for smoother and quicker conversions. Training for those responsible for inputting documents pays off.

Checklist 5.2: Characteristics of an Electronic Document Management System

Input

❏ Protected, read-only

❏ Distributed

❏ Capacity for interaction, such as query and response forms

❏ Compatible with "tickler" software

❏ Specialized training

Access

❏ Link or jump readily between applications

❏ Link or jump readily between documents

❏ No special user password required

❏ Usage can be monitored

❏ Multiple computing platforms, if needed

❏ Compatible with company standard software

❏ Usable from/to remote sites

❏ Handles simultaneous users without queuing or slowing

Continued

❏ Reliable communications networks

❏ Terminals in common areas

Viewing

❏ Compatible with users' hardware and software, including graphics

❏ WYSIWYG (what you see [on the screen] is what you get)

❏ Text emphasis, such as underline, bold, italics

❏ Special characters, such as dashes, slashes

❏ Document number, date, and screen or page number

❏ Passive notification of revisions

❏ Addition, revision, and cancellation screens

❏ Automatic update of addition, revision, and cancellation screens

Searching

❏ Context specific

❏ Language relationships

Continued

Access

Several considerations for choosing a standardized, online system involve viewer access. The common denominator of the features is people-friendly access, which means compatibility, comfort, speed, and reliability. These features emphasize easy and fast movement between related applications and from document to document.

The best online systems allow users to link or jump readily between applications and documents, for example, from a standard operating procedure produced in a word processing program to an approval authority database. An intranet link can be constructed between the part of a procedure that specifies a form and the part of an approval authority database that lists the approval required for that specific form. Another example applies to a hierarchy of quality system documentation compliant with ANSI/ISO/ASQ Q9001-2000: links between the quality system manual, standard operating procedures, and work instructions. Recent versions of popular word processing software feature document links. Some of the most challenging links or jumps, however, are between unrelated systems, such as material handling or accounting systems and standard operating procedures.

To encourage users to access documents, and to avoid costly maintenance, avoid issuing special passwords for viewing. Either have a common password for all users (especially on a system where limited access is desired for some information), or configure a system to require no password.

To obtain data for continuous improvement to documentation, for example, to learn which documents are accessed and how often, include a feature that tallies usage by document group and specific document, such as all standard operating procedures or just procedure X. Intranet-based systems can be programmed readily to record and compile the number of visits to sites and pages.

Although desktop computers are moving toward operating seamlessly across platforms, such as PC and Macintosh, standardized hardware reduces time and cost of processes associated with access, for example, delivering training and preparing published instructions. Web-based systems generally disregard or minimize the impact of disparate platforms on access to information.

Another feature of a world-class documentation system is standard software, whose benefits extend beyond the electronic document management system. However, merged and reengineered organizations, understandably, sometimes are reluctant to adopt standard, organization-wide software, because of the inconvenience and initial investment of resources needed for conversion.

Successful document management systems address an organization's need for remote site access. As organizations expand globally, remote access becomes an increasingly frequent need. Internet and remote intranet access are options. Some organizations access documentation through telecommunications systems that have protected call-back features. CDs distributed by conventional channels can substitute for online access, but their use involves considerable regular maintenance.

Online systems should be able to handle multiple users simultaneously without slowing access. Organizations are wise to investigate the limits of their existing and proposed telecommunications resources, hardware, and software. Systems that work well for organizations with 50 employees sometimes fail with several hundred or several thousand. Benchmarking with similarly configured organizations often can provide the most helpful data for selecting the best system.

Easy, fast, and dependable online access can be no better than the weakest link in an organization's communications network. Functions that require close to 100 percent uptime, such as visitor authorization in a secure facility, will want to consider the reliability of communications in planning a system or deciding whether to retain backup hard copy at users' locations—for example, at plant entrances or emergency and disaster recovery control rooms.

A final consideration of access relates to common viewing stations. Although office workers generally have access to a personal or easily shared computer terminal, specialized manufacturing facilities, outdoor locations, and other work sites may prohibit close-at-hand electronic access. One solution is to install terminals in protected common areas where employees can access online documents. Cafeterias and break rooms, libraries, field office trailers, and central corridors are a few locations where employees can have common access.

Viewing

System features that allow all users to view information as intended are the most satisfactory and the most economical to maintain. Whenever special processes need to be implemented for just some users, the resulting variability introduces opportunities for errors and requires additional maintenance activity. For instance, two different sets of instructions may have to be written and maintained for viewing intranet documents at workstations that can display sophisticated graphics and those that cannot. The next best situation to standardized viewing capabilities is accommodating those differences, for example, embedding alternative directions where the graphics were intended to be seen. Unacceptable systems permit some stations to display a document as intended, and others to fill a screen with gibberish instead. People-friendliness is the common denominator of features for viewing documents, just as it is with access.

Printing

❏ To e-mail

❏ By document

❏ By screen

❏ Hard copy on demand (discouraged wholesale printing)

❏ Document number, date, and page

❏ Disclaimer

Storage

❏ Cost

❏ Transmission ease

❏ Protection

❏ Audit trails

❏ Retrieval ease

Logistics

❏ Usability

❏ Cost:

  ❏ Conversion

  ❏ Purchase

  ❏ Upgrades

❏ Electronic coordination and approval

❏ Alternatives for limited access

Systems Support

❏ Internal

❏ Outsourced

❏ Contract

Seldom do entire organizations purchase or upgrade their computers at the same time, except for small organizations and start-ups. Therefore, online documents usually are viewed through a variety of hardware and sometimes software. Graphics, such as logos and diagrams, that are legible on one monitor may be fuzzy, slow to appear, or not viewable at all on another. System standardization may require adding memory, upgrading video cards or software, or other modifications to handle graphics satisfactorily. Where upgrades are not feasible, care should be taken when inputting documents to ensure that the least sophisticated equipment can display all document features. That may mean simplifying some documents or document formats.

WYSIWYG (pronounced *whizzy wig*) stands for What You See Is What You Get. It means that a printed document looks exactly like it appears on a screen. Some systems do not deliver WYSIWYG to all workstations. Although not as common as a few years ago, screen-to-printout mismatches are still frustrating and can lead to withdrawal of support for online document systems. Documents sent through e-mail systems occasionally also have WYSIWYG difficulties, particularly in automatic features such as page numbering.

A system should be able to display emphasized text using, for example, bold, underlined, or italicized type. PDF documents, described earlier, are one solution. Intranet-based systems, generally, are another.

Special characters, such as dashes and slashes, may interfere with some system programming, but usually are not a problem with popular desktop applications.

Document numbers and revision dates on every page or screen, and page or screen numbers of total pages or screens (such as "page 2 of 4"), help viewers manage documentation. If a person needs to leave a screen temporarily, for instance to answer a telephone call, they can resume viewing activity quickly without needing to press keys to find out where they were.

Another helpful feature is to notify viewers passively when a document is revised, a new document is added, or an existing document is deleted. Passive notification means the user doesn't have to query the system to learn of changes. E-mail notification is one vehicle for this feature. E-mailed distribution can be customized according to document subject. For example, notice of revisions to documents in one manual, such as calibration procedures, can be sent only to employees involved in calibration processes. This feature is especially useful for reviewing a document prior to online publication; only key personnel receive notification of the changes to be reviewed. Alternatively, the entire document may be sent electronically to selected reviewers.

Inclusion of addition, revision, and cancellation screens aids viewers who may be unable to access the system for a considerable period of time, such as during vacations, leaves, or travel. Intranets can display such screens and link them directly to the referenced documents or to explanations for their cancellation. Rolling 12-week windows have worked well for many organizations. These screens and links usually are updated weekly, but can be updated according to the volume and frequency of changes. To reduce maintenance activity, screens and links can be programmed to update automatically as documents are revised on the system.

Searching

A few years ago, employees had to enter keywords for each document into the system one by one, and retrieval was limited to individual words or phrases. Software now has powerful search engines that are sensitive to context and language relationships. For example, by typing in the word *retail* and excluding *Retail Division*, a user can display all documents that address a company's retail issues, but not the many documents that include Retail Division, such as in the document headers of a Retail Division procedures manual. Viewers no longer have to guess the exact words the writer used in a document; instead, the system can display documents containing synonyms or other related terms. Software can locate information hierarchically related to entered words. For instance, if *banana* is entered, it can display information about *fruit* (more general) or about *plantains* (more specific), a type of banana. Programs can even show the various weighting of different documents—in other words, can arrange them by likely relevance. The best systems not only display documents, but zero in on places in the documents, paragraphs, and sentences where the searched information can be found.

Many Internet and intranet browsers offer excellent search capabilities. Some can be used to search an entire document system; others are organized by topic or by document subgroups (see Appendix C, Resources, Software, Web Site Searching).

At the most basic level, documents can be searched using common word processing software. However, organizing them as master documents with subdocuments allows greater search capabilities, for example, searching only certain sections within a manual. The biggest disadvantage to searching with word processing software alone—and the disadvantage is considerable—is the inability to search across an entire manual or document system.

Printing

Printing on demand and to a variety of media is an important system feature and is readily available through nearly all software. However, the capability to print out a whole manual with a mouse click may be counterproductive. Consideration should be given to configuring the system to restrict wholesale printing, especially when an organization is converting from a hard copy to online system. Printing out entire manuals provides neither the access, cost, or other benefits of online, nor the advantages of well-organized published hard copy manuals.

Capabilities should include printing by document, page, and screen, and printing to e-mail (sending documents as attachments). Systems should also have the ability to print automatically the document number, date, and page on each page printed out. Without that information, obsolete individual pages may find their way into reports and correspondence and compromise document integrity.

Automatically printing disclaimers can be useful in protecting an organization from reliance on obsolete documentation. A disclaimer printed at the foot of every page, for example, can state the prevailing relationship between the printed and online page and can affirm that the printout is effective only for a specified period of time (such as 24 hours).

Storage

Document management systems should meet several requirements, including cost, transmission ease, protection, audit trails, and retrieval ease.

Efficient systems transmit documents electronically from desktop to central or remote storage, usually across a network, thereby minimizing handling costs. Nearly all contemporary systems feature easy point-and-click file transfers to a storage server. On-site servers can be short-term repositories, and hardware at remote sites can meet long-term storage needs. Often—especially for smaller organizations—the server is little more than a high-capacity desktop computer, thereby containing system costs.

Sound document management systems require the preservation of document integrity, including restricted ability to add, revise, and delete documents. They also provide protection in the event of a disaster, such as fire or flooding. Saving files to floppy disks kept near a hard drive may be convenient, and unfortunately is one of the most common kinds of storage systems, but it is risky. The frequency of backing up documents depends on the volume and frequency of revisions. Regularly scheduled daily or weekly backups work well for organizations with fairly dynamic documentation systems. Organizations undergoing major reorganization or process improvements also benefit from frequent backups. The more automated the procedure, the greater the likelihood of consistent backups (see chapter 9 for more information on storage).

Maintaining document audit trails is another critical feature of a document management system. Earlier revisions and both merged and deleted documents can be archived automatically by the system and are retrievable within a reasonable time frame. To meet the requirements of ANSI/ISO/ASQ Q9001-2000, and good business practice, archived documents should be marked clearly or identified electronically to avoid confusing them with current documents, and history files should be traceable forward and backward.

Retrieval from electronic document storage can eliminate the requirement for multiple file copies and can introduce other efficiencies. For example, large organizations often issue organization charts by department. To facilitate retrieval, because of investigations or other litigation activity, they are often duplicated and filed both by department and date. Typical investigations need to determine the reporting structure in place at a given time, but some need to trace a particular department's reorganizations. Electronic databases require only single entries of the charts and permit sorting and retrieval either by date or department or some other attribute. Electronic retrieval should be fast and reliable.

Logistics

Practical considerations for an electronic document management system include usability (see chapter 4); reasonable costs for conversion, purchase, and upgrade; electronic coordination and approval; and alternatives for areas with limited access.

A system with the most sophisticated search capabilities and numerous features may be frustrating and costly if users require prolonged training. Such a system often also drains IS help desk resources. Organizations should also consider the expense of converting their existing document systems; the cost of purchasing hardware, software, and licensing agreements; and the often overlooked estimated expense of upgrades. Questions to ask include: How often are upgrades issued, and how extensive and expensive have they been in the past?

Another practical consideration is document coordination and approval. Typically, company documents require review and approval of several functions. A policy on employee training, for example, may be reviewed by HR, quality assurance, contracts, and purchasing functions. The hard copy approval process could be both paper- and time-consuming. Revisions are duplicated and mailed with a cover/response page. Reviewers comment or mark up the hard copy, usually duplicate and file their input, and mail the revision. Document coordination personnel compile responses and then reconcile differences among reviewers by telephone or meeting, or they mail a new revision.

With electronic coordination and approval, document revisions are placed online and reviewers are notified through the online system, usually by e-mail. Reviewers can comment directly on the system and can view and respond to other reviewers' responses. Software allows reviewers to post electronic "sticky notes" directly on the online documents. The more sophisticated systems permit electronic approval of the final document, which is then published on the system.

Finally, organizations that have limited or no access to conventional electronic distribution or display should consider the practicality of alternative distribution, such as CDs. Systems that allow easy information transfer to alternative document delivery are worth seeking for such organizations.

Systems Support

Organizations that have an internal information systems function often can provide the technical support to install, customize, and manage an online document storage and retrieval system. Frequently, however, internal IS functions are challenged to meet existing demands and are unavailable to take on the project. Two alternatives to internal support include outsourcing the application or temporarily hiring consultants to establish the system, who then turn it over to internal personnel to manage. The following list of major activities typically requested of IS personnel could be a blueprint for organizations seeking the same kind of support:

- Assign an IS department project manager to coordinate support for accessing and searching documents on the intranet.

- Consult with the documentation improvement team to schedule activities that result in online, searchable access to the streamlined documents by a given date.

- Install server software and all software needed by at least one representative in each function for browsing, searching, displaying, and printing documents.

- Advise the documentation improvement team on access alternatives for limited-access areas, for example, disks or CDs.

- Establish and document uploading procedures, including for new or revised documents and cancellations.

- Advise the documentation improvement team on procedures and provide necessary support for e-mail notification of new or revised documents and cancellations.

- Establish and maintain hot line support during the installation of the online system. Maintain data and provide reports of problems and questions to be used to continuously improve the system and indicate training and online help requirements.

- Train users in accessing and searching documents. Train personnel to upload documents.

- Maintain data on document hits.

- Establish procedures for electronic archiving, and recommend offsite storage for disaster recovery.

E-MAIL POLICY

Successful businesses today use e-mail to communicate with employees, customers, suppliers, and others. Companies use e-mail systems to transmit memos, policies, purchase arrangements, forms, and many other kinds of transactions and documents.

However, the same e-mail system that delivers information reliably and immediately (or nearly so!) also can introduce liability—ranging from mild confusion to legal and economic disaster. How well does your organization manage its e-mail? Or does it manage it at all? Is your e-mail a catastrophe waiting to happen?

This section addresses when it is appropriate to use e-mail, and when it's not; e-mail access and privacy; and managing and retaining records of e-mail messages. The section also offers guidelines for e-mail etiquette.

Use E-mail Appropriately

An organization furnishes e-mail services to help employees conduct business. Therefore, the organization's e-mail policy should emphasize business uses, for example, purchasing arrangements, meeting notices and minutes, memos, general business announcements and bulletins, procedures, forms, work schedules, and similar types of messages and documents. The organization may set the same limitations on personal use of e-mail that exist for telephone, fax, and carrier-delivered mail. Many organizations specify limits for using e-mail for personal communications, such as work-related social events like employment anniversaries and holiday parties. Whatever the policy, communicate it clearly, and apply and enforce it consistently.

What kind of e-mail has no place on a company's e-mail system? For one, any highly personal messages, such as gossip or love letters. Another bad idea is using e-mail for communications about employee performance or discipline. These highly sensitive issues should be discussed in person, for both professional and legal reasons. And a third e-mail no-no is any kind of negative remark about a product or service—either the company's own or a competitor's. Each of these examples could lead to embarrassing or expensive legal or regulatory activity. A good rule of thumb is to ask yourself how you would feel if the message were announced on the six o'clock news. If you'd rather not see or hear it broadcast, then leave it out of your e-mail.

Not-So-Private Messages

E-mail users often are surprised to learn that their messages are far from private. Network administrators usually have access to the messages, and immediate supervisors often do as well. Even using the delete key, contrary to what many people think, may not destroy an e-mail message. In fact, it is usually easy to retrieve a so-called deleted message from the e-mail "trash bin," and utility software often can find and reconstruct messages generally thought gone forever.

Do employers look at their employees' e-mail messages? In a poll reported in the November 1996 issue of *On Q* magazine, 36 percent of executives said they peek at employees' e-mail

("Speaking of Quality"). Do they have the right? Many think so. According to the same article, the auditors and consultants interviewed believe that if computers are designated for company-related purposes, and employees are told that anything on the computer system is subject to examination, then it is okay for bosses to read their employees' e-mail.

Now let's look at e-mail from a lawyer's perspective. In an article on the "Peril of the E-mail Trail," Jacobson, Lowenbaum, and Koski (1995) write that e-mail "is increasingly viewed by plaintiff's lawyers as a great source of 'smoking gun' evidence." The authors explain that people often send hasty, explicit messages assuming they are temporary. An e-mail message can last for months or years, saved on the recipient's computer or the company's backup media, or on a hard drive even after being "deleted." Keep in mind that e-mail messages, like other company documents, may be subject to discovery proceedings in legal actions, which can result in sizable judgments against the company.

Managing E-mail

One of the biggest frustrations of using e-mail is being unable to easily find a message or attached document again. Companies that store word-processed documents in a largely disorganized way are even more likely to do so with e-mail.

Managing e-mail effectively involves selecting a system that can meet users' needs for immediacy, formality, accountability, access, security, and permanency (when desired). This means that users should consider how the system can organize messages and attachments. Further, users should look at the system's editing and display capabilities; for example, they should ask if the software has a spelling checker and if it automatically identifies the author, recipient, date, or other desired information.

Other considerations for managing e-mail include the need for acknowledging receipt of a message; for any legal or contractual conditions that require original signatures; compliance with security standards, such as password protection; or other measures to authenticate a message. (Of course, technology is speeding along, offering many products that capture signatures electronically. See the last section of this chapter.) Additionally, consider whether the company needs to limit the distribution of confidential messages or draft documents (The University of the State of New York/The State Education Department 1997).

Preparing for an emergency or maintaining business continuity in the event of a disaster, such as flood, earthquake, tornado, or hurricane should include provisions for your e-mail system. Provisions should also be made for other threats to the security of the system, such as computer hardware and software failure, media deterioration (for example, CD-ROMs do not last as long as most people believe), telecommunications failures, and human error, sabotage, or vandalism.

Smart companies realize the importance of having an up-to-date records retention program that addresses e-mail issues, a current records retention schedule, and procedures that ensure compliance. Systematically destroying e-mail records is not the same as selectively destroying records that might be subject to subpoena. A documented program for destroying e-mail records has saved more than one company from legal or financial ruin.

Checklist 5.3: E-mail Etiquette

❏ Proofread.

❏ Be concise.

❏ Limit distribution.

❏ Consider system differences.

❏ Identify yourself.

❏ Be careful with humor and sarcasm.

❏ Don't send e-mail in anger.

❏ Don't use all capital letters.

❏ Be careful what you put in print.

E-mail Etiquette

Because it is so easy to generate and transmit an e-mail message so quickly, many of us have a sorrowful story of pressing the "send" button before it should have been pressed (or pressing it when it *never* should have been pressed!). So before you send your next e-mail message, consider the following guidelines.

Proofread. Spelling and grammar errors are distracting and may project an unwanted image.

Be concise. Busy people are more likely to read brief messages, and short paragraphs are easier to comprehend onscreen.

Limit distribution. Send copies only to those who need to have the message delivered to them individually. Consider using a bulletin board, the Internet or an intranet, or other electronic communication vehicle to reduce the number of copies distributed. Each copy means someone has to read, think about, and disposition the message.

Consider system differences. Some e-mail systems break up lines exceeding 72 characters and many don't handle emphasis, such as bold, italics, and underlining. Graphics also are often a problem for many systems. Learn the system capabilities of your recipients and write messages accordingly.

Identify yourself. In your messages, include your name and affiliation and any other information that may help the recipient deal with your message. Be sure to include your e-mail address because some systems do not automatically display it. To save time, if your system permits, use an automatic signature that includes identifying information.

Be careful with humor and sarcasm. Label or otherwise identify messages meant to communicate humor. E-mail messages have no voice cues to help recipients interpret messages as intended. Use keyboard punctuation to show humor or other emotions (such as smiley faces). But avoid sarcasm, because it is easily misinterpreted.

Don't send e-mail in anger. Angry messages can be taken out of context and become destructive. Communicate anger personally or even better, sleep on it and decide in the morning if you still want to convey anger.

Don't use all capital letters. Messages sent completely in capital letters come across as angry, rude, or sharp.

Be careful what you put in print. Think twice about transmitting personal information or abusive, harassing, or bigoted messages. Any of these kinds of messages may be damaging for a long time to come.

THE CASE FOR IMAGING

As long-term storage of hard copy records becomes more and more costly, businesses are turning to electronic imaging to capture, retain, and retrieve information. In the most basic terms, digital images of documents are comprised of tiny picture elements (pixels), which can be manipulated electronically. Imaging systems can reduce the cost of handling hard copy documents by saving filing time and space, and retrieval time. Images commonly are captured from electronic sources, such as software and e-mail, and from hard copy by scanning, although other capture devices, such as video, fax, and X-ray also are used.

Is electronic imaging too good to be true? The answer is both "no" and "yes." It can be a reasonable alternative to hard copy document processing, especially if an organization's storage costs are high in relation to its labor costs (converting hard copies to electronic images can be labor-intensive), if document access speed is critical to business goals, and if knowledgeable personnel are available to ensure that storage media remain compatible with retrieval hardware and software and are stable over time. Imaging from electronic source documents generally is cost-effective if source documents are indexed fully and consistently. If not, the cost of imaging from electronic documents can approach the expense of imaging hard copies. Imaging from existing electronically indexed hard copies can be a reasonably priced effort. Imaging hardware and software vendors sometimes promote their products and services without communicating clearly all the costs of implementing a system. Frequently, organizations are surprised by the staff power required to scan existing documents into the system. Where organizations can store essential records inexpensively (for example, using off-site warehouses or outsourced facilities) and users can live with retrieval time in hours, not minutes, hard copy storage may make more sense economically. And sorry stories abound where organizations stored imaged documents on tapes and disks and other devices for which retrieval software or hardware was no longer available, or the storage media deteriorated over time. For imaging to work, someone in the organization needs to be responsible for monitoring the equipment, software, and storage media and advising when conversions to other products would be prudent.

Checklist 5.4: Considerations for Electronic Document Imaging

❏ Storage costs are high in relation to labor costs.

❏ Fast access to documents is critical.

❏ Knowledgeable personnel are available to monitor equipment, software, and media availability and condition.

6

Measured Improvement

Solutions presented in this chapter address documentation challenges such as:

- How to measure the satisfaction of documentation customers

- How to achieve zero defects

- What to do when documentation is too old

- How to reduce processing time

- How to reduce volume

- How to estimate the cost of documentation

Every major improvement effort, when initiated, strains resources. Like any successful invest-ment, returns come later. Although some process improvements pay off immediately, more take at least a few weeks, and sometimes months, to show results. Organizations baseline current processes, and that diverts personnel away from other assignments. Teams meet to identify causes and trends and generate solutions. Whether preparing for ANSI/ISO/ASQ Q9001-2000 registra-tion, adding pizzazz to a user's guide to attract customers, or redesigning a forms management system, change consumes resources, especially when documentation ownership has been entrenched in an organization for years and reaches far into other functions, such as quality assur-ance, media, or purchasing. How can an organization justify embarking on a major documentation improvement effort?

The answer is in the nature of today's marketplace, whether global or intradivision or any-thing in between. The pressure is constant to improve processes. Customers expect higher qual-ity and lower costs. That is as true for a documentation contractor as it is for a company that processes pickles. And measurement is nothing more than a tool to both judge and adjust a course for improvement.

Further, several clauses of ANSI/ISO/ASQ Q9001-2000 require measurements for continual improvement, including 8.1 c), 8.4, and 8.5.1. Clause *8.1 c) Measurement, analysis and improvement, General* states:

> *The organization shall plan and implement the monitoring, measurement, analysis and improvement processes needed to continually improve the effectiveness of the quality management system.*

8.4, Analysis of data states:

> *The organization shall determine, collect and analyse appropriate data to determine the suitability and effectiveness of the quality management system and to evaluate where continual improvement of the effectiveness of the quality management system can be made. This shall include data generated as a result of monitoring and measurement and from other relevant sources.*

8.5.1, Continual improvement states:

> *The organization shall continually improve the effectiveness of the quality management system through the use of the quality policy, quality objectives, audit results, analysis of data, corrective and preventive actions and management review.*

A formula was created to help management (engineering) see the temporary effect of improvement investing. It illustrates increased workload—which translates to expense—of organizations going through change, even though the change will eventually result in reduced workload and expense.

$$W(X, T) = W{-}(X) + W'(X, T)$$

W = Workload

X = Organization

T = Time

> *The workload of a given organization at any time (W) is equal to a steady state workload under quiescent conditions (W–) plus a variable workload attributable to turbulent conditions (change) (W').*

Acknowledging the initial but temporary investment in increased workload and expense, this chapter describes processes contributing to improved documentation nimbleness and presents metrics to monitor progress—from baseline data to world-class achievement in customer satisfaction, defect-free documents, and currentness. Then processes, metrics, and improvements are presented for cycle time, volume, and cost.

CUSTOMER SATISFACTION

In chapter 2, customers—including external customers, users, and subject matter owners—were among the five sources of need described for documentation. Customer satisfaction is also an important feature of popular quality initiatives, such as ANSI/ISO/ASQ Q9001-2000 and Six Sigma (see chapter 7). How do we measure customer satisfaction? How do we express improvement?

One way is to give feedback sheets to customers each time a product or service is delivered and then compile the responses and examine the data for common threads. The neighborhood soup and salad restaurant presents a postage paid card with a dinner check. The furnace repair person leaves the same kind of card. Each time a documentation consulting firm completes a project, it sends a feedback sheet with the invoice. The automobile dealer's service manager calls an Internet distributor for computer hardware, and software transmits a simple questionnaire by e-mail. An S&P team sends a simple check-off form when it works with subject matter owners to produce or revise their procedures and other documents (see chapter 2). The team tracks feedback quarterly and finds opportunities to improve service.

When S&P employees for a large company built senior management commitment for their online document management system, they sent a memo to every major function and division head. They asked for feedback. These internal customers, they found, wanted a longer lead time before hard copy manuals were eliminated. However, the S&P team also gained support for the project.

IS department staff developed the organization's intranet to measure document hits (the number of times each screen is viewed). They reported the information monthly to the S&P team, which used the data to help shape decisions about documents needed online.

Improvement-conscious software manufacturers install help line databases that reveal trends in customers' trouble calls. With enough callers for a problem spot, the company can either improve its software or revise its Web help function or user manual.

ZERO DEFECTS

In terms of rework cost and loss of customer satisfaction and image, documentation defects are no different than for any other product or service. Many people believe it is impossible to achieve zero defects. Like any product or service, establishing clear goals according to customers' needs comes first. Then metrics are established, strategies planned and implemented, and results achieved. Defects in documentation include typos; but they also include content inaccuracy, misfiled or otherwise inaccessible records, and lost forms. Every defect translates into wasted money and time, such as responding to messages about the defect, lost confidence that becomes lack of support, and expenses for consumables such as paper and other media.

This section focuses on proofreading processes and metrics that helped a documentation team achieve zero defects, primarily in text quality and content accuracy.

Proofreading

To some, three proofreaders for every document seems like overkill. To an organization that knows the cost of rework, confusion, distraction, and even mild annoyance caused by defective documentation, three seems just right.

The following is a funny but true story about a company bulletin about quality. The company's quality division called to alert a documentation function that a bulletin had to be published by 4:00 p.m. the same day. The caller insisted on walking the draft over to the function, which was about a quarter mile away. Huffing and puffing, the anxious caller came with bulletin in hand. "I'd like to look it over first," the documentation manager told him. "No," he said. "Our division manager already looked it over and signed it, and we don't have time. We have to get this printed and distributed by the afternoon mail run."

With a quick glance at the copy, the manager spotted two errors immediately. Reading that page and the second one carefully produced three more. By now the caller was visibly impatient.

The manager asked, "There was no time to proofread this bulletin, but there is time to fix the mistakes and run back to get a new signature?" By the way, the title of the bulletin was "Total Quality."

Before adopting Nimble Documentation® processes, the same company gave their policies and procedures to S&P writer and editor Bill to proofread. Bill was an excellent proofreader; but nobody else was. So Bill spent a good part of his workday proofreading coworkers' documents. And the people who word processed the drafts always assumed Bill would catch their errors. The arrangement was a perfect example of the traditional inspector-at-the-end-of-the-production-line model.

Bill's team largely had maintained existing processes for more than 25 years and balked at changing work processes. Gradually, as the organization attracted attention for its growing practice of continuous measurable improvement, pride overtook resistance. Key to the transformation, which later landed the team a zero-defects award, was a proofreading system that held all participants who added value to a document responsible for the document's quality, starting with the word processing person. In many offices, the person who does word processing is expected to submit a draft to be proofread by someone else. Here, every person was responsible for the quality of their own work, and everyone functioned as a receiving inspector. Staff corrected defects early and received feedback early to help detect, correct, and prevent recurring defects. Soon, Bill no longer was the only skilled proofreader. Everyone was.

This is a good place to address the sometimes controversial issue of having word processing personnel prepare documentation. Hardly an office exists where a writer, editor, engineer, manager, or other document generator isn't preparing a document for publication, whether on the Web or hard copy. Except for very brief or informal documents, it is wise and cost-effective to have specially trained word processing professionals rather than other staff do the final formatting. For one, word processing specialists are skilled in the sophisticated features of word processing software that can save time and reduce errors. Second, who is generating the drafts, designing, or supervising while writers, editors, engineers, and supervisors spend hours adjusting margins or working with other document formatting features? And last, can competitive organizations continue to afford compensating highly paid personnel for work that is better accomplished by others? It is satisfying to produce a finished document. It introduces closure to sometimes abstract, vague, and elusive assignments. However, unless the therapeutic effect upon document generators to final format a document is more important than time, quality, and cost efficiencies, documentation functions should seriously consider assigning work to word processing specialists.

Although requiring more than one proofreader for each procedure may seem unnecessary and wasteful, eliminated rework proved its worth for one documentation team. (The quality community reminds us that an error corrected during processing costs 10 times the price of an error prevented. And the cost once the product is delivered—document published—is 100 times!)

The system included a document cover sheet (synopsis sheet) that identified the staff responsible for proofreading: word processing person (proofreader one), writer and editor (proofreader two), and second writer and editor (proofreader three). A major part of the system was a check-list for countable errors (developed by the team) and monthly metrics charting the team's progress. The checklist, an application of a widely known quality control tool, was designed after pilot data showed defect trends. For example, errors were more likely in text outside the body of a procedure or bulletin, such as a document number or title. Proofreaders tallied any errors they found. Each used a different color pen and gave feedback to the others. The proofreading improvement effort also included training sessions with a corporate communications editor, and later, desk instructions.

In less than a year, average monthly defect rates dropped from more than two per page to fewer than one per 20 pages, and those defects tended to be extremely minor, such as the number of spaces between sentences. As defects approached zero, the system was modified to sampling pages at increasing intervals, with no significant increase in errors. Because of the feedback and training, error-free work became the organizational standard, staff members became more skilled in producing error-free work the first time, and cycle time decreased for processing documents.

You may be asking, "What about spellcheck?" or "So what is the big deal over a few typos?" The spellcheck feature was part of the proofreading process, but was inadequate. Some features today address some of the checklist entries, such as duplicate words (*the the*), but many errors still pass through spellcheck filters. For example, popular word processing software sometimes misses punctuation or format inconsistencies or word transpositions. Right on cue, during the preparation of the manuscript for this book, we were replacing the hyphenated word *on-line* with the unhy-phenated *online* (as words become more commonplace they tend to lose their hyphens). We were tempted to use the global find-and-replace feature (often called *Replace all*) of the word process-ing software, but decided it was too risky. Shortly into the find-and-replace activity, the word *production-line* came up, with the *on-line* part of *production-line* highlighted! Grammar checkers do identify some problems, such as noun-verb agreement, but also suggest that so many correct constructions are incorrect that many documentation specialists usually find it better not to use them. For accuracy, nothing yet beats word-by-word review performed by a skilled proofreader.

For large companies especially, any error could result in many telephone calls, which take staff time to respond to. Errors also tarnish the image of the documentation function, which is more than merely a cosmetic concern. That's not to say a typo has the same effect as a display advertisement seen in a regional newspaper, like the one featuring a sale on hosiery, unfortunately listed as *Pestilence*, when what it probably meant was *Resilience*! However, even when the typo potential is not as sorrowful, a reputation for professionalism and skill goes a long way to obtain-ing support and commitment for resources to maintain and improve service. Customer trust is at stake. Even a minor typographical error, if repeated, plants a question in customers' minds: If they're sloppy about typos, are they sloppy about content, too? Pride in workmanship also can contribute to sustained quality.

Every documentation function that adopts a similar system will have different countables, depending upon the nature of the documents, skills of the staff, and improvement goals. Figure 6.1 shows the tally sheet that worked for one function.

The same function developed proofreading desk instructions to document its processes and help train new staff. Figure 6.2 is a copy of the S&P function's proofreading desk instruction. Figure 6.3 shows proofreading desk instructions after an online system was implemented and the organization

Month _____

First proofreader												
Second proofreader												
Third proofreader												
CONTENT											**TOTAL**	
Missing information												
Inaccurate information												
Clarity (phrase or sentence)												
Unclear referent												
Poorly organized paragraph												
Wrong word												
Other content defect												
SPELLING												
Title misspelling												
Heading misspelling												
Body misspelling												
Name misspelling												
Footnote misspelling												
Other misspelling												
MECHANICS												
Doubling												
Roman/Arabic numerals												
Inconsistent hyphenation												
Noun-verb disagreement												
And/or												
Capitalization												
Pagination												
Inconsistent use of colon												
Inconsistent use of period												
Inconsistent headings												
Inconsistent underline												
Transposition												
Unnecessary *Denotes revision*												
Other mechanics defects												
FORMAT												
Uneven margins												
Brackets												
Misaligned paragraph number or letter												
Letter spacing												
Line spacing												
Form of date												
Other format defects												
PAGE TALLY												

Figure 6.1 S&P proofreading defect classifications.

1. The writer and editor receives a hard copy or electronic file, or both, of the new or revised document draft. (Note: The writer and editor may be helping to originate or revise a document. Also, where a document already exists on the S&P system, the writer and editor transfers the document to their desktop to make changes to it.)

2. For minor changes, the writer and editor edits the document and may make those changes, which are then submitted to the word processing person electronically to format and finalize on the S&P system.

   For major changes or new documents, the writer and editor edits and submits the redlined hard copy or electronic file, or both, to the word processing person for keying and formatting on the S&P system.

3. The writer and editor notifies the word processing person that the document is ready for finalization.

4. The word processing person copies the document submitted by the writer and editor to the S&P system.

5. The word processing person proofreads the document and submits it to the writer and editor for proofreading.

6. The writer and editor proofreads the document and forwards it to the second writer and editor to proofread.

7. The writer and editor submits the document to the originator or executive for approval.

Figure 6.2   S&P proofreading desk instructions.

The following instructions provide guidance to the S&P Department for proofreading procedures, bulletins, and statements of responsibility (SORs) before release, to ensure accuracy and clarity.

Word Processing Persons

1. After completing word processing and before printing out a hard copy for proofreading, run spellcheck. Proofread the document. If only minor corrections are detected during proofreading, make them on the draft copy but do not make corrections on the electronic file until the writer and editor has also proofread the document (this reduces the number of correction cycles).

2. When the writer and editor indicates a copy is needed for approval, incorporate the final changes, run a final spellcheck, proofread and mark corrections, and return the package to the writer and editor for proofreading. After the writer/editor has proofread the document, incorporate the accumulated changes.

Writers and Editors

1. Proofread all drafts, using S&P standard editing marks or electronic revision marks, and return the drafts to the word processing person to incorporate changes.

2. To obtain a final copy of the document for approval, perform the following:

   a. Have a second writer and editor proofread and edit the document (using a different color).

   b. If changes are minor, submit the document (with completed Synopsis Sheet) to final proofreader for review and approval.

Figure 6.3   S&P proofreading instructions (for online publication).

c. Note: If the document is an Attachment or Maintenance Revision, a Synopsis Sheet is not required. The final proofreader indicates approval on the Data Processing and Review Record (DPRR).

d. If changes are extensive, have the word processing person incorporate changes before submittal to final proofreader. (Use discretion in deciding whether a second proofreading is necessary.)

e. After the final proofreader's review, submit the document to the word processing person for incorporation of final changes.

f. After the final proofreader's approval and incorporation of final changes, submit the document and Synopsis Sheet to the designated executive for approval.

3. When the copy is received from the information provider with confirmation on the DPRR that it has been uploaded, proofread the following items:

a. The document, comparing it with the hard copy or marked electronic file, to be sure all the information is accurate. Also confirm keyword accuracy, using a copy of the key word list supplied by the information provider and comparing it with the keywords written on the DPRR. [Or proofread meta data for intranet documents.]

b. Changes to the Table of Contents.

c. Changes to the 12-week screen.

S&P Leader

Reviews documents received from writers and editors and indicates approval by signing and dating the Synopsis Sheet (DPRR for Attachments and Maintenance Revisions).

Information Providers

After the document is uploaded, proofread the document, comparing it to the hard copy, or marked electronic file, for accuracy and confirming that all screen information is correct. Also, confirm that keywords [or meta data] are accurate by comparing them with the keywords written on the DPRR.

Information providers should also proofread changes to the Table of Contents and changes to the 12-week screen [which can be automated].

Figure 6.3 S&P proofreading instructions (for online publication) *(continued)*.

saw the need to control errors that slipped in before and during uploading processes. Both systems were adopted before installing software that features online group editing and revision. Workflow and document control software currently automates may of the steps described following.

CURRENTNESS

Blink, and technology zooms by. Yet company policies and procedures often grow mold. Worse, cumbersome and obsolete documentation snubs customers and suffocates employees—and may be a resource bomb waiting to be detonated by the next legal challenge.

Maintaining current documentation balances between the need for up-to-the-minute documents and available resources. When laws change, documents such as a city's no-smoking policy may need to change immediately. And establishing an annual review cycle for all policies and procedures helps prevent document obsolescence. A document that is worth keeping is worth keeping up to date. But if an organization is fairly stable, and processes do not change much, adopting a review cycle of 24 months or perhaps even 36 months may be adequate.

Design metrics to baseline the currentness of policies, procedures, and other documents. Then regularly collect data and chart the organization's progress toward eliminating the oldest documents, assuming critical ones are reviewed first. Naturally, after a major documentation improvement effort, all of the documents will be current. Establish objectives to continue to monitor currentness and raise red flags when documents begin to age. In many organizations, documentation is a low priority, at least until audits or legal claims strike. So use currentness metrics to nudge subject matter experts to review documents to keep them up to date. Or invest in document management software that computes currentness and other metrics and generates charts automatically. Figure 6.4 shows metrics for currentness of policies and procedures at the start of a major improvement project.

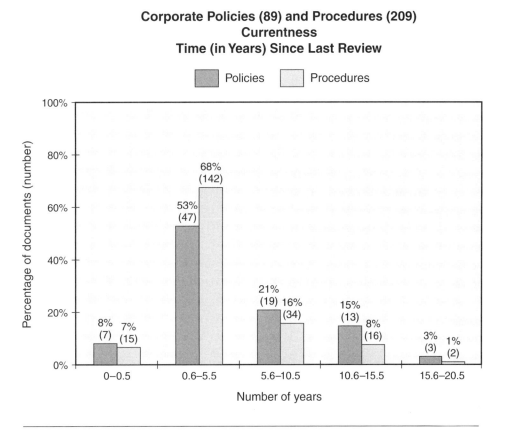

Figure 6.4 Metrics for currentness.

CYCLE TIME

Documents that take a long time to write, edit, coordinate, and publish frustrate writers and users. Keeping track of processing cycle time may reveal some surprises and may spur staff into searching for non-value-added processes and ways to improve the documentation management system. If nothing else, the metrics bring attention to functions that tend to delay the review process and motivate them to place a higher priority on reviewing drafts. Some organizations are using document management systems that take advantage of optical scanning technology. Documents, including records, have bar graphs that when scanned at transfer points in the process generate cycle time data on demand.

A corporate team benchmarked coordination time for policies and procedures with several companies in Southern California, mostly in the defense electronics industry, and researched industry data. Documents took a whopping average of six months to coordinate. In the cycle time chart, another corporate team superimposed the industry data on its achievement in reducing coordination time for corporate policies and procedures (see Figure 6.5). What harm can come from a six-month average? Laws and regulations change. Companies reorganize. Customers' requirements change. Competition increases. It behooves a documentation function to process and publish directive documentation quickly.

Another team at a different company tracked document backlog during a major documentation conversion to an online system. These metrics helped the team members plan their work and respond to customers. The actual data are unavailable; however, metrics for sample data are presented in Figure 6.6.

Subject matter experts told a support team they needed to upload documents more quickly. The support team baselined the cycle time for uploading documents and charted its metrics. By identifying value-added and non-value-added activities, and obtaining additional technical training, the team members succeeded in reducing the average uploading time from about 2.5 *days* to about 30 *minutes* (see Figure 6.7). The customers were pleased.

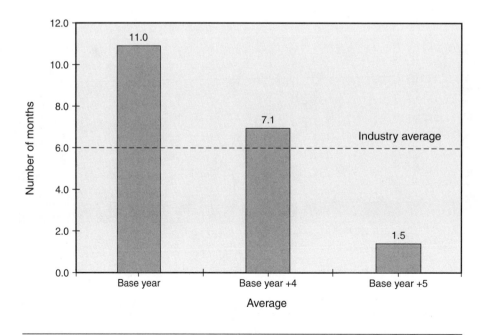

Figure 6.5 Corporate policies and procedures: coordination and approval.

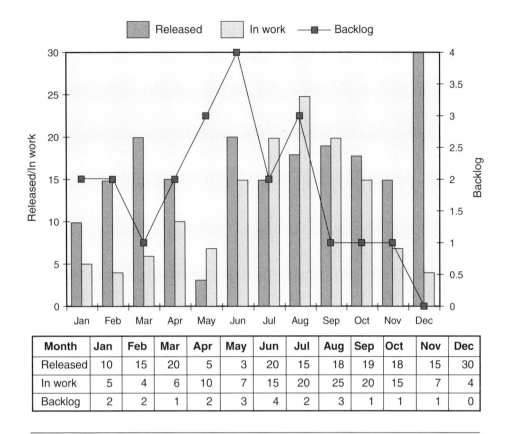

Month	Jan	Feb	Mar	Apr	May	Jun	Jul	Aug	Sep	Oct	Nov	Dec
Released	10	15	20	5	3	20	15	18	19	18	15	30
In work	5	4	6	10	7	15	20	25	20	15	7	4
Backlog	2	2	1	2	3	4	2	3	1	1	1	0

Figure 6.6 Sample data: items released, in work, and backlog.

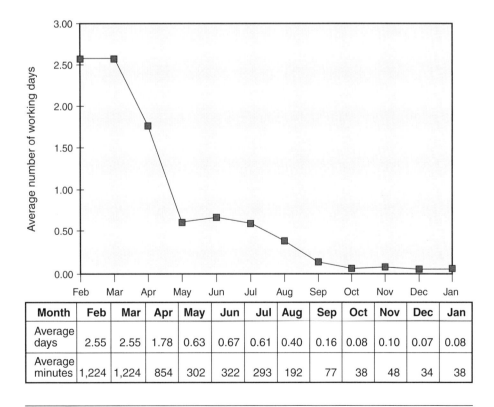

Month	Feb	Mar	Apr	May	Jun	Jul	Aug	Sep	Oct	Nov	Dec	Jan
Average days	2.55	2.55	1.78	0.63	0.67	0.61	0.40	0.16	0.08	0.10	0.07	0.08
Average minutes	1,224	1,224	854	302	322	293	192	77	38	48	34	38

Figure 6.7 Average monthly cycle time for uploading documents.

VOLUME

Documentation, whether hard copy or online, is expensive to maintain. More documents are more expensive to maintain. More also increase liability. The potential for successful grievances and lawsuits goes up as volume increases. However, even if litigation is unsuccessful, businesses pay dearly. The compensation clock keeps ticking while staff research and prepare defenses. And documents that employees fail to follow are mine fields waiting for footsteps. Documents are easy targets for auditors. So, typically, many procedures are written in direct response to audit findings. Over time, the procedures accumulate. Manuals get fat.

Monitoring the number of documents—hard copy or electronic—and pages—including Web pages—and estimating the costs of processing and maintaining them provide important feedback for improvement. Data provide incentives to control volume and, therefore, maintenance costs and liability. Regularly reported volume metrics also motivate teams to continue their zeal in applying the litmus test to all requests for new documents or for expansive revisions to existing ones. Figure 6.8, which shows a simple chart for measuring the continuous reduction of an organization's product operations procedures, is an example of volume metrics.

World-class documentation functions generate volume metrics at the start of their documentation streamlining effort (baseline chart) and at regular intervals thereafter. Baseline metrics that include current volume and targets for reducing volume keep the goal in view of progress (see Figure 6.9).

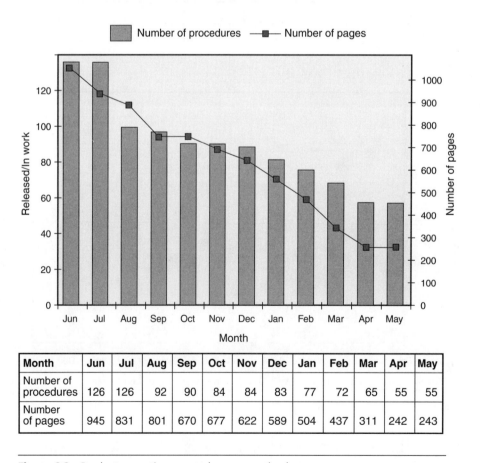

Month	Jun	Jul	Aug	Sep	Oct	Nov	Dec	Jan	Feb	Mar	Apr	May
Number of procedures	126	126	92	90	84	84	83	77	72	65	55	55
Number of pages	945	831	801	670	677	622	589	504	437	311	242	243

Figure 6.8   Product operations procedures manual volume.

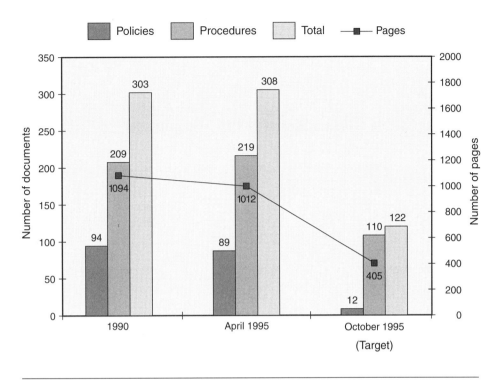

Figure 6.9 Baseline and target volume metrics.

COST: THE ICEBERG MODEL

Organizations considering an online document management system often cite cost as a reason to reject or postpone converting their hard copy system, or converting their LAN-based electronic file system to a Web or intranet system. They name the following costs: hardware, software, telecommunications, technical support, text conversion, training, and other expenses. A counter argument usually includes saving paper and printing costs. It might also include the expense of internal distribution or mailing services to satellite sites. The online argument, however, rarely includes the hidden costs.

Think of an iceberg. The really dangerous part is beneath the surface of the water. The part you don't see can do the most damage, whether we are talking about icebergs or documentation system costs (see Figure 6.10). Revisions to hard copy documents are particularly costly. With each revision, someone drafts a change notice or revised document. Then the person word processes the draft notice or revision (or drafts and word processes at the same time). Then someone copies the revision and someone distributes the copies to gain approval of all the functions involved in the change. The processes are repeated after comments arrive regarding the proposed revision. Once the final copies are distributed, someone removes and discards the obsolete copy from each manual and then files the new document. Think of the cost of these hidden processes. But there's more.

Before the draft ever gets to the word processing stage, someone has to research the changes to see if they conflict with or impact other existing information. So they have to search other manuals and documents manually or file by file if the documents are merely Word files on a LAN.

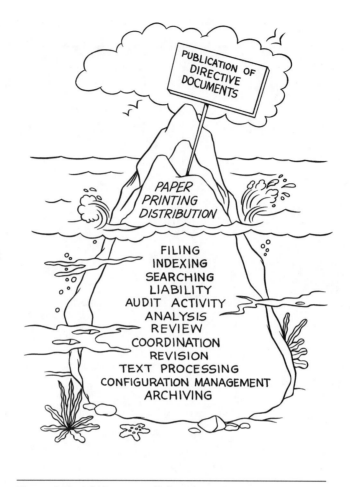

Figure 6.10   Hidden costs of documentation systems.

Someone has to update the index. In many organizations, copies of draft revisions awaiting review and final document copies both dive to the bottom of the in-basket stack. Reviewing drafts tends to have a low priority. However, maintaining manuals tends to have an even lower priority. Therefore, many manuals wait to be updated, and the result is increased liability and sometimes increased audit activity because of the delays. For all of the hidden factors, the break-even point of converting to an online document management or Web system may be closer than most people realize.

Suppose an organization has an online document management system. Is the true (read complete) cost known to add, revise, or even cancel a document? (Yes, cancellations can be costly.) Many companies pay for their documentation function with general administration funds and may not source expenses down to the level of the function. Even the organizations that do source expenses to that level seldom measure the cost of processing a document. Knowing little about the cost of processing an average document is a considerable disadvantage for introducing and implementing improvement initiatives. And the ignorance bypasses one of the biggest incentives to streamlining a documentation function: cost. Cost metrics for documentation can support decisions to outsource or insource (see chapter 10).

Figure 6.11 is a list of costs that can help a company compute the true expense of its corporate policies and procedures and that can be adapted to compare the cost of an existing hard copy system against an online one. It can be used also to discourage the addition of a document of questionable need. Not all listed items apply to a given organization and other items may apply. The list assumes that hard copy documentation is produced with a computer and printer, not a typewriter. The expense of some items will vary depending on whether hard copy or electronic. Hard copy documents might require only office suite, operating system, and telecommunications software. Electronic document management systems might also require imaging, document control, and Web page editing software.

Cost of Documentation

Product or process

- Writing*
- Paper
- Print cartridges or ribbons
- Correction supplies (for example, white-out liquid)
- Word processing*
- Editing*
- Editing and proofreading supplies (for example, pens)
- Fasteners (for example, binders, clips, and staples)
- Distribution (for example, postage and shipping and burdened salaries for internal delivery staffing, collating, and shrink-wrapping)
- Telecommunications equipment (for example, cables and modems)
- Software (both initial purchase and upgrades)
- Filing, archiving, and records management equipment and supplies (for example, cabinets, sorting equipment, labels, and file folders)
- Filing, archiving, and records management*
- Indexing*
- Liability
- Audit activity*
- Content analysis*
- Coordination, including hard copy or e-mail notification*
- Review and approval*
- Revision maintenance (for example, marking tables of contents and inserting and deleting documents)*
- Configuration management*

Figure 6.11   Cost of documentation.

- Management*

- Facility space

- Utilities (for example, lighting, gas and electric, and water)

- Janitorial and maintenance supplies

- Janitorial and maintenance*

- Office furniture

- Information retrieval*

- Answering inquiries, including help*

- Improvement initiatives, including maintaining metrics*

- Audit*

* Represents burdened salaries or contractor fees

Figure 6.11   Cost of documentation (*continued*).

Part III

Application

7

Quality Initiatives

Solutions presented in this chapter address documentation challenges such as:

- What are the document and records requirements and implications of ANSI/ISO/ASQ Q9001-2000?

- How does the Baldrige Award compare with ANSI/ISO/ASQ Q9001-2000?

- What documentation and records are implied by Baldrige Award criteria?

- How can a documentation center of excellence (COE) implement TQM?

- What is Six Sigma and what does it have to do with documentation?

At a seminar on ISO 9000, the facilitator asked participants to identify their number one obstacle to becoming registered. Greater than 90 percent said documentation. According to the 1880 respondents of a 1996 survey of ISO 9000-registered firms, conducted by Irwin Professional Publishing and Dun & Bradstreet Information Services, "the greatest barriers to achieving registration were document development (57.9 percent) and procedure creation (41.0 percent) ("ISO 9000 for Quality's Sake" 1996).

Every major quality initiative—for example, ANSI/ISO/ASQ Q9001-2000 and the Baldrige Award—requires or implies documentation to communicate, control, monitor, or evaluate quality. Documentation serves as a keeper of process decisions. Its role is to provide guidance for consistent ways of operating. It enables employees to learn and be reminded of acceptable ways to fulfill work assignments. Documentation also can be a diagnostic tool that helps organizations target priorities for improving processes.

Documentation can demonstrate compliance with stated requirements or criteria. For ISO 9001, for example, effective quality policies, operating procedures, work instructions, and other documentation can convince auditors that processes are in place. For the Baldrige Award, documentation can show examiners that an organization delivers performance excellence. Other quality standards, regulations, and requirements—such as QS-9000, the FDA, and military specifications—demand accurate and current documentation to affirm safety, purity, protection, durability, and other attributes. World-class organizations can settle for nothing less than documentation that fulfills its purpose, yet is cost-effective and fast to create, access, and maintain, and responsive to organizational and market change. To illustrate the role of documentation in quality initiatives, this section presents an overview of each of three quality initiatives, their documentation requirements or implications, and how total quality management (TQM) relates to a documentation function. The solutions are the same as for other Nimble Documentation®: a zero base; hierarchy, structure, format, and style that facilitate access and minimize resource consumption; standardized processes; and measured continuous improvement.

ANSI/ISO/ASQ Q9001-2000

ANSI/ISO/ASQ Q9001-2000 is a standard for quality management and quality assurance that applies to virtually all businesses and organizations, including manufacturing, service, public agencies, and others. The standard grew from the International Organization for Standardization started in Geneva, Switzerland, in 1946. (Although some writers attribute the term *ISO* to an acronym for the Swiss organization, most trace ISO to the Greek word *isos*, which, loosely translated, means *equal* or *consistent*.)

Why are organizations putting so much time, energy, and resources into becoming registered to ANSI/ISO/ASQ Q9001-2000? Mostly, to gain six major benefits:

- Customer satisfaction
- Access to global markets
- Marketing edge
- Reduced costs and time
- Perceived quality
- Heightened staff morale

An organization's customers may demand ANSI/ISO/ASQ Q9001-2000 registration, especially if the customer itself has achieved registration. Even agencies of the U.S. government, such as the National Aeronautics and Space Administration (NASA), are registered. ISO 9001 registration is mandatory for many European companies, stemming from European Union demands. To compete, other major traders in world commerce are doing the same. Splashy brochures and giveaways at trade shows and building banners proclaim ISO 9001 registration to attract business. For example, at conventions, companies affix stickers to their marketing materials and display congratulatory signs for their ISO 9001 registration. Sales representatives are overheard to say that their companies may seek registration just because their competitors have.

The discipline required of quality management and operating processes can lead to greater efficiency and can save organizations time and dollars. Rework, waste, confusion, and inconsistencies all generate needless expense. Although ISO 9001 registration is not an assurance of quality products or services, this seal of approval gives that impression (and product and service quality nearly always improves with ISO 9001 assessment and registration). Most organizations form teams to help them achieve registration. The common goal, the camaraderie, being listened to and paid attention to, knowing how to do a job, and receiving training—all these elements of ISO 9001 teams—tend to contribute to a more satisfied and productive workforce.

ANSI/ISO/ASQ Q9001-2000 is comprised of eight sections. The first three address general considerations and the remaining five correspond to major groups of quality system processes, as follows:

1. Scope

2. Normative reference

3. Terms and definitions

4. Quality management system

5. Management responsibility

6. Resource management

7. Product realization

8. Measurement, analysis, and improvement

Where does ANSI/ISO/ASQ Q9001-2000 fit in the family of quality efforts? Is it just another quality initiative? Does an organization abandon current quality standards to embrace ISO 9001? Does it discard plans to seek the Baldrige Award? Is ISO 9001 just a stepping-stone to Six Sigma?

Seeking any of these quality initiatives usually leads to the same result: improved quality. And several clauses link ISO 9001 and the Baldrige Award. Baldrige, however, is a single point. Once it is given, it's given. Further, the Baldrige Award means more to U.S. customers than to other nations, although many other countries have national quality awards, as do individual U.S. states. Additional features distinguish the two quality initiatives; however, both sets of criteria require or imply documentation to support processes. Figure 7.1 shows ISO 9000 in a continuum of quality initiatives from no quality system to a world-class quality system. Documentation for the Baldrige Award and Six Sigma is addressed in greater detail later in this chapter.

What are the documentation requirements of ANSI/ISO/ASQ Q9001-2000? First, the standard requires an organization to define and document its quality policy. Individual sections of the standard specify documented procedures and records. To achieve ANSI/ISO/ASQ Q9001-2000 registration, most organizations develop a quality system manual as their first tier documentation. This

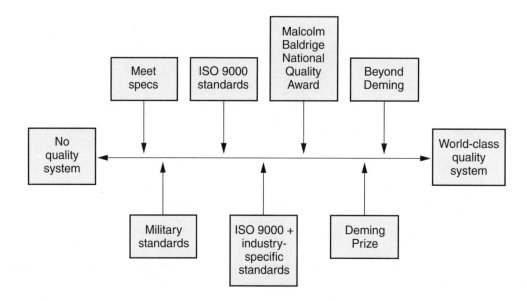

Source: Adapted from John Kerr. *An Insider's Guide to ISO 9000.* Newport Beach, CA: IMPAC Integrated Systems, Inc. n.d. Used with permission.

Figure 7.1   A continuum of quality initiatives.

manual communicates the organization's philosophy of and commitment to quality. Typically, organizations develop a second tier of operating procedures that implement the quality policy and define activities or processes. A third tier may include work instructions, that is, steps on using equipment, entering data for transactions, and similar detailed guidance. ISO 9001-compliant documentation may be in any media, hard copy or electronic.

The most nimble quality system manuals are organized according to ISO 9001 clauses and seldom include more than 20 pages. Manuals that combine quality policy with operating procedures, naturally, will be longer. Some organizations merge operating procedures with work instructions in one manual. The level of detail in the documentation depends on the experience and skills of employees and the complexity of the processes. No specification in ANSI/ISO/ASQ Q9001-2000 dictates the hierarchy, structure, or format of required documentation. However, a common hierarchy is shown in Figure 7.2.

Commonly, the first tier quality system manual refers to each clause of the standard by clause number. For example, the organization's quality policy statement, signed by a senior executive, is placed in the quality system manual under the heading *5.1 Management commitment, b) establishing the quality policy* or *5.3 Quality policy.* Similarly, the kind of information contained in purchase orders and other purchasing documents is defined in the quality system manual under *7.4.2 Purchasing information.* Where a lower-tier document details processes of the quality system required according to ISO 9001, that document is noted in the quality system manual. For example, in the manual under *7.5.3 Identification and traceability,* a paragraph refers by number and name to the company's traceability operating procedure. For company XXX, the operating procedure reference might be *XXXP 7-5 Production and Service Provision.* Depending on the company's quality system documentation hierarchy, structure, and format, work instructions may

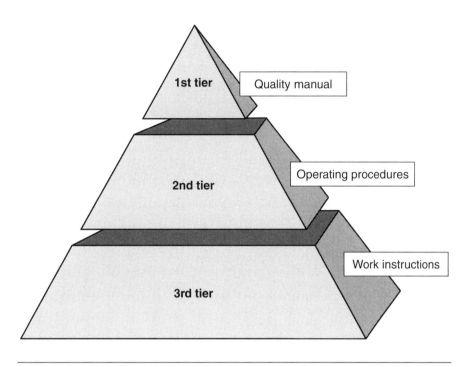

Figure 7.2 Common hierarchy for ISO 9001-compliant documentation.

be referenced in a related operating procedure. The most user-friendly documentation systems number related documents, or their parts, similarly. For example, a work instruction for receiving product identification is numbered *XXXWI 7-5-3A Receiving Product Identification*.

ANSI/ISO/ASQ Q9001-2000 requirements also specify records and data for control and verification. One definition of documentation is *recorded information*. And records, for many, mean *recorded evidence, proof*, or *verification*. The definitions of documentation and records overlap. The standard, however, is clear on requiring both. Forms are information templates that, completed, can serve as records, for example, evidence of employee training. Captured data, such as measurements driven by software-managed machinery, can also serve as records.

Many ANSI/ISO/ASQ Q9001-2000 clauses specify or imply documentation and data or records or both. Table 7.1 shows ANSI/ISO/ASQ Q9001-2000 clauses that specify or imply documentation and data and records. Typical placement for documenting how a company meets the requirements is shown in parentheses; however, the best documentation placement for a given company depends on many factors, including the number of documentation tiers, complexity of product or service, and experience and skill of personnel. Unlike the 1994 version of the standard, ANSI/ISO/ASQ Q9001-2000 uses the word *procedure* without the modifier *documented* in only a couple of instances. Table 7.1 excludes those instances because they are not clearly requirements for documentation. Also, the chart generally omits reference to work instructions as typical documentation placement because companies vary widely in the scope and volume of work instructions needed for their processes. The term *procedures* rather than *procedure* is used when more than one operating procedure is customary; however, the number of related procedures varies from company to company and site to site.

Applying the principles of zero-based documentation to ANSI/ISO/ASQ Q9001-2000 requirements and a mind-set of continuous improvement can yield some streamlined solutions.

Table 7.1   ANSI/ISO/ASQ Q9001-2000 clauses that specify or imply documentation, data, and records.

Note: Parentheses indicate typical means of fulfilling the documentation requirement or implication. Plural Operating procedures means more than one document typically is published to fulfill the requirement or implication.

Number	Section and Clause	Documentation and Data Requirement or Implication	Records Requirement
4.1	**General requirements**	Documented quality management system and a) Ensured availability of information necessary to support the operation and monitoring of quality management system processes (Quality system manual, data)	
4.2	**Documentation requirements**		
4.2.1	**General**	a) Documented statements of quality policy and quality objectives b) Quality manual c) Documented procedures d) Documents needed to ensure effective planning, operation, and control of processes (Quality system manual, quality policy, operating procedures, plans, data)	Records (see 4.2.4)
4.2.2	**Quality manual**	a) Quality manual, including scope of quality management system, including details of and justification for any exclusions b) Documented procedures or reference to them c) Description of the interaction between quality management system processes (Quality manual, operating procedures)	
4.2.3	**Control of documents**	Controlled quality management system documents Documented procedure to define the controls needed to: a) Approve documents for adequacy prior to use b) Review and update and re-approve documents c) Ensure identification of changes and current revision status of documents d) Ensure that relevant versions of documents are available at points of use e) Ensure that documents remain legible and readily identifiable f) Ensure that documents of external origin are identified and their distribution controlled g) Prevent unintended use of obsolete documents, and apply suitable identification if documents are retained (Operating procedure)	Controlled records
4.2.4	**Control of records**	Documented procedure that defines controls for identification, storage, protection, retrieval, retention time, and disposal of records (Operating procedure)	Records to provide evidence of conformity to requirements and of the effective operation of quality management system; legible, readily identifiable, and retrievable records
5.1	**Management commitment**	Top management established: b) Quality policy c) Quality objectives (Quality policy, quality objectives in quality manual)	

Continued

Number	Section and Clause	Documentation and Data Requirement or Implication	Records Requirement
5.3	Quality policy	Top management assurance that quality policy: a) Is appropriate to purpose of the organization b) Includes commitment to comply with requirements and continually improve effectiveness of quality management system c) Provides framework for establishing and reviewing quality objectives d) Is communicated and understood within the organization e) Is reviewed for continuing suitability (Quality policy, quality manual, data)	
5.4	Planning		
5.4.1	Quality objectives	Top management assurance that quality objectives, including those needed to meet requirements for product [see 7.1a)], are established at relevant functions and levels within the organization; measurable quality objectives consistent with the quality policy (Quality objectives in quality manual, data)	
5.4.2	Quality management system planning	Top management assurance that: a) Quality management system plans are carried out to meet general requirements (4.1) and quality objectives b) Integrity of quality management system is maintained when changes are planned and implemented (Plans, quality objectives)	
5.5	Responsibility, authority, and communication		
5.5.1	Responsibility and authority	Top management assurance that responsibilities and authorities are defined and communicated (Quality manual, operating procedure, job descriptions, statements of responsibility)	
5.5.2	Management representative	Top management appointment of manager who: b) Reports performance of quality management system and need for improvement (Reports, data)	
5.6	Management review		
5.6.1	General	Top management review of the quality management system, including assessment of improvement opportunities and need for changes, including quality policy and quality objectives (Quality policy, quality objectives)	Records of management reviews
5.6.2	Review input	Information on: a) Audit results b) Customer feedback c) Process performance and product conformity d) Status of preventive and corrective actions e) Follow-up actions from previous management reviews f) Changes that could affect the quality management system g) Improvement recommendations (Data, reports, surveys)	

Continued

Number	Section and Clause	Documentation and Data Requirement or Implication	Records Requirement
5.6.3	**Review output**	Decisions and actions related to: a) Improvement of effectiveness of quality management system and processes b) Improvement of product related to customer requirements c) Resource needs (Data, reports)	
6.2	**Human resources**		
6.2.2	**Competence, awareness, and training**		Records of assessment and of education, training, skills, and experience
7.1	**Planning of product realization**	Determine: a) Quality objectives and requirements for product b) Need to establish processes, documents, and provide resources specific to the product c) Verification, validation, monitoring, inspection, and test activities (Plans)	Evidence that the realization processes and resulting product meet requirements
7.2	**Customer-related processes**		
7.2.2	**Review of requirements related to the product**	Review product requirements (Drawings, plans, specifications)	Results of requirements reviews and any actions arising from reviews
7.2.3	**Customer communication**	Customer communication that includes: a) Product information b) Inquiries, contracts, or order handling, including amendments c) Customer feedback, including complaints (Letters and other correspondence, product specifications, contracts, purchase orders, sales orders)	
7.3	**Design and development**		
7.3.1	**Design and development planning**	Determine: a) Design and development stages b) Review, verification, and validation for each stage c) Responsibilities and authorities for design and development Update planning output as design and development progresses (Plans)	
7.3.2	**Design and development inputs**	Determine inputs relating to product requirements, including: a) Functional and performance requirements b) Statutory and regulatory requirements c) Any information derived from previous similar designs d) Other requirements essential for design and development (Plans, laws, statutes, regulations)	Input records

Continued

Number	Section and Clause	Documentation and Data Requirement or Implication	Records Requirement
7.3.3	Design and development outputs	Outputs that: a) Meet input requirements for design and development b) Provide information for purchasing, production, and service provision c) Contain or reference product acceptance criteria d) Specify product characteristics essential for safe and proper use (Drawings, specifications)	
7.3.4	Design and development review		Results of design and development reviews and any necessary actions
7.3.5	Design and development verification		Verification results and any necessary actions
7.3.6	Design and development validation		Validation results and any necessary actions
7.3.7	Control of design and development changes	Approved design and development changes (Drawings, specifications)	Results of reviews of design and development changes and any necessary actions
7.4	Purchasing		
7.4.1	Purchasing process	Criteria for selection, evaluation, and re-evaluation of suppliers (Operating procedure, list of suppliers)	Records of evaluation results and any necessary actions
7.4.2	Purchasing information	Product description, including, where appropriate, requirements for: a) Approving product, procedures, processes and equipment b) Qualifying personnel c) Quality management system (Purchase orders, sales orders, contracts)	
7.4.3	Verification of purchased product	Establish inspection or other activities to ensure that purchased product meets specified purchase requirements Where verification will be at supplier's premises, intended verification arrangements and method of product release (Operating procedure and purchase orders, sales orders, contracts)	
7.5	Production and service provision		
7.5.1	Control of production and service provision	Control conditions for planning and carrying out production and service provision, as applicable: a) Availability of information that describes product characteristics b) Availability of work instructions c) Use of suitable equipment d) Availability and use of monitoring and measurement devices e) Implementation of monitoring and measurement f) Implementation of release, delivery, and post-delivery activities (Plans, operating procedure)	

Continued

Number	Section and Clause	Documentation and Data Requirement or Implication	Records Requirement
7.5.2	**Validation of processes for production and service provision**	Validate processes where output cannot be verified by subsequent monitoring or measurement. Arrangements include, as applicable: a) Criteria for process review and approval b) Approval of equipment and qualification of personnel c) Use of specified methods and procedures d) Records requirements e) Revalidation (Operating procedure, equipment specifications, employee files)	Validation records
7.5.3	**Identification and traceability**	Identify product and product status (Labels, tags)	Where traceability is required, records of unique identification of product
7.5.4	**Customer property**	Identify, verify, protect, and safeguard customer property (Labels, tags)	Records of lost, damaged, or unsuitable customer property
7.5.5	**Preservation of product**	Identify, handle, package, store, and protect product (Labels, signs, tags)	
7.6	**Control of monitoring and measuring devices**	Determine the monitoring and measurement to be taken and devices needed to prove that product conforms to requirements. Where necessary to ensure valid results c) Identify measuring equipment and determine calibration status Assess validity of previous measuring results for nonconforming equipment Confirm ability of computer software to satisfy intended application, when software is used (Plans, labels, tags, data)	Calibration and verification records
8.1	**[Measurement, analysis and improvement] General**	Plan monitoring, measurement, analysis, and improvement processes needed to: a) Demonstrate product conformity b) Ensure conformity of quality management system c) Continually improve effectiveness of quality management system Determine methods and extent of use (Plans)	
8.2	**Monitoring and measurement**		
8.2.1	**Customer satisfaction**	Monitor information relating to customer perception of whether the organization has met customer requirements (Surveys, questionnaires)	
8.2.2	**Internal audit**	Conduct internal audits to determine whether quality management system: a) Conforms to plans and to ANSI/ISO/ASQ Q9001-2000 requirements Plan an internal audit program Define audit criteria, scope, frequency, and methods Define responsibilities and requirements for planning and conducting audits and for reporting results and maintaining records (Operating procedure, plans, ANSI/ISO/ASQ Q9001-2000 standard, reports)	Records of internal audits

Continued

Number	Section and Clause	Documentation and Data Requirement or Implication	Records Requirement
8.2.3	**Monitoring and measurement of processes**	Monitor and, where applicable, measure quality system management processes Demonstrate ability of processes to achieve planned results (Data, plans)	
8.2.4	**Monitoring and measurement of product**	Monitor and measure product characteristics according to plans to verify that product requirements have been met (Plans)	Evidence of conformity with acceptance criteria and indication of the persons authorizing product release
8.3	**Control of nonconforming product**	Identify and control product that does not conform to product requirements to prevent its unintended use or delivery Define controls and related responsibilities and authorities for dealing with nonconforming product (Labels, tags, signs, operating procedure)	Records of the nature of nonconformities and any subsequent actions taken, including concessions obtained
8.4	**Analysis of data**	Determine, collect, and analyze data to demonstrate the suitability and effectiveness of quality management system and to evaluate opportunities for continual improvement of the effectiveness of the system, including data generated as a result of monitoring and measurement and from other relevant sources (Data)	
8.5	**Improvement**		
8.5.1	**Continual improvement**	Continually improve quality management system through the quality policy, quality objectives, audit results, data analysis, corrective and preventive actions, and management review (Quality policy, quality objectives in quality manual, data, reports)	
8.5.2	**Corrective action**	Define requirements for: a) Reviewing nonconformities (including customer complaints) b) Determining the causes of nonconformities c) Evaluating the need for action to ensure that nonconformities do not recur d) Determining and implementing action needed e) Records of the results of action taken f) Reviewing corrective action taken (Operating procedure)	Records of the results of corrective action taken
8.5.3	**Preventive action**	Define requirements for: a) Determining potential nonconformities and their causes b) Evaluating the need for action to prevent occurrence of nonconformities c) Determining and implementing action needed d) Records of results of action taken e) Reviewing preventive action taken (Operating procedure)	Records of results of preventive action taken

Individual Training Plan and Record

Employee name:_____ Employee number:_____

Last   First   Middle initial

Education, training, or certification	Required	Elective (Check one)	Date required	Date completed
Example: B.S. Finance		✔		6/15/1999
Example: WCQMS Employee Awareness	✔		7/31/2001	7/30/2001

Instructions:

For required training, enter the name of the training, check the *Required* box, and enter the date by which training needs to be completed. After training is completed, enter the date training was completed.

For elective training, enter the name of the training, check the *Elective* box, and enter the date training was completed.

WXY Form 6.2.2 Rev. 09/12/2000

Figure 7.3 Individual training plan and record.

For example, a quality system improvement team at a credit monitoring and reporting service used a combined training plan and record. The hybrid document fulfilled two requirements of ANSI/ISO/ASQ Q9001-2000 section *6.2.2 Competence, awareness and training:* (a) determine the necessary competence for personnel performing work affecting product quality and e) maintain appropriate records of education, training, skills and experience. Figure 7.3 shows how the company's Individual Training Plan and Record let supervisors and employees identify both required and elective training needs. Instructions are printed directly on the form, which is numbered corresponding to the ANSI/ISO/ASQ Q9001-2000 clause. The revision date is printed on the form, as well. A related operating procedure only references, but doesn't duplicate, the form. Filed in each employee's personnel file, the form also becomes a record of completed training. Only one document is processed and maintained. An increasingly popular alternative to printed records is software featuring a database whereby supervisors and others with a need to know can access training assignments and records electronically. Many software packages designed specifically for ISO 9001 implementation contain that feature. Plenty of other opportunities, like these, exist for translating ISO requirements into Nimble Documentation.®

Organizations seeking registration to ANSI/ISO/ASQ Q9001-2000 are wise to first assess their existing quality system processes and corresponding documentation. Trained internal personnel or consultants can perform a preliminary gap analysis to match processes and documentation, including records, against the standard. Findings generated by the analysis should specify any major and minor nonconformities in both processes and documentation. Recommendations should be specific.

For more information on ANSI/ISO/ASQ Q9001-2000 requirements, see Appendix C, Resources or browse the Web. The American Society for Quality (ASQ) maintains a Web site at www.asq.org, where you can link to other Web sites for ISO 9001 information. ASQ's monthly magazine, *Quality Progress*, and other publications devoted to quality frequently include articles about ISO 9001.

Figure 7.4 places the quality initiative's documentation requirements in perspective.

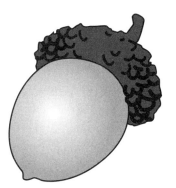

- If it moves, **train** it!

- If it doesn't move, **calibrate** it!

- If it isn't **documented,** it doesn't exist!

- If it isn't **authorized,** it didn't happen!

Source: Ann Niese, course notes, *Implementing ISO 9000*, presented at California State University, Long Beach, CA, 6–20 May 1995. Used with permission.

Figure 7.4 ISO 9000 in a nutshell.

THE BALDRIGE AWARD

John Kerr, in "But Is It Better than Baldrige?" presents four distinctions between ISO 9000 and the Baldrige Award.

1. ISO is not anyone's personal philosophy; it's an internationally ratified, bona fide *standard*.

2. ISO 9000 is easy to understand. "People see the short-term value in getting organized," says consultant Bob Bowen.

3. Where the Baldrige Award preoccupies contestants with goal-setting, ISO 9000 certification is the tool that opens the door to continuous improvement practices.

4. The Baldrige Award uses self-assessment, with a board of examiners screening for best practices. With ISO 9000, you document your process and the assessors come in to see if you've applied your documentation.

The 2001 Baldrige National Quality Criteria Program for Performance Excellence features a memo from Harry Hertz, director of the program, that emphasizes business challenges. He writes:

'Business as usual' really means challenge and change. Whether your business challenges are e-commerce and the Internet economy, globalization, rapid innovation, outsourcing and supply chain management, cost reduction, or just maintaining your competitive advantage, the Baldrige Criteria can help you address them. (National Institute of Standards and Technology 2001: www.quality.nist.gov)

Established by Public Law 100-107, the Malcolm Baldrige National Quality Improvement Act of 1987 was signed by President Ronald Reagan. Its purposes were to promote the awareness of quality excellence, to recognize quality achievement of U.S. companies and other organizations, and to publicize successful quality strategies. It is given annually to a manufacturing company, or subsidiary; service company, or subsidiary; small business; and education and health care institution. Where ISO 9001 registration verifies an *organization's* consistent, reliable quality system, the Baldrige Award advertises a *nation's* business quality as well as organizations'.

The award is conferred through a four-stage process. First, organizations submit a comprehensive application, which is reviewed and evaluated by a board of examiners. The application summarizes the company's practices and performance. Applications that score well in the first stage are subjected to a consensus review and evaluation. At the third stage, examiners visit the sites of applicants that score well in stage two. At stage four, a panel of judges review applications and recommend candidate award recipients to the Secretary of Commerce. After it is determined that an applicant will not move to the next stage of consideration, each applicant receives a feedback report. Prepared by the board of examiners, the reports target key gaps, reinforce company strengths, and help applicants learn new and better ways to evaluate suppliers, customers, partners, and even competitors.

Unlike ISO 9001, the Baldrige Award's seven examination criteria only indirectly refer to documentation. For example, they require demonstration that an organization's operational requirements address regulatory and other legal requirements. The organization must show excellence through its action plans. It must show how the organization obtains objective and reliable information on customer satisfaction. Its information and data must support key business operations and business strategy. Demonstration of an organization's performance management can be translated into documentation.

The zero-based approach and measured improvement features of Nimble Documentation,® on the other hand, correspond directly to the Baldrige Award criteria. Firms or departments that provide documentation (for instance, technical editing and word processing businesses or S&P functions), could benefit from the Baldrige Award criteria to evaluate and improve their own processes. Section *2.2, Strategy Deployment*, for example, examines how key strategic action planning translates into effective performance management and includes performance measures. Consider documentation metrics to fulfill these criteria such as customer satisfaction, zero defects, currentness, cycle time, volume, and cost. These indicators, discussed in chapter 6, could contribute to an effective performance management system for a documentation COE (see chapter 10) or other Nimble Documentation® function. The Baldrige Award criteria category *5, Human Resource Focus*, examines how a workforce is enabled to develop and use its full potential and how it aligns with performance objectives. Compare this category to COE self-directed team goals and performance, accountability, and evaluation. Each addresses a working environment conducive to full participation. Or look at the Baldrige Award criteria category *6, Process Management*. This category examines customer-focused design, product, (National Institute of Standards and Technology 2001) service delivery, key business, and support processes.

The foundation of zero-based documentation is its sources of need, including customers. The litmus test questions ask about customers' needs (see chapter 2). Baldrige award section *6.2, Business Processes*, and *6.3, Support Processes*, address continuous improvement (chapter 6). The Baldrige Award category *7* is *Business Results*; consider the documentation cost model (chapter 6). Performance management is the heart of the Baldrige Award. It is also the heart of Nimble Documentation® processes.

Following are the seven Baldrige Award criteria categories for performance excellence.

1. Leadership

2. Strategic Planning

3. Customer and Market Focus

4. Information and Analysis

5. Human Resource Focus

6. Process Management

7. Business Results

Each criterion requires some form of documentation, or evidence or record of conformity. Information and data from many sources (for example, from employees and customers) thread through the criteria. At the least, applicants for the award need to prepare extensive documentation to be reviewed by a board of examiners.

Table 7.2 shows a few Baldrige Award criteria categories as examples of documentation requirements or implications for written evidence. Common placement for documenting an

Table 7.2 Examples of Baldrige Award criteria and documentation requirements and implications.

Item	Heading	Documentation Requirement or Implication
1.2	**Public Responsibility and Citizenship**	How the company addresses the current and potential impacts on society. (Policies or procedures)
2.1	**Strategy Development**	How the company sets strategic directions for its competitive position, and how strategy development leads to an action plan. (Plans)
3.2	**Customer Relationships and Satisfaction**	How the company provides information to enable customers to seek assistance, conduct business, and voice complaints. (Procedures)
4.1	**Measurement and Analysis of Organizational Performance**	Selection, management, and use of information and data to improve the company's overall performance, including comparative information and data.
4.2	**Selection and Use of Comparisons and Information and Data**	Comparative information and data include benchmarking and competitive comparisons.
5.2	**Employee Education, Training, and Development**	How the company's education and training address key action plans and needs. (Objectives and procedures)
5.3	**Employee Well-Being and Satisfaction**	How the company maintains a work environment that supports employee well-being, satisfaction, and motivation. (Procedures and surveys)
6.1	**Product and Service Processes**	How new, significantly modified, and customized products and services are designed. (Procedures)
7.4	**Organizational Effectiveness Results**	Results of productivity, cycle time, and supplier and partner performance. (Data)

organization's compliance with the criteria is shown in parentheses; however, organizations use a variety of formats to document Baldrige Award criteria, including policies and procedures, annual reports, and formal plans.

SIX SIGMA

Six Sigma, the third quality initiative discussed in this book, was developed and implemented at Motorola Corporation in 1986. In 1988, Motorola also became one of the first companies to receive the Baldrige Award.

Essentially, Six Sigma is a highly disciplined process that helps an organization focus on selecting improvement projects that are based on customer requirements and the bottom line. The intent is to improve customer satisfaction and achieve quantifiable improvements to profitability. According to Harry K. Jackson, Jr., director of the Management Sciences Institute, the average Six Sigma project saves an organization $50,000 to $200,000 per project per year (2001).

Six Sigma offers a formal infrastructure and an approach that uses the DMAIC quality process:

D   Define

M   Measure

A   Analyze

I   Improve

C   Control

Sigma is a statistical term for measuring variability around the mean in a normal distribution, traditionally plus or minus three sigma. Assuming normalcy, a Six Sigma implementation can mean for an organization close to 100 percent in-process yields and defects below 0.002 parts per million. For example, in manufacturing, the process could be used to measure the number of sub-standard products. In a service industry, it could quantify completion delays.

The central idea behind Six Sigma is: If you can measure the number of defects in a process, you can figure out systematically how to eliminate them and get as close to zero defects as possible. Potential benefits of implementing Six Sigma include but are not limited to:

- Increased profitability

- Workforce reduction

- Optimal cycle time

- Maximum equipment uptime

- Improved customer satisfaction

- Improved capacity and output

- Reduction in total defects, rework, and scrap

- Increased product and service reliability

- Decreased work-in-progress (WIP)

- Improved process flow

- Improved administrative and service systems

To fully reap the benefits of Six Sigma, organizations must implement Six Sigma in all aspects of their operations.

The initiative is implemented through an executive directive to reduce variability in every company process and with every employee participating. An organization must establish an achievable, quantifiable quality goal, such as 3.4 parts-per-million defects (plus or minus six sigma).

Typically, employees attend a day-long course explaining the initiative. Each employee assesses their job function with respect to how they can improve the organization. Teams report on progress monthly and provide interim—commonly, twice a month—reports to the implementation leader, who could be an outside consultant or specially trained employee. The leader, who has had much training, usually is assigned full-time to lead the organization's improvement efforts. He or she measures and tracks actual versus scheduled milestones to keep the implementation moving forward.

Precise, clear documentation is critical to implement Six Sigma successfully. For example, the implementation team maintains an improvement book to document all efforts related to the process. The book is archived as a record and is made available to other teams. The book can also fulfill documentation requirements of quality standards such as ANSI/ISO/ASQ Q9001-2000 and QS-9000.

The process requires regular reviews, such as team presentations, as well as formal audits to ensure progress as planned. Full implementation of Six Sigma, particularly in large companies, can take many years. A five-year implementation is common.

Six Sigma documentation requirements and implications, all of which lend themselves to a nimble approach, include:

- Executive directive
- Vision
- Measurement indexes

- Quality goals
- Progress metrics
- Implementation plans

TOTAL QUALITY MANAGEMENT

Some say the *t* in *total quality management* really stands for *transformation*. A way to think of TQM is permeating the achievement of quality purposefully, rather than accidentally, through the pores of an organization. But, unlike ANSI/ISO/ASQ Q9001-2000, TQM is not a model. It is a philosophy. TQM continues where ISO 9001 leaves off. David S. Huyink, past chair of the ISO 9000 Quality Consortium, sees ISO 9001 as "a model with an embedded philosophy" and TQM as a "philosophy that can be expressed through a model such as the Malcolm Baldrige National Quality Award criteria" (1996, 615).

TQM focuses on continuously providing products that meet customer expectations at competitive prices—it is built on a quality foundation but sports a business spin.

John J. Hudiburg, former chairperson and chief executive officer of Florida Power and Light, describes the three most important factors for successful TQM.

First is a strong, visible, and consistent commitment by top management. This needs to be constantly emphasized and reinforced as a key success factor for the company. Second is a strong commitment to education and training of all employees. And last, it must be profoundly understood that there has to be a concrete system in place to make it happen, a systematic way of encouraging all employees to do their best. (Hudiburg 1991, 185)

Whereas many ISO 9001 clauses specifically *require* quality system documentation for compliance, Baldrige Award criteria *imply* documentation, primarily in the shape of plans and records, and other information formats, and as evidence of meeting the criteria. Six Sigma implies documentation, such as measurement indexes and implementation plans. TQM, however, does not indicate documentation at all.

TQM is addressed in this book not as a requirement or implication of documentation, but rather as a way an organization *does* documentation. Consider that TQM philosophy mirrors the elements of a documentation COE, as shown here:

- All plans and actions are responsive to demonstrated needs, including customers'
- Focus is on strategic business goals
- Leadership is committed to managed change

- Excellence is built into every aspect of the organization

- All employees participate

- Employees are skilled in examining and improving processes continuously

- Optimum performance is expected from every department and every employee

- Employees are highly trained

- Cross-functional teams are important

From a corporate S&P department to a technical writing and editing firm, TQM means quality for a documentation business. Consider each of the elements of TQM in terms of a documentation COE.

All plans and actions are responsive to demonstrated needs, including customers.' Customer service feedback sheets, focus group meetings with document owners to plan the format of procedures, the litmus test for streamlining documentation systems, improving uploading cycle time to meet managers' requirements—each of these are examples of TQM applied to a documentation function.

Focus is on strategic business goals. Flowing down company goals to function, team, and individual objectives points performance in the right direction.

Leadership is committed to managed change. Management supports transforming an organization into self-directed teams and provides resources for their success.

Excellence is built into every aspect of the organization. Examples include nonglare lighting, zero-defects forms, current bulletins, and lightning turnaround time for uploading.

All employees participate. The secretary becomes the leader of the team to overhaul organization charts, a plaque is awarded for 100 percent participation in continuous measurable improvement training.

Employees are skilled in examining and improving processes continuously. Staff members learn how to flowchart, establish and maintain metrics, and use fishbones for problem solving—living improvement.

Optimum performance is expected from every department and every employee. Word processing personnel are accountable for proofreading their work, and managers volunteer for 180-degree performance evaluations to learn how to listen better.

Checklist 7.1: Total Quality Managed Documentation Function

- ❏ Plans and actions responsive to needs

- ❏ Focus on strategic business goals

- ❏ Leadership committed to managed change

- ❏ Excellence built in

- ❏ All employees participate

- ❏ Employees skilled in examining and improving processes continuously

- ❏ Optimum performance from everyone

- ❏ Highly trained employees

- ❏ Cross-functional teams

Employees are highly trained. Uploaders become network certified writers, editors train on improved document management software, and word processing personnel learn to use style sheets and macros.

Cross-functional teams are important. The approval authority team brings in representatives of finance, legal, HR, and other functions to improve the approval authority system.

Despite the fact that TQM does not specify or imply documentation, the TQM model mirrors the elements of a documentation COE and can be applied to reinforce the introduction of quality improvement processes.

8

Other Applications

Solutions presented in this chapter address documentation challenges such as:

- Why a disclaimer belongs in an employee handbook

- How to make a user manual people-friendly

- Why measured improvement is important for safety program documentation

- How to keep ISO 14001 documentation lean

- What other documentation applications can benefit from the nimble approach

The basic elements of Nimble Documentation®—meeting customers' requirements and other sources of need, helping organizations respond quickly to changing market and workplace conditions, maintaining only documentation that fulfills a demonstrated need, and fixing documentation that causes problems—apply very well to a wide variety of documentation for world-class organizations. This chapter shows how the approach works for employee handbooks, user manuals, safety program documentation, and ISO 14001 requirements. The chapter also briefly describes the approach's value to other applications, such as QS-9000 and TL 9000.

EMPLOYEE HANDBOOKS

Say *employee handbook* and what comes to mind? For many, a picture emerges of bureaucratic policies, rules, and procedures. Small business owners who left larger companies because they were weary of all the regulations may be reluctant to establish employee rules. Managers of other organizations may see written policies as invitations for employee abuse. It doesn't have to be that way. In fact, some policies are legally required, such as preventing sexual harassment and discrimination. Further, spelling out workplace guidance sets a good foundation for growth. New companies, such as garage-born dot-coms that can get by without much formal direction, find employees bumping into one another when the work population grows. They yell "unfair" when employees are treated differently by different supervisors. They yell "unfair" louder to regulatory agencies and courts. Written policies can prevent misunderstandings, confusion, and duplicated effort, and they can reduce exposure to legal challenges and judgments. Employee handbooks allow employees to concentrate on core business. But how do the features of Nimble Documentation® apply to employee handbooks?

Start with customers. Ask: Who are they? What do they want to know? What laws and contractual requirements translate into employee issues? What harm could come to the organization if a proposed document or piece of information were omitted? What harm could come if it were *included?* And, finally, ask: How can an organization improve an existing handbook, for example, to lower costs, facilitate access, and keep information up to date?

These are the same basic questions to ask of quality manuals, procedures, forms, records, and other documentation. The answers to these questions, the litmus test of documentation plus inquiry into continuous process improvement, form the backbone of a world-class employee handbook.

Federal and state laws in the United States; national, provincial, and regional laws elsewhere; and municipal statutes dictate some of the information to be included in employee handbooks. Workers compensation regulations and rules about smoking, alcohol, and drugs at the workplace all have a place in the handbooks. You will see work hour rules; vacation, attendance, and leave policies; disability and disciplinary procedures; codes of conduct; and insurance provisions. In some handbooks, policies are written regarding personal appearance, direct deposit banking, and performance evaluations. Not surprisingly, employee policies often stretch across the greater portion of comprehensive company policies and procedures manuals. Companies that maintain data on specific handbook topics typically report that users research employee policies, such as sick leave, more than any other general set of topics.

A very large electronics firm converted its hard copy manuals to a Web-based system. During the testing phase, an improvement team was collecting information on the number of hits each Web document received. The team intended to check each document against litmus test questions. If no one ever viewed a particular document, and communicating the policy in writing was not required by law or contract, the team considered omitting the policy from the new system. Every time a user looked at a Web page, the system registered the view as a hit and compiled usage statistics on the document. Overwhelmingly, the most popular documents were employee policies. Workers wanted to know about benefits, but they also searched for information on layoffs, the company's performance appraisal rating system, and the policy prohibiting smoking in company buildings.

The same team recommended canceling an administrative guidebook and a supervisors' reference book, which included obsolete and duplicate employee policies. The company, which at the time was reorganizing and undergoing massive changes in the workforce and in its programs, decided the HR function could no longer keep the information in these books current. The function recognized the potential liability of obsolete and conflicting documentation, especially concerning employee benefits and procedures. Changes in personnel laws also contributed to the obsolescence. Few other areas of documentation these days change as frequently as employee policies.

Nimble Documentation® means information that is required or wanted, error-free, current, easy to access, responsive to changing conditions, and volume and cost conscious. The team delivered.

The recommendations in this book for user-friendly formats and styles (chapter 3) and for a user manual index (hard copy or online search engine) apply to employee handbooks as well (see the User Manuals section of this chapter).

Another consideration for an employee handbook is a disclaimer. When is a contract not a contract? The answer is when it says so. World-class organizations avoid spending valuable resources on defending themselves. Attorney Susan K. Krell of Jackson, Lewis, Schnitzler & Krupman, Hartford, Conn., writes in *The Personnel Law Update* (1995) about an employee who successfully sued a company claiming that the company handbook was an "implied contract" that conferred specific rights that the company violated.

This is not the first time a company has found itself incurring unintended liability because of its policies and procedures manual. That handy resource can lead to big headaches if it's not worded properly. Krell suggests including a prominent disclaimer that states the handbook, manual, or online collection of policies is *not* a contract, that it is provided only for informational purposes, and that the information may be revised at any time at the sole discretion of the company.

One disclaimer that is brief and clear was published by Hughes Aircraft Company in its online Company Policies and Practices Manual.

The policies, practices, and procedures set forth in this Company Policies and Practices Manual are guidelines for supervision. They are not intended to confer contractual rights of any kind upon any employee, or to create contractual obligations of any kind for the Company. The Company may revise, delete, or supplement any policy, practice, or procedure in this Company Policies and Practices Manual at any time in its sole discretion. (Hughes Aircraft Company, Company Policies and Practices Manual, 1996. Reprinted by permission.)

A disclaimer, a company may find, is more important for an employee handbook, or employee policies in a comprehensive manual, than in any other kind of business documentation.

To get a head start on developing an employee handbook, consider readily available resources. Software catalogs and retailers routinely advertise several employee handbooks available on disk or downloadable from a Web site. Libraries and bookshops carry sample manuals. Also, firms such as the Independent Small Business Employers of America publish hard copy options for handbooks along with a customizable CD or diskettes. Any of these aids can be a catalyst for an organization that is having difficulty generating an employee handbook (see Appendix C, Resources). The most challenging and time-consuming part of the effort, however, is customizing these documents, which often means structuring and facilitating interviews or focus groups with key personnel. In any case, it is advisable to seek professional legal advice before publishing an employee handbook.

USER MANUALS

User manuals are the first thing we see when we unpack a new computer or VCR, but the last thing we turn to when we are in trouble. What is it about them that makes user manuals so intimidating?

The best ones reduce users' frustrations—and time responding to SOS calls, faxes, and e-mail. Can user manuals serve as goodwill ambassadors? It's possible.

Questions similar to those posed for employee handbooks guide the development of user manuals along the Nimble Documentation® path. Who are the customers? What do they want to know? What harm could come if a proposed piece of information or step were omitted? What harm could come if it were included? How can an organization improve an existing user manual, for example, to reduce costs, facilitate access, and keep information current with changing technology?

Informal correspondence with many users over the years indicates the benefits of the following features; however, the best way to create a good user manual is to get customers' direct feedback. How do you do that? One way is to maintain help line databases. Document trouble calls and maintain statistics. Discover the kind of problems that plague users again and again. Then, draft a revised manual to clarify the problem areas. Conduct a usability study (see chapter 4) and pilot the draft with lay users. Eliminate unnecessary instructions that might distract readers and contribute to a manual's intimidating bulkiness.

Include tips on undoing steps, particularly for long sequences of instruction. "Undo" instructions are a godsend. All humans at least occasionally press the wrong key or overlook a step. Help users undo missteps. Include call-out boxes, marginal notes, and other highlighted instructions. The true story of the *any* key teaches us not to assume anything (see chapter 2).

Modular or play script formats suit user manuals well for several reasons. One, step-by-step instructions written in these formats are easy to follow, and two, *if–then* decision points stand out (see chapter 3). It doesn't hurt that these formats also project a high-tech image. Graphics, especially screen captures, help users relate instructions printed in the manual to what they see on their monitors. But perhaps the best user manual isn't a manual at all. Online help delivers help at the point of need. Help is just a click away with popular help software such as ForeHelp, RoboHelp, and True Help.

If prizes were awarded to documentation that frustrates users, one would have to go to inadequate indexes. How many times has each of us looked in a user manual for help, known the instructions we needed were in there because we found them before, and still could not locate the information we needed!

If you are responsible for writing a user manual, test drive the draft index with people who are unfamiliar with the product. Gather all the terms that they could use to look up the same information. Here is a case in point. At least seven different terms are used for logging off a computer, depending on the operating system and application: *close, bye, end, exit, logout, logoff,* and *quit.*

Include synonyms, terms that are more general, and more specific words. Don't be afraid of redundancy. Remember that few people read an index like a novel. They read only the entries they need. For example, include *search* as well as *find, preferences* as well as *options.* List subheadings by themselves as well as under other terms. For example, list *smart quotes* as an individual entry as well as *smart* indented under *quotes.* Be generous with cross references. If you are using the indexing feature of word processing software, use it only as a foundation. Modify the draft index to make it more comprehensive and user-friendly.

Finding information in a well-equipped user manual can be faster than getting a colleague's response to a user's voice mail message or a technical support person's live voice.

SAFETY PROGRAMS

Like employee handbooks and user manuals, documentation for safety programs benefits from the nimble approach. In this case, legal requirements serve as some of the customers, because they must be satisfied to maintain an organization's good business health. Other customer requirements may be contractual. For example, a construction company may be obligated by written agreement to provide safety training to workers at a building site. Also, employees are customers because they use procedures manuals, training records, and other safety program documentation.

Some states, such as California, require companies to establish and maintain programs to ensure a safe and healthy environment for their employees. An injury and illness prevention program that complies with the California Codes of Regulations specifies documentation components, such as a code of safe practices. The code includes supervisor and employee responsibilities, working conditions, and protective equipment; records of formal inspections to verify compliance with the codes; records of workplace-related accident, near-miss, and illness investigations and corrective action; and employee training records.

Nimble Documentation® for safety programs, like other policies and procedures, adopts a zero-based approach (see chapter 2). Only information required by law, contract, or prudent business practice is included. Only information that can harm an organization if omitted is documented. Language and graphics that potentially could confuse users are left out. Safety program records are maintained and stored according to the specifications of an integrated records retention program. Documentation includes forms necessary to meet program requirements, such as accident investigation, employee safety suggestion, employee training, and hazard evaluation and abatement. Figures 8.1 and 8.2 present sample forms for a group safety training session and hazard evaluation and abatement, respectively. They were prepared for an educational agency.

The organization's approval authority system assigns responsibilities for the safety program, including establishing policy. For example, the program itself is approved by the highest level operations officer or designee. A safety coordinator verifies accident investigations and evaluates safety hazards, and both employees and supervisors verify that employees have completed required safety training.

[LMN Logo]
Group Safety Training Session

Date of training: _____   Trainer: _____

Type of training: I & IP: _____   Hazard communication: _____

Training schedule: Initial: _____   Refresher: _____   New assignment: _____

The following employees have attended the training session indicated above. Training was conducted according to training procedure 6.2.2A. The signature of each employee verifies that he or she has attended this training session.

Employee name (please print)	Employee number	Employee signature
1.		
2.		
3.		
4.		
5.		
6.		
7.		
8.		
9.		
10.		
11.		
12.		
13.		
14.		
15.		

_____
Signature of safety trainer

LMN Form 6.2.2A Rev. 11/20/2002

Figure 8.1   Group safety training session form.

[LMN Logo]
Hazard Evaluation and Abatement Form

Date of inspection: _____ Inspector: _____

Department: _____ Location: _____

General Observations

1. **Housekeeping**
   (   ) Acceptable   (   ) Corrective action needed   (   ) Not applicable

   _____

   _____

   _____

2. **Fire extinguishers**
   (   ) Acceptable   (   ) Corrective action needed   (   ) Not applicable

   _____

   _____

   _____

3. **First aid and emergency response equipment**
   (   ) Acceptable   (   ) Corrective action needed   (   ) Not applicable

   _____

   _____

   _____

4. **Electrical**
   (   ) Acceptable   (   ) Corrective action needed   (   ) Not applicable

   _____

   _____

   _____

Page 1 of 2
LMN Form 6.2.2B Rev. 12/4/2002

Figure 8.2 Hazard evaluation and abatement form.

5. **Material handling and storage**
   ( ) Acceptable   ( ) Corrective action needed   ( ) Not applicable

   _____

   _____

   _____

6. **Equipment**
   ( ) Acceptable   ( ) Corrective action needed   ( ) Not applicable

   _____

   _____

   _____

7. **Exits**
   ( ) Acceptable   ( ) Corrective action needed   ( ) Not applicable

   _____

   _____

   _____

8. **Personal protective equipment**
   ( ) Acceptable   ( ) Corrective action needed   ( ) Not applicable

   _____

   _____

   _____

9. **Storage areas**
   ( ) Acceptable   ( ) Corrective action needed   ( ) Not applicable

   _____

   _____

   _____

Completed by:_____   Date: _____

Page 2 of 2
LMN Form 6.2.2B Rev. 12/4/2002

Figure 8.2 Hazard evaluation and abatement form *(continued)*.

The plain vanilla text format (see chapter 3) is common for hard copy safety manuals and usually is adequate and economical to write and maintain. Whatever format is adopted, step-by-step instructions for handling safety emergencies should be especially quick to access and easy to follow. Many organizations now have their safety manuals on an intranet. Some convert the manual directly to HTML, but others maintain the manual online as individual PDF files. The advantage is that individual safety policies and procedures can be printed for easy hard copy reading. In an emergency or disaster that precludes use of the online system, critical information on hard copies printed earlier off the system can be accessed.

Measured improvement to an organization's safety program documentation could encompass some of the same elements as other documentation. Useful metrics include indicators of defect-free writing; currentness; processing time, which is particularly important for investigating and correcting workplace hazards and injuries; training; volume; and cost (see chapter 6).

Because laws and regulations change, and organizations may restructure frequently, establishing and maintaining regularly scheduled safety documentation reviews are important. Speedy processing time for investigating and correcting problems prevents subsequent accidents, injuries, and illnesses. Metrics that capture processing time support improvement efforts objectively and eliminate sometimes divisive hearsay. Well-maintained and regularly reviewed safety training records provide feedback on employees who have been trained and those who need to be scheduled for training. Volume metrics tend to keep documentation trim. Finally, organizations that know the cost of their processes, including safety documentation, can investigate alternatives. For example, regularly measured costs allow an organization to compare the expense of preparing and revising documentation by internal documentation staff, by a safety function or department, by the general administrative function, or by an outside contractor (outsourcing). Without cost metrics, objective improvement decisions are hard to come by, and organizations tend to keep the status quo—even if the status quo is needlessly expensive.

Features of nimble indexes for safety manuals, hard copy or online, are the same as for user manuals. For example, *glasses* should be listed as a stand-alone entry and should also be listed under *protective equipment*, under *eye care*, and as *safety glasses*. Pilot-test browsers to be sure they find information and modify content or meta data to ensure intended results.

ISO 14001

ISO 14001, a standard for environmental management systems, is another application whose documentation requirements and implications can benefit from the nimble approach. This section presents an overview of the standard, then addresses its documentation issues.

As communications technology continues to expand, the world continues to shrink. World-class companies are constantly finding better and faster ways to communicate and, as they march toward a global economy, more and more are finding it is just as easy to do business in Brussels as it is in Burbank. The problems crop up when companies want to do business in both Brussels *and* Burbank.

ISO 14001 was developed to provide a structure for environmental management that would be accepted globally and could be integrated with organizations' overall management activity. Another goal of the standard was to provide assurance that environmental performance would meet the many and sometimes confusing array of regulatory, audit, and other environmental management requirements. Creation of the standard has also been in response to public concern over industrial impact on both the local and world environment. The growing sentiment is that organizations should take responsibility for their own deeds.

With the potential to replace regional and national environmental requirements that impede international commerce, ISO 14001 also can reduce the costs associated with compliance with multiple systems—a particular benefit for multinational firms. The scope of ISO 14001 is broad, and some international suppliers are feeling pressure to comply.

ISO 14001 is similar to ISO 9001 in that both are comprehensive standards. Also like the ISO 9000 series, the 14000 series includes guidelines. Prudent businesses are adopting the standard to reduce potential environmental liabilities before they become problems and are promoting awareness among employees of the connection between their jobs and environmental compliance.

ISO 14001 features six major environmental management system requirements:

1. General requirements

2. Environmental policy

3. Planning

4. Implementation and operation

5. Checking and corrective action

6. Management review

Documentation, as in ANSI/ISO/ASQ Q9001-2000 and other quality initiatives, is a critical component of ISO 14001. Several clauses of the standard clearly specify documentation, such as *environmental objectives and targets; roles, responsibility, and authorities; information, in paper or electronic form, to (a) describe the core elements of the management system and their interaction and (b) provide direction to related documentation; and documented procedures* (ASQC, ISO, and ANSI 1996). Other ISO 14001 clauses imply documentation, or, at least, can be fulfilled through documented policies, procedures, and records (see Table 8.1). Documentation also can be a primary vehicle for promoting employee awareness of the system and for establishing a history of responsible environmental management.

Environmental management documentation may be integrated into an organization's standard management and operating policies and procedures or it may stand alone. Many processes that affect quality and are specified in quality system documentation also apply to environmental management. However, many organizations integrate their quality system documentation into standard management and operating policies and procedures. ISO 14001 does not specify how an organization meets its documentation requirements and should not justify more manuals if existing documentation can accommodate environmental management. In fact, the introduction to the standard itself addresses the option of complying with ISO 14001 requirements by adapting existing

Table 8.1 ISO 14001 requirements and implications for documentation and records.

Note: The term *implied documentation* means documented procedures or other publications (hard copy or electronic) typically are used to demonstrate and communicate the information that can fulfill these requirements.

Number	Section and Clause	Documentation Requirement or Implication	Records Requirement
4.2	ENVIRONMENTAL POLICY PLANNING	Documented environmental policy.	
4.3.1	Environmental aspects	[Implied documentation] Procedure to identify the environmental aspects of controlled activities, products, or services that can significantly impact the environment.	
4.3.2	Legal and other requirements	[Implied documentation] Procedure to identify legal and other environmental requirements.	
4.3.3	Objectives and targets	Documented environmental objectives and targets at every relevant function and level within the organization.	
4.4	IMPLEMENTATION AND OPERATION		
4.4.1	Structure and responsibility	Documented roles, responsibility, and authority.	
4.4.2	Training, awareness and competence	[Implied documentation] Procedures for importance of conformance, significant environmental impacts of work activities and benefits of improved performance, roles and responsibilities in achieving conformance, and potential consequences of nonconformance.	
4.4.3	Communication	[Implied documentation] Procedures for internal communication. Documented procedures for communication from external interested parties.	Recorded decisions on processes for external communication on its significant environmental aspects.
4.4.4	Environmental management system documentation	Information, in electronic or hard copy media, to: • Describe core elements of the environmental management system and their interaction • Guide related documentation	
4.4.5	Document control	[Implied documentation] Procedures to control required documents to ensure they: • Can be located • Are reviewed periodically, updated when needed, and approved by authorized personnel • Are available in current version at all locations where essential environmental management system activities are performed • Are promptly removed from use when no longer current, or otherwise protected against unintended use • If obsolete, are retained for legal or other purposes and properly identified Documents shall be legible, dated, kept orderly, readily identifiable, and retained for a specified period. [Implied documentation] Procedures and responsibilities to create and modify documentation.	

Continued

Number	Section and Clause	Documentation Requirement or Implication	Records Requirement
4.4.6	Operational control	Documented procedures for situations where absence could lead to deviations from environmental policy, objectives, and targets; stipulated operating criteria. [Implied documentation] Procedures related to significant environmental aspects of goods and services used by the organization, and procedures and requirements communicated to suppliers.	
4.4.7	Emergency preparedness and response	[Implied documentation] Procedures to identify potential emergencies, and the organization's planned preparation and response to accidents and emergency situations, and for preventing and mitigating associated environmental impacts.	
4.5	**CHECKING AND CORRECTIVE ACTION**		
4.5.1	Monitoring and measurement	Documented procedures to regularly monitor and measure key characteristics of operations and activities posing potential significant impact to the environment. Documented procedure to periodically evaluate compliance with relevant environmental legislation and regulations.	Records of performance, relevant operational controls, and conformance to organization's environmental objectives and targets. Calibration and maintenance records of monitoring equipment retained according to organization's procedures.
4.5.2	Nonconformance and corrective and preventive action	[Implied documentation] Procedures to define responsibility and authority for handling and investigating nonconformance, acting to mitigate impacts, and to initiate and complete corrective and preventive action. Record in documented procedures any changes implemented as a result of corrective or preventive action.	
4.5.3	Records	[Implied documentation] Procedures to identify, maintain, and dispose of environmental records, including training records and results of audits and reviews. Documented retention times for records.	Records shall be legible, identifiable, and traceable to involved activity, product, or service; stored and maintained so they are readily retrievable and protected against damage, deterioration, and loss. Maintain records to demonstrate conformance to requirements of the standard.
4.5.4	Environmental management system audit	[Implied documentation] Procedures for periodic environmental management system audits. Procedures shall address scope of the audit, frequency and methodologies, responsibilities and requirements for conducting the audit, and methods for reporting results.	
4.6	MANAGEMENT REVIEW		Documented management reviews of the environmental management system to ensure its continuing suitability, adequateness, and effectiveness, and to identify opportunities for continual improvement.

management system elements. Further, ANSI/ISO/ASQ Q9001-2000, *Introduction, 0.4 Compatibility with other management systems*, states:

> *This International Standard has been aligned with ANSI/ISO/ASQC Q14001-1996 in order to enhance the compatibility of the two standards for the benefit of the user community.*
>
> *This International Standard does not include requirements specific to other management systems, such as those particular to environmental management, occupational health and safety management, financial management or risk management. However, this International Standard enables an organization to align or integrate its own quality management system with related management system requirements. It is possible for an organization to adapt its existing management system(s) in order to establish a quality management system that complies with the requirements of this International Standard.* (ASQ 2000, xi)

Organizations are beginning to take advantage of the purposeful alignment compatibility, for example, by developing a single, combined quality-environmental system manual.

Forms can fulfill some of the records requirements of ISO 14001 (clause 4.5.3), and approval authority for environmental management transactions can meet structure and responsibility requirements (clause 4.4.1). Documentation functions may wish to pay particular attention to clauses *4.4.5, Document control*, and *4.5.3, Records*.

How do the features of Nimble Documentation® apply to ISO 14001? Their applicability is fundamentally the same as for company policies and procedures, employee handbooks, user manuals, and safety program documentation. A source of need in this case is *interested parties*, defined in the standard (Definition 3.11) as "individual or group concerned with or affected by the environmental performance of an organization" (see clause *4.3.3, Objectives and targets*). This could include employees, the general public, regulatory agencies, and many other parties. Another source of need that must be satisfied are legal requirements (see clause *4.3.2, Legal and other requirements*). The litmus test of Nimble Documentation® along with the focus on sources of need, is implied by clause 4.3.3.

> *When establishing and reviewing its objectives, an organization shall consider the legal and other requirements, its significant environmental aspects, its technological options and its financial, operational and business requirements, and the views of interested parties.* (ASQC, ISO, and ANSI 1996, 3)

An important feature of Nimble Documentation® applies to ISO 14001. The standard was designed to allow for a wide range of documentation associated with an environmental management system, but also to minimize the documentation burden placed on compliant organizations. In fact, the standard itself nearly paraphrases a central tenet of zero-based documentation: Documented procedures are required only "where their absence could lead to deviations from the environmental policy and the objectives and targets" (ASQC, ISO, and ANSI 1996, 4).

A world-class organization's financial, operational, and business requirements would not be met by environmental management documentation that was unnecessary or by the omission of documentation that was. And it behooves such an organization to continue to improve existing environmental management documentation, for example, to lower costs, facilitate access, and keep information up to date.

ADDITIONAL APPLICATIONS

Applying the zero-based approach and the litmus test to directive documentation and maintaining continuous measured process improvement can help an organization satisfy its sources of need, including legal and other requirements; improve quality; and save time and resources. In this chapter, Nimble Documentation® processes were shown to apply to employee handbooks, user manuals, safety programs, and ISO 14001. In the next chapter, the approach will be shown to apply equally as well to documentation relatives, such as records, forms, and approval authority systems. What other documentation would benefit from becoming more nimble? Documentation required to comply with other standards is an obvious candidate.

QS-9000, the quality requirement unveiled by the big three auto makers (Chrysler, Ford, and General Motors) in 1994, expands ISO 9001 requirements. It adds three sector-specific requirements: the production part approval process, continuous improvement, and manufacturing capabilities. QS-9000 also includes customer-specific requirements for each of the three auto makers. Documentation requirements of the standard are the same as ISO 9001's, plus warrants (an industry standard document), controlled drawings and design changes, preliminary process performance results for critical characteristics, appearance approval reports, inspection results, laboratory test reports, process flow diagrams, and many others. Some have estimated the QS-9000 documentation requirements at three times ISO 9001's. Should an organization become QS-9000 registered? Both General Motors and Chrysler mandated that its suppliers become registered to the standard by 1997. At press time, Ford had not required its suppliers to be QS-9000-compliant.

Should a supplier adopt the Nimble Documentation® approach? Because the auto makers by definition are their suppliers' customers, or a source of need, it would make no sense for prudent suppliers to ignore the standard—a voice of the customer. Furthermore, no supplier can remain globally competitive buried in documentation that needlessly constrains processes, is costly to maintain, or exposes the supplier to liability. Likewise, no supplier should do without documentation whose absence would be harmful, or should have documentation that could hurt.

Telecommunications, like the auto industry, has adopted an industry-specific quality standard. TL 9000 is a set of requirements for a quality management system and performance measurements for suppliers of telecommunications hardware, software, and services. The Quality Excellence for Suppliers of Telecommunications (QuEST) Forum established TL 9000 to foster continued improvements to the industry's products and services, including service reliability. Comprised of telecommunications service providers, suppliers, and liaisons, the QuEST Forum publishes, distributes, and maintains the *TL 9000 Quality Management System Requirements Handbook* and the *TL 9000 Quality Management System Measurements Handbook*. The QuEST Forum created and developed TL 9000 to eliminate the need to conform to multiple telecommunications quality management standards.

TL 9000, like QS-9000, builds on an ISO 9000 foundation, specifically, ANSI/ISO/ASQ Q9001-2000. Also, like QS-9000, TL 9000 promotes industry-wide consistency and efficiency and can reduce redundancy and improve customer satisfaction.

TL 9000 compliance extends many benefits to telecommunications customers, subscribers, and suppliers, including:

- Continual improvement of service to subscribers

- Enhanced relationships between organizations and their customers

- Common requirements for quality management

- Efficient management of external audits and site visits

- Uniform measurements

- Overall cost reduction and increased competitiveness

- Better management and improved performance

- Industry benchmarks

Several components form the TL 9000 structure:

- ANSI/ISO/ASQ Q9001-2000

- Common TL 9000 Requirements

- Hardware, Software, and Services Specific Quality Management System Requirements

- Common TL 9000 Measurements

- Hardware, Software, and Services Specific Quality Management System Measurements

Because of their common foundation, minimum documentation requirements for TL 9000 are virtually identical to other quality management standards, such as ANSI/ISO/ASQ Q9001-2000 and QS-9000, and also ISO 14001, an environmental management system standard:

- Quality policy

- Quality objectives

- Quality manual

- Documented procedures

- Other documents needed for effective process planning, operation, and control

- Controlled records

To develop and maintain TL 9000-compliant documentation that minimizes maintenance burden, adopt the Nimble Documentation® approach. Identify sources of need, then check all documents or potential documents, or parts, against the litmus test.

Other industries that require documentation to comply with regulations and specialized quality standards include healthcare, food, pharmaceuticals, energy, government, education, and hospitality.

When you think of documentation that can help an organization become more competitive—trim, flexible, accessible, and responsive to change—think of presentation software, such as Microsoft PowerPoint (see chapter 4). Think of proposals, training manuals, and reports; think of performance evaluations, memos, and letters. Then apply the methodology of Nimble Documentation.®

9

Documentation Relatives

Solutions presented in this chapter address documentation challenges such as:

- How to develop a records retention program that minimizes both liability and expense

- The benefits of automated forms

- How to minimize the time and expense of processing forms

- How to streamline an approval authority system

- The legality of digital signatures

A world-class documentation system integrates directive document relatives. Inconsistent, disorganized, or bloated records, forms, and approval authority systems can muddle or clog an otherwise nimble system of policies, procedures, and work instructions. On the other hand, by applying the zero-based approach (see chapter 2), these related components can strengthen and simplify business processes and they can reduce or conserve operating expenses. Quality standards, such as ANSI/ISO/ASQ Q9001-2000, require documented, managed records relating to the quality of an organization's products or services (see chapter 7). An environmental management system standard, such as ISO 14001, specifies or implies records maintenance, retention, and disposition (see chapter 8). Also, prudent business requires a controlled records retention system to contain the costly runaway records proliferation that often results from an organization's information explosion. Well-structured and sensibly managed company forms can make it easier for internal and external customers to communicate with an organization and maneuver through administrative transactions quickly. Authorization for document control or committing company funds or other resources is a legal requirement; adopting a system that communicates that authority readily and clearly is smart.

This chapter presents the foundation for a practical and legally accepted records retention program and describes a popular seven-step method for developing a program that shares features with the zero-based approach to documentation. The chapter also addresses efficient forms and elements of a trim, responsive approval authority system, including the use of digital signatures.

RECORDS

"Our records have grown out of control. Each year we create or receive mounds of paper records, generate stacks of computer printouts and produce cabinets full of microfilm and other duplicate records. The next year the volume increases even more." In *Records Retention Procedures* (1995), Donald S. Skupsky presents a convincing case for companies to establish a consistent, organized, and economical records retention program. The information explosion has created a records explosion. Companies keep records indefinitely as protection against litigation, but ironically end up supporting their adversaries' cases with subpoenaed information that should have been destroyed long ago. To the legal argument for a strong records retention program, Skupsky adds the costs of space, staff, equipment, and supplies for unnecessary or risky records and the need to readily access valuable and current information. His case is compelling. So much so that two new standards for records retention are being developed as we go to press: *Developing and Operating a Records Retention Program, Part I and Part II.* The proposed *Part I* will provide "guidance to organizations in setting up a retention program as a component of an overall records management program." *Part II* promises to "expand upon the basic elements outlined in [Part I] and "address the specific issues, nuances, and requirements necessary for addressing electronic records in a retention program." (www.arma.org/publications/standards/workinprogress.cfm)

ANSI/ISO/ASQ Q9001-2000 is another good reason to establish a nimble, comprehensive records retention program. As shown in Table 7.1, ISO 9001 certification requires records maintenance in many areas, such as section *4.2.1* and *4.2.4, Documentation requirements, General* and *Control of records*, respectively; *5.6.1, Management review, General*; *6.2.2, Human Resources, Competence, awareness and training*; and *7.4.1, Purchasing process.* (For an in-depth analysis of ISO 9000 records requirements, although based on the 1994 series of ISO 9000 standards, see Eugenia K. Brumm's book *Managing Records for ISO 9000 Compliance*, 1995.) Referencing applicable records directly in quality system documents or linking to them online, such as in operating procedures, saves users' time.

Traditionally, a records retention program establishes retention schedules for each of up to thousands of individual entries. Usually, the program and retention schedule access are designed around precise record titles and the department responsible for each record. The problem is that when companies reorganize or departments simply change names (a common occurrence in firms subscribing to continuous process improvement and in mergers and acquisitions), records are difficult to locate. Staff members are challenged by obsolete, inaccessible records and companies are faced with high maintenance costs.

Skupsky's solution is four integrated files or reports: (1) legal research index, (2) legal group file, (3) records retention schedule, and (4) records listing with retention periods. The beauty of

Skupsky's method is that by classifying information into logical units, it can be processed economically as grouped data rather than individual data points.

The legal research index is organized by legal group code and subject and by the laws regarding retention. Table 9.1 shows the jurisdiction, the location where the law applies (Jur.); citation, the 14-digit code used to identify laws, from *Legal Requirements for Business Records* (LRBR Code); subject of the law; legal group code; legal period of retention; and the records affected and agency responsible for administering the law. Second is the legal group file, which classifies and codes laws into related groups and assigns a retention period for each group. Table 9.2 shows the legal group, subject, description, legal requirements, legal considerations, and total retention period for legal purposes. Next, the records retention schedule places related records into coded categories, and includes descriptions, retention periods, retention periods for copies, and offices responsible for the categorized records (see Table 9.3). Last in Skupsky's retention method is a

Table 9.1 Sample legal research index.

Jur.	Citation	LRBR Code	Subject	Legal Group	Legal Period	Records Affected/Agency
US	26 CFR 1.6001-1	US 226-0970-00	tax income	ACC000	IND	accounting records Internal Revenue Service
US	26 CFR 31.6001-1	US 226-1090-00	tax employment	ACC000	4	payroll records Internal Revenue Service
US	26 CFR 31.6001-2	US 226-1100-00	tax employment	ACC000	4	payroll records Internal Revenue Service
US	26 CFR 31.6001-4	US 226-1130-00	tax employment	ACC000	4	payroll records; unemployment taxes Internal Revenue Service
US	26 CFR 31.6001-5	US 226-1150-00	tax employment	ACC000	4	payroll records Internal Revenue Service
US	26 CFR 301.6501(A)-1	US 226-1870-00	tax income— assessment general	ACC000	AS3	accounting records Internal Revenue Service
US	26 CFR 301.6501(C)-1	US 226-1880-00	tax income— assessment fraud	ACC000	ASIN	accounting records Internal Revenue Service
US	26 CFR 301.6501(E)-1	US 226-1890-00	tax gift— assessment understatement by 25%	ACC000	AS6	accounting records Internal Revenue Service
US	26 CFR 301.6501(E)-1	US 226-1890-00	tax income— assessment understatement by 25%	ACC000	AS6	accounting records Internal Revenue Service
US	26 CFR 301.6532-1(A)	US 226-1960-00	tax income— suit	ACC000	LA2	accounting records Internal Revenue Service
US	26 CFR 301.6532-2	US 226-1970-00	tax income— suit	ACC000	LA2	accounting records Internal Revenue Service
US	29 CFR 5.5	US 229-0040-00	contract federal— payroll	ACC000	3	payroll records Labor, Department of
US	29 CFR 516.5	US 229-0300-00	employment payroll records	ACC000	3	payroll records Labor, Department of: Wage and Hour Division
US	29 CFR 1620.22(B)	US 229-0910-00	limitation of actions wages, recovery of	ACC000	LA3	payroll records Equal Employment Opportunity Commission

Source: Donald S. Skupsky, *Records Retention Procedures*, Englewood, CO: Information Requirements Clearinghouse, 1995. Used with permission.

Table 9.2 Sample legal group file.

Legal Group	Subject	Description	Legal Requirements	Legal Considerations	Total
ACC000	Accounting/Tax General	Includes tax assessment or specific tax requirements for accounts payable, accounts receivable, etc. **Legal Requirements:** Minimum TX: TTC 111.0041 Maximum US: 26 CFR 31.6001-1 Selected US: 26 CFR 31.6001-1 **Legal Considerations:** Minimum US: 26 USC 6532 Maximum US: 26 CFR 301.6501(C)-1 Selected US: 26 CFR 301.6501(E)-1 **Selected Legal Retention Period**	**3** **4** **4**	**LA1** **ASIND** **6**	**6**
ACC100	Accounting/Tax Capital Acquisitions	Includes depreciation, capital gains and losses, and repairs for capital property **Legal Requirements:** Minimum US: 26 CFR 1.167(E)-1 Maximum US: 26 CFR 1.167(E)-1 Selected US: 26 CFR 1.167(E)-1 **Legal Considerations:** Minimum US: 26 CFR 301.6501(A)-1 Maximum US: 26 CFR 301.6501(C)-1 Selected US: 26 CFR 301.6501(A)-1 **Selected Legal Retention Period**	**ACT** **ACT** **ACT**	**AS3** **IND** **6**	**ACT+6**
ADV000	Advertising Packaging/ Labeling	Includes laws related to promotions, introductory offers, product size advantages, etc. See MAN100 for product liability considerations. **Legal Requirements:** Minimum US: 16 CFR 502.101 Maximum US: 16 CFR 502.101 Selected US: 16 CFR 502.101 **Legal Considerations:** Minimum TX: 16.003 Maximum TX: 16.003 Selected TX: 16.003/LIABILITY CONCERNS **Selected Legal Retention Period**	**1** **1** **1**	**LA2** **LA2** **ACT+2**	**ACT+2**

Source: Donald S. Skupsky, *Records Retention Procedures*, Englewood, CO: Information Requirements Clearinghouse, 1995. Used with permission.

Table 9.3 Sample records retention schedule.

Retention code	Retention Category Descriptive/Cross Reference	Legal Group	Retention of Official Records				Retention of Copies	Office of Record
			Legal	User	Other	Total		
ACC1000	Accounting Accounts Payable/Receivable Records related to payment of financial obligations and receipt of revenues. Includes vouchers, vendor invoices and statements; payroll and payroll deductions; government contracts and grants, contributions, and other income.	ACC000	6	3	0	6	MAX1	Accounting
ACC1010	Accounting Journals/Ledgers Records used to transfer charges between accounts and for summarizing account information. Final, annual records only.	ACC000	6	10	0	10	MAX1	Accounting
ACC2000	Accounting Capital Property Includes purchase and sales of property and equipment, depreciation, improvements, etc. Includes financial obligations associated with capital expenditures, purchase of land, buildings, equipment, furnishings, motor vehicles; material transfers, work orders, additions or improvements to building or equipment, property reporting.	ACC100	ACT+6	ACT	0	ACT+6	MAX5	Accounting
ACC9900	Accounting General Records related to accounting records not previously covered. Includes accounting reports, control documents; system input, maintenance and changes.	NONE	0	3	0	3	MAX1	Accounting

Source: Donald S. Skupsky, *Records Retention Procedures,* Englewood, CO: Information Requirements Clearinghouse, 1995. Used with permission.

records listing, with retention periods, that flows down from the coded schedule (see Table 9.4). Figure 9.1 can help developers determine the scope of legal research required for a records retention program (Skupsky, 1995).

The seven-step method for developing a records retention program shares features with the zero-based approach to documentation. The method's nimbleness lies in its purposeful approach, that is, retaining records only if and as long as required by several sources of need, for example, customers—including executives, accounting, legal functions, and other administrative functions—and laws. Skupsky's method also reduces development and maintenance costs by grouping and coding records with similar requirements and by avoiding assigning individual records to departments. The seven steps follow, but readers should refer to *Records Retention Procedures* (Skupsky, 1995) for details on developing a nimble, comprehensive records retention program.

1. *Complete preliminary procedures.* Obtain approval and support for the program. Inventory existing records maintained by the organization. Determine organizational structure activities, business locations, and regulatory agencies.

2. *Research laws.* Review applicable laws; include legal counsel.

Table 9.4 Sample records listing with retention periods.

Department/Location Record Series	Record Code	Retention Category	Legal Group	Retention of Official Records				Retention of Copies	Office of Record	Status
				Legal	User	Other	Total			
Accounting										
Accounts Payable										
accounts payable	ACC-00-01	ACC1000	ACC000	6	3	0	6	MAX1	Accounting	Official
accounts payable invoices	ACC-00-02	ACC1000	ACC000	6	3	0	6	MAX1	Accounting	Official
accounts payable ledgers	ACC-00-03	ACC1010	ACC000	6	10	0	10	MAX1	Accounting	Official
amortization records	ACC-00-04	ACC1000	ACC000	6	3	0	6	MAX1	Accounting	Official
bills	ACC-00-05	ACC1000	ACC000	6	3	0	6	MAX1	Accounting	Official
cash disbursements	ACC-00-06	ACC1000	ACC000	6	3	0	6	MAX1	Accounting	Official
commission statements	ACC-00-07	MIS1000	NONE	0	1	0	1	MAX1	Various	Official
cost accounting records	ACC-00-08	ACC1000	ACC000	6	3	0	6	MAX1	Accounting	Official
cost sheets	ACC-00-09	ACC1000	ACC000	6	3	0	6	MAX1	Accounting	Official
cost statements	ACC-00-10	ACC1000	ACC000	6	3	0	6	MAX1	Accounting	Official
credit card charge slips	ACC-00-11	ACC1000	ACC000	6	3	0	6	MAX1	Accounting	Official
credit card statements	ACC-00-12	ACC1000	ACC000	6	3	0	6	MAX1	Accounting	Official
debit advices	ACC-00-13	ACC1000	ACC000	6	3	0	6	MAX1	Accounting	Official
donations	ACC-00-14	ACC1000	ACC000	6	3	0	6	MAX1	Accounting	Official
expense reports	ACC-00-15	ACC1000	ACC000	6	3	0	6	MAX1	Accounting	Official
invoices	ACC-00-16	ACC1000	ACC000	6	3	0	6	MAX1	Accounting	Official
petty cash records	ACC-00-17	ACC1000	ACC000	6	3	0	6	MAX1	Accounting	Official
property taxes	ACC-00-18	ACC1000	ACC000	6	3	0	6	MAX1	Accounting	Official
purchase requisitions	ACC-00-19	FIN8000	NONE	0	3	0	3	MAXI	Finance	Official
royalty payments	ACC-00-20	ACC1000	ACC000	6	3	0	6	MAXI	Accounting	Official
travel expenses	ACC-00-21	ACC1000	ACC000	6	3	0	6	MAXI	Accounting	Official
unemployment insurance payments	ACC-00-22	ACC1000	ACC000	6	3	0	6	MAXI	Accounting	Official
vouchers	ACC-00-23	ACC1000	ACC000	6	3	0	6	MAX1	Accounting	Official
workers compensation insurance payments	ACC-00-24	ACC1000	ACC000	6	3	0	6	MAX1	Accounting	Official
Accounts Receivable										
accounts receivable	ACC-10-01	ACC1000	ACC000	6	3	0	6	MAX1	Accounting	Official
accounts receivable ledgers	ACC-10-02	ACC1010	ACC000	6	10	0	10	MAX1	Accounting	Official
cash books	ACC-10-03	ACC1010	ACC000	6	10	0	10	MAX1	Accounting	Official

Source: Donald S. Skupsky, *Records Retention Procedures,* Englewood, CO: Information Requirements Clearinghouse, 1995. Used with permission.

1. General Business Activities
- ☐ Business Organization
  - ☐ Corporation
  - ☐ Corporation, Professional
  - ☐ Partnership
  - ☐ Partnership, Limited
  - ☐ Sole Proprietorship
- ☐ Employment/Personnel
- ☐ Tax/Accounting
- ☐ _____

2. Record Locations
- ☐ Country
  - ☐ United States
  - ☐ Canada
  - ☐ _____
- ☐ States/Provinces
  - ☐ _____
  - ☐ _____
  - ☐ _____
- ☐ Local Government
  - ☐ _____
  - ☐ _____

3. Regulatory Agencies
- ☐ Federal
  - ☐ Agriculture
  - ☐ Defense
  - ☐ Energy
    - ☐ Federal Energy Regulatory
  - ☐ Environmental Protection Agency
  - ☐ Federal Deposit and Insurance Corp.
  - ☐ Health and Human Services
  - ☐ Housing and Urban Development
  - ☐ Labor
    - ☐ Employment and Training
    - ☐ Employment Standards
    - ☐ Equal Employment Opportunity
    - ☐ Occupational Safety and Health
    - ☐ Wage and Hour
    - ☐ _____
  - ☐ Securities and Exchange Commission

3. Regulatory Agencies (cont.)
- ☐ Federal (cont.)
  - ☐ Small Business Administration
  - ☐ Transportation
  - ☐ Treasury
    - ☐ Alcohol, Tobacco, and Firearms
    - ☐ Internal Revenue Service
  - ☐ _____
  - ☐ _____
- ☐ State/Local
  - ☐ Labor
  - ☐ Revenue
  - ☐ _____
  - ☐ _____
  - ☐ _____
  - ☐ _____

4. Industry
- ☐ Agriculture
- ☐ Banking
- ☐ Communications
- ☐ Construction
- ☐ Education
- ☐ Health Care
- ☐ Manufacturing
- ☐ Petroleum
- ☐ Transportation
- ☐ Utility
- ☐ _____
- ☐ _____

5. Products/Activities
- ☐ _____
- ☐ _____
- ☐ _____

6. Other Regulated Areas
- ☐ Advertising
- ☐ Consumer Protection
- ☐ Environment
  - ☐ Air Pollution
  - ☐ Land/Water Pollution
  - ☐ _____
- ☐ _____
- ☐ _____

Source: Donald S. Skupsky, *Records Retention Procedures,* Englewood, CO: Information Requirements Clearinghouse, 1995. Used with permission.

Figure 9.1 Determining the scope of legal research.

3. *Extract key legal information.* Use relevant laws from the Legal Research Index, which is easier to review than the laws' full text.

4. *Assign applicable laws to groups and determine legal retention periods.* Assigning to legal groups the hundreds of laws that typically affect an organization's records retention eliminates the need to refer to each law individually.

5. *Develop the retention schedule.* Identify the functional retention categories that correspond to the records inventory. Fewer than 100 categories usually will suffice. Define the types of records covered by each category. Determine initial user retention periods and any other retention periods. Assign legal groups to the functional retention categories. Indicate the total retention category, which is the longest of the legal, user, or other retention periods. Determine the office responsible for maintaining official records for the total retention period. Other groups will maintain records according to the period indicated for copies.

6. *Assign a functional retention category to each record listed in the inventory.* The records retention period for the category becomes the period for the record series. Generate a report with records retention periods.

7. *Revise the four integrated retention files and reports (legal research index, legal group file, records retention schedule, and records listing with retention periods).* Develop procedures on records destruction, documentation, program revision, training, and any other implementation issues. Distribute the draft schedules and procedures for review. Prepare the records retention program manual and obtain approval.

Following Skupsky's seven-step method fits a handle around records retention requirements, but it does not address the other essential elements of archiving documentation: prevention, preparation, and recovery of damaged or lost documentation, and the more mundane issue of document history files.

It takes only one experience crashing a hard disk with critical or hard-to-reconstruct information for most people to start backing up document files routinely. Unfortunately, many people's idea of data protection is to copy files to a floppy disk and keep it in a cabinet or drawer. Some keep the backups right next to the computer. It is not difficult to imagine that some disasters will affect all property at the same location. Maybe a crashed hard disk won't damage a floppy disk, but a fire can burn the computer *and* the backup near it. Earthquakes in California, Mexico, and Japan; hurricanes in North Carolina; floods in Missouri; power surges in France—no site is safe from natural or human-caused disasters. A sensible program will protect important information and assist in recovery in case damage or loss cannot be prevented.

Checklist 9.1: Steps for Developing a Zero-Based Records Retention Program (drawn from Skupsky, 1995)

☐ Complete preliminary procedures.

☐ Research laws.

☐ Extract key legal information.

☐ Assign laws to groups; determine legal retention periods.

☐ Develop retention schedule.

☐ Assign functional retention category to each record.

☐ Revise the four integrated retention files and reports.

For office backups, devices such as tape systems and Zip drives offer convenient document backup storage. A Bernoulli drive is another, removable alternative. Each of these systems works better than an assortment of floppy disks, and each is faster and easier to transport. But documentation functions also need to establish remote storage capabilities in the event of wider ranging disasters.

A reciprocal arrangement works well for some organizations, whereby a function mails documentation copies regularly, say, weekly, to an off-site location more than a couple of hundred miles away. The recipient function does the same. Each time a new backup arrives, the old one is rotated out. Some companies transfer backed-up files electronically. With the reciprocal system, the potential for lost documentation is no greater than one week's worth. Every company documentation function should have a written procedure for recovering information in an emergency (the procedure should be stored at more than one site, of course). Sound online document management systems include regular backups and remote rotating storage.

Another important consideration for records is audit trails. Hansel's trail of crumbs became a lifeline for the storybook character and his sister. Indexed history files serve the same purpose for organizations. Auditors or legal specialists research files to determine the company policies and practices that were in effect at a given time. Records may be subpoenaed by former employees who claim the company acted wrongfully. Suppliers request reviews of purchase orders. Often, the outcomes of litigation depend on the integrity of the history files. The economy of locating obsolete documents quickly contributes to an organization's financial good health. A history or audit trail becomes especially important when major reorganizations or documentation streamlining efforts rearrange or delete documents or parts of them.

To preserve a clear audit trail, maintain a matrix of documents and their revisions by number and topic and information deleted from them. Notate an organization chart matrix with old and new names for an organization or their parts. Maintain a master (and a backup of the master) of each document revision. To avoid obsolete copies being mistaken for current versions, stamp every obsolete hard copy master with words such as *History files* or *Reference only*. Protect electronic history masters from revision.

FORMS

Think of a form as an information template, an efficient vehicle for gathering the same kind of information from many sources. A nimble form does not surprise its users. It does not cause confusion or waste its users' time. A nimble form is clear. The best are self-explanatory. The next best include instructions on the reverse side, if hard copy; on the front, if generated by computer; linked to online instructions, if data entry is online; or supported by online help. Instructions on the form, or the form's Web page, help avoid detours to a procedures manual.

To facilitate information entry, processing, and retrieval, maintain the expected order of fields or elements. For example, if an organization's standard memorandum lists *date* first, then *to*, next *from*, and finally *subject*, maintain that order for all memos. Employees expecting to see the date first will be able to quickly file and retrieve documents chronologically. If they expect to see the subject last, they can thumb through a pile of memos briskly, scanning for a topic. If a group of forms requires the last name first, but a single form asks for the first name first, many people will complete the form incorrectly or cross out, white out, erase, or re-enter information. Or they may rip up or clear the form and start again. In any case, extra resources will be spent when they don't have to be.

Forms are standardized to facilitate compiling information. Sure, a user can write a freehand letter or e-mail message to carry the same information as a form; however, a bit of information omitted that a recipient requires will generate additional processing time. For example, a letter might not include a needed social security number. Then the recipient has to correspond, requesting more information, and the user has to correspond again. Placing a social security number field on a standardized form decreases the correspondence. Placing the field in an expected location on the form and clearly asking for the information further minimizes processing time.

Completed forms also serve as records and allow future users to locate information in history files faster.

Today, competitive organizations use forms that are automated at least to some extent. At the most basic level, form masters are created through word processing or other computer software or are purchased, copies are printed, and users complete the forms by typewriter or by hand. At the next level of automation, a copy is generated—printed—on demand and completed by typewriter or hand. Automation at the third level means a form is generated by computer and completed by computer. Standard word processing packages include a forms template function. Transactions conducted through forms can be approved by hand signature. Forms automated at the fourth level may be password approved or authorized by digital signature. Also, information can be linked electronically to other automated forms and systems, for example, creating a paperless system that can eliminate opportunities for error by eliminating data re-entry. Some systems use voice data entry and voice recognition for approval. The most sophisticated systems automatically "read" information electronically and process it from multiple sources, such as Web pages, e-mail, software applications such as databases, and scanned hard copy.

A forms improvement team at a large company initiated an electronic forms library. Before the improvement, individuals throughout the company were re-creating company forms on their computers. To assist their customers, the forms control staff planned to capture already created forms and add them to the online forms library. The team sent out notices to each division asking employees to share copies of their forms. The team reviewed the forms it received and selected and enhanced employees' versions to add to the library. After the forms were organized and indexed on a server, the team publicized their availability and instructions to access them.

Many organizations have a problem with too many forms. Or, there are too many form errors or omissions. The zero-based documentation approach works well for streamlining forms. First, apply the litmus test (questions one to four, following). Then ask about a nimbler way (question five).

1. Is the form required by law?

2. Is the form specified by contract?

3. Is the form needed according to prudent business practices?

4. Will any harm come to the organization if the form is eliminated?

5. Will any harm come to the organization if the form is retained?

Checklist 9.2: Considerations for Nimble Forms

❒ Ensure the form's name shows its purpose.

❒ Maintain expected order of fields.

❒ Don't hide small but critical fields.

❒ Make the form clear without instructions.

❒ If instructions are needed, print them on the form, not in a separate procedure, or fully automate the form.

❒ Position field names clearly with their corresponding fields.

❒ Use a single form for multiple duty.

❒ Identify each form with a number and revision date, keyed to other documentation.

❒ Avoid referencing names and telephone numbers.

❒ Conduct a usability test on the form and revise the form if necessary.

If the form is needed but employees are burdened by confusing navigation bars or field titles far from fields, then the form requires staff to expend more resources, including time, than necessary. Conduct usability testing, if necessary, to minimize resource requirements (see chapter 4).

If the answer to each of the first four litmus test questions is "no," cancel the form. If at least one question warrants a "yes," and the answer to question five is "yes" or "maybe," consider revising the form.

Following are a few ways to minimize the time and dollars spent on processing a form:

- *Name the form so its purpose is clear.* "Administrative Request" is too vague. Be more specific.

- *Maintain the expected order of fields.* Use organization-standard headers. Sequence fields logically, for example: chronological, most important information to least, or highest value item field to least value.

- *Avoid hiding small but essential fields where they may be overlooked.* A social security number field between two large comment boxes is easy to miss. Emphasize the field, for example, by surrounding it with space, using bolder text, or repositioning it to a more prominent location on the form.

- *Design the form to be clear without instructions.* However, if instructions are required, print them on the form itself, not in a procedure manual, or fully automate the form, including data entry and processing. Help users find information quickly.

- *Position field names clearly with their corresponding fields.* Don't make users guess whether they need to write above a field name or below it (or to the left or to the right of it). The disputed ballots in the 2000 U.S. presidential election are a glaring and unfortunate departure from nimble forms. Voters, confused by the location of candidates' names on the ballots, may have miscast their votes, which may have determined the forty-third president of the United States.

- *Use a single form for multiple duty.* An HR department of a large company required four separate forms to process an employee transfer request: one for payroll, one for employee relations, one for the equal opportunity office, and one for the career development office. Much of the same information was required for each form. A single form could have been used to feed information into a database accessible by each of the four functions.

- *Identify each form with a number and revision date*. Key the form number to other documentation covering the same function or process, such as an ISO 9001-compliant quality system manual, standard operating procedures, or records (or all of these).

- *Avoid referencing individuals' names or telephone numbers, except if the form is online or otherwise economical to revise, or if the information is hard to find elsewhere.* Organizations change. Rerouting forms to other individuals or placing multiple telephone calls is expensive and delays transactions. Consider including linked e-mail addresses, but update e-mail addresses regularly to avoid dead end e-mails or error messages.

- *Conduct a usability test on the form and revise the form if necessary*. Ask users who are unfamiliar with the form to test it. Observe the users and ask for feedback as they are testing the form. Revise the form if usability is unsatisfactory. Re-test the revised form with a new group of users.

APPROVAL AND DIGITAL SIGNATURES

Big, long-established companies tend to accumulate administrative processes that have outgrown their usefulness. After awhile, nobody remembers why a process is required. For example, no one can figure out why six signature lines foot a standard company form, when only the last approver seriously reviews the transaction authorized by the form. Everyone else assumes the person who signs just below their signature will do it. When questioned about signature line strata, people say, "That's the way we've always done it." Some small or new companies, not knowing a better way, emulate the established giants. Or, sometimes, upstarts, for example, new dot-com businesses, have no consistent administrative processes in place, which is equally harmful. By trying to avoid anything that sounds bureaucratic, some firms—usually the ones most proud of their entrepreneurial culture—miss out on the benefits of standardized management and operating systems. For many organizations, approval authority is an archaic administrative process and often a terrific candidate for streamlining.

This section addresses approval authority systems first and then presents information on electronic signatures and digital signatures, and the distinction between them, and their legality.

Approval Authority Systems

A cross-functional team at one company tested its belief that the multiple layers of signatures specified by forms for business transactions were rubber stamps and added little value to the authorization process. The team designed pilot projects in two functions to streamline transactions authorized by signed forms: finance and HR. The team interviewed transaction owners, those responsible for activity as a result of receiving a fully signed form. The results indicated that greater than 75 percent of the forms studied could be eliminated and, on the remaining ones, levels of authorization could be deleted completely or reduced significantly with no compromise in meeting legal, contractual, or prudent business requirements and no harm to the company (four steps of the litmus test for approval authority systems). Executive

Checklist 9.3: Considerations for Charts of Approvals

❏ Accessibility

❏ Date

❏ Scope

❏ Clarity

❏ Conditions for designees

❏ Conditions for alternates

❏ Method for indicating approval

❏ Acceptable formats (such as forms, POs)

❏ Authority for chart's contents

management supported pushing down administrative decisions closer to the operational level and eliminating unneeded higher layers of authorization. What manager wouldn't be grateful for a smaller stack of forms to approve?

The complexity of an approval authority system depends largely on the scope and complexity of an organization's products and services and the standards and regulations of its industry. But it also depends on the organization's leadership style or management culture. Whatever the complexity, however, the system should be communicated clearly to all participants and accessible by all who need to use it.

Many companies have placed their approval authority systems online. Organizations link their directive documents and forms via their intranet. That way, with a click on a link an employee can find out who is authorized to approve a transaction specified in an operating procedure and they can authorize the transaction via an electronic form using a password or other electronic signature instead of a handwritten signature.

For more traditional hard copy systems, a chart of approvals should be included in standard operating procedures or a policies handbook. Figure 9.2 shows a simple chart prepared for a small, young but rapidly growing service business. It communicates authority to approve transactions yet avoids administrative wastefulness and congestion. Note that formats for approving transactions are not limited to forms (Figure 9.2, paragraph 2.3).

Another chart of approvals (Figure 9.3), from an educational agency's policies and procedures handbook, identifies the executive and senior management positions by level and indicates the levels authorized to approve transactions listed by function or process. This chart was particularly important to the agency because it communicated information about forms consolidated from the merger of two organizations.

Digital Signatures and Electronic Signatures

A discussion of approval authority systems would be incomplete without mentioning completely automated forms transmission. Generating forms electronically and then printing them out for a signature wastes valuable resources. One way to automate forms is to use encryption keys, which must be delivered or picked up (private key management) or distributed electronically, for example by e-mail (public key management). In simple terms, digital signatures are encrypted and decrypted, and both the message and the originator are authenticated.

[XYZ LOGO]	**Chart of Approvals**	**Operating Procedure**
		Number: XYZP 1-2-1 Date Issued: August 7, 2001 Page: 1 of 2

1.0 SCOPE

Applies to all employees at all XYZ Corporation facilities.

2.0 PROCEDURE

2.1 The personnel or functions designated in the chart below, or their designees, are authorized to approve specified transactions or commit company funds according to indicated condtions. Designees are authorized in writing.

2.2 Alternates are authorized to approve specified transactions or commit company funds only in the absence of the designated personnel or functions. Alternates may not authorize designees.

2.3 Written signatures or electronic passwords indicate approval. Formats for approval include, but are not limited to: forms, letters, memoranda, contracts, and purchase orders.

Transaction	Approval Authority	Alternate	Comments/Conditions
Compensation Increases	Compensation Committee		After Dept. Mgr. recommends
Contracts	President	Exec. VP	
Copy–[Confidential] Reports	Dept. Mgr.		After Copy Committee recommends
Corrective/Preventive Action	Dept. Mgr.		
Employee Discipline	Dept. Mgr.		
Employee Suggestions	Dept. Mgr.		
Expense Reimbursement	(See comments)		Required, in sequence: 1. Staff; 2. Dept. Mgr.; & 3. President or Finance Exec.
Facilities Upgrades/Construction	President	Exec. VP	After Facilities Mgr. recommends
Hiring	Dept. Mgr.	HR Mgr.	
Leaves	Dept. Mgr.	HR Mgr.	
Performance Appraisal	Dept. Mgr. & Compensation Committee		Both required
Project Authorization Request (PAR)	President	Exec. VP	After Dept. Mgr. approves
Promotion	Compensation Committee		After Dept. Mgr. recommends

Property
  Purchasing–Capital
  Purchasing–Office Supplies
	Exec. VP
	Dept. Mgr.		

Figure 9.2 Example A of chart of approvals.

[XYZ LOGO]

Operating Procedure

Chart of Approvals

Number: XYZP 1-2-1
Date Issued: August 7, 2001
Page: 2 of 2

Transaction	Approval Authority	Alternate	Comments/Conditions
Receiving	Reception		
Safety	HR Mgr.		
Security–Locks	Facilities Mgr.		
Shipping	Admin. Asst.		
Telephones, 800 numbers	Facilities Mgr		
Termination	Dept. Mgr.	HR Mgr.	
Training	Dept. Mgr.		
Transfer–Interdepartment	Transferring & Receiving Dept. Mgrs.	Both required	
Travel	Dept. Mgr.		
Vacation	Dept. Mgr.		

I. A. Prove, Vice President, Administration

Figure 9.2 Example A of a chart of approvals *(continued)*.

Chart of Approvals

The following table indicates the authority to approve requests or specific documents committing Agency resources.

Key:

A – Chief Executive Officer
B – Chief Financial Officer
C – Deputy Director
D – Director, Administration and Finance
E – Contracts and Administrative Services Manager/Controller
F – Program Manager
G – Project Director

An X indicates authority to approve requests or commit Agency resources. No employee may approve his/her own request.

Form	Authority Levels							Comments
	A	**B**	**C**	**D**	**E**	**F**	**G**	
Business Operations								
Timesheets	X	X	X	X	X	X	X	
Local/Non-Local Expense Reports	X	X	X	X	X	X	X	
Mileage Reports	X	X	X	X	X	X	X	
Purchase Requests	X	X	X	X	X	X	X	
Purchase Orders	X	X		X				
Travel Authorizations	X	X	X	X	X	X	X	
Statements of Work Completed (Consultant)	X	X	X	X	X	X	X	
Requests for Space/Relocation	X	X	X	X				
Check Requests (only by prior authorization)	X	X	X	X	X			
Office Assignments	X	X						
Contracts for Services (Consultant)	X	X		X				
Relocation Expenses	X	X	X	X				1
Personnel Operations								
Leaves of Absence	X	X		X				1

Figure 9.3 Example B of chart of approvals.

Form	A	B	C	D	E	F	G	Comments
Notices of Appointment (Exempt)			X					1
Notices of Appointment (Non-Exempt)			X					1
Requests for Regular Employee	X	X	X	X				1
Requests for Temporary Employee	X	X	X	X	X	X	X	2
Timesheet Revisions	X	X	X	X				
Personnel Action Notices	X	X	X	X				1
Overtime Authorizations	X	X	X	X	X	X	X	
Proposals, Grants, and Contracts (Refer to Proposal Development Procedures.)								
Intent to Propose (ITP)	X		X					
Proposals	X		X					
Contracts and Grants[3]	X	X		X				
Teaming Agreements	X	X		X				
Equity Expenditure Request	X	X		X				
Subcontracts	X	X						
Financial								
Investments	X	X		X				
Leases and Rental Transactions	X	X		X				
Attorney Fees	X	X	X	X				
Bad Debt Settlements and Charge-off of Delinquent Accounts	X	X	X	X				
Disposal of Agency-Owned Assets	X	X	X	X				

1. Signature approval of the Deputy Director of Human Resources is required in addition to any other indicated level.
2. Signature approval of Controller is required in addition to any other indicated level.
3. Only officers of the Agency are authorized to sign any document that legally binds the Agency. This includes contracts, memoranda of understanding, letters of agreement, maintenance agreements, purchase orders, etc.

Figure 9.3   Example B of a chart of approvals *(continued).*

Figure 9.4 diagrams how the keys work. Standards for encryption keys already exist and widely-used applications are being developed. Several repositories exist for public key certificates that contain information identifying each user. Others can then retrieve certificates electronically from the repositories to authenticate digital signatures.

David G. Propson writes in "Everything You Wanted To Know About Digital Signatures, But Were Afraid To Ask" (2001) that in the Fall 2000, U.S. President Bill Clinton enacted a law that made digital signatures equivalent to handwritten ones. The law has started to streamline many common administrative processes, from approving timesheets to contracts. But many of us do not understand the difference between digital signatures and electronic signatures. And newspaper articles and magazine features often confuse the two.

Propson explains the difference. An *electronic signature* is the broader term. It can mean anything from attaching an automatic signature to an e-mail message to signing an electronic tablet connected to a cash register at a retail shop. A *digital signature*, on the other hand, confirms the identity of the signer. The digital signature is backed by a digital certificate that contains a code unique to the signer. An encrypted file, which verifies the identity of the signer, is attached to the code. The code is used to produce the digital signature. All of this happens to confirm that the

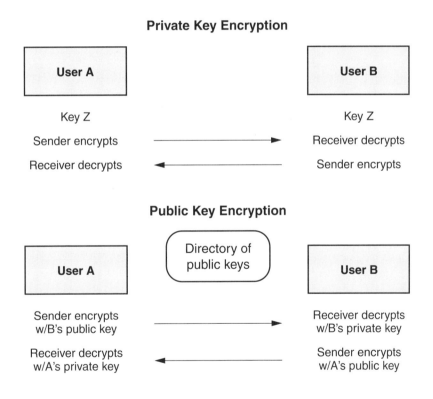

Source: Kibbee Streetman, "Who Holds the Keys to Encrypted Electronic Documents?" *Technologies for Managing Information*, 1, no. 4 (May 1996). Used with permission.

Figure 9.4　Private key encryption and public key encryption.

signer is who they claim to be. Today digital signatures can be used for legally binding documents, although other hurdles need clearing to create a national, consistent policy, and to refine the technology. Further, the technology for using other electronic signatures is being developed and in some cases, already is in use, such as fingerprinting and retinal scanning.

10

Documentation Center of Excellence

Solutions presented in this chapter address documentation challenges such as:

- What are the basic characteristics of a documentation center of excellence (COE)?

- What are the benefits and drawbacks of outsourcing and insourcing documentation services?

- What skills are needed by empowered documentation staff?

- How do you develop effective self-directed documentation teams?

- What characterizes the most effective focus groups for writing procedures?

- What is the role of training in a documentation COE?

- What factors contribute to accountability?

- What is the relationship between a documentation COE and team performance evaluation?

A center of excellence (COE) is a way to bring together a company's capabilities to produce a peerless, specialized product or process. COEs exploit the synergy of top talent working together and the economies of standardized facilities and equipment. Design COEs traditionally cluster engineering expertise to focus on a single product or family of products or processes. Production COEs typically consolidate state-of-the-art manufacturing capabilities. Administrative COEs, such as purchasing functions, take advantage of volume processing and streamlined resources. A documentation COE is no different. It draws together expertise, facilities, and equipment, for example, trained teams, hub-arranged offices, and standardized software, to deliver Nimble Documentation.®

This chapter, the last in the *Application* topic group, defines a documentation COE and presents options for organizations that wish to establish, improve, or contract for documentation services. First, COE characteristics are described, then the advantages and disadvantages of outsourcing and insourcing the function are illustrated. Next is a discussion of the skills required for COE personnel and then exploration of self-directed documentation teams. The chapter also identifies personnel roles and responsibilities, and training. Finally, it addresses accountability for the function and performance evaluation.

CHARACTERISTICS OF A DOCUMENTATION COE

Whether deployed by an internal documentation organization, a documentation consultant or outsourcing firm, or document "owner" (function or staff responsible for content), a documentation COE displays four basic characteristics. It is:

- Responsive to customers and other sources of need

- Streamlined

- Empowered

- Quality managed

Consider each of the four COE characteristics followed by examples of how organizations have demonstrated those characteristics.

Responsive to customers and other sources of need. Responsive documentation requires continuously assessing customers' needs (such as readers, users, and subject matter owners) and legal and other requirements. Assessments include questionnaires and surveys, hot line call analyses, Web site hits, and piloted instructions. Analytical reports that show quickly and clearly the benefit to the reader or to the goals of the reader's organization are responsive documentation. Responsiveness is easier user access to information, lower cost of an online versus hard copy documentation system, or improved technical service speed and accuracy. Regularly reviewing legal and other requirements and maintaining regular contact with representatives of standards and audit organizations also help to ensure responsiveness to need.

- *Assess customer requirements*. A team of writers and editors asked users if they wanted to be included in e-mail notification of new, revised, or canceled company bulletins. They sent messages to users whose names were on hard copy distribution lists.

- *Provide access*. A process improvement team gave presentations and held question and answer sessions at division staff meetings to learn how operating procedures could be made more accessible. A county probation department trained its managers and supervisors to write court reports with facts and numerical data presented early in the reports to help judges quickly reach the most important information.

- *Simplify.* A quality engineer and documentation manager co-facilitated a focus group of document owners to eliminate redundant sections of the company's quality system procedures.

- *Contain or reduce costs.* A cross-functional team reengineered a forms system and drastically cut warehouse floor space and leasing costs, and later, other costs associated with hard copy forms.

- *Respond with speed and accuracy.* An organization chart function with vocal support of executive management shaved days off the average turnaround time for preparing and distributing charts.

The county probation department contracted to train its managers and supervisors to write analytically. One of the goals was to achieve a customer or "you" attitude in memos, court reports, performance evaluations, and other strategic documents. In this public system, heavy workloads and limited resources mean every piece of writing must connect quickly with a customer's needs. Showing the benefit to the reader, the "you" attitude saves the reader time, and often rescues a document from needless return cycles, or worse, the bottom of a pile (see chapter 6).

Streamlined. Nimble organizations streamline their processes by eliminating non-value-added activities and unneeded documentation (see chapter 2) and by standardization (see chapter 5). Manufacturing organizations historically have streamlined their processes through a variety of initiatives, including time and motion studies, quality circles and other tools for improvement, and standardized production. Organizations have begun to turn their attention to administrative functions, such as documentation, as prime candidates for streamlining. Following are a few documentation streamlining initiatives implemented at one company. Employees:

- Reduced volume, simplified language, and consolidated written procedures of four merged divisions in conjunction with the company's strategic initiative to streamline all directive documents.

- Reduced the volume of organization charts and their processing cycle time. The company structure was changing rapidly. Charts for lower level organizations, especially, were almost always obsolete, often before they were published. The function responsible for organization charts imported a facilitator from the quality division to help a team streamline chart processing and drive responsibility for lower-level charts down to the organizations. The results were a 46 percent decrease in volume and an approximately equal reduction in average cycle time to publish a chart from draft to distribution.

- Increased inventory turns for forms. The forms inventory system was revamped by a cross-functional team comprised of forms administration, purchasing, and graphic arts staff. The team reduced warehouse floor space from 3250 to 479 square feet, a savings of approximately 85 percent. Outsourcing the system to a forms management company provided additional benefits. Later, the team fully automated most forms with a Web based system and eliminated the costs associated with all but a handful of hard copy forms.

Empowered. Technology has been fairly impressive for managing documentation, but no factor is more critical to Nimble Documentation® than empowered personnel.

World-class organizations recognize that company chiefs can know less than five percent of each company operation. A well-trained workforce that has clearly defined roles and responsibilities takes initiative toward meeting organizational goals, is held accountable for performance, and is the difference between an organization that competes successfully and one that watches on the sidelines.

Much like *reengineering*, the term *empowerment* has been misunderstood, overused, and misapplied. To many, it means unled and unmanaged employees, permissiveness, carte blanche, and anything goes. This is not empowerment for world-class documentation.

One definition of empowerment is "having the authority and responsibility to make the decisions and take the actions necessary to improve your work" (The Forum Corporation 1992). To be empowered, individuals must have:

- The skills to do their job

- The commitment to satisfy their customers

- A strong positive attitude

- The willingness to accept accountability for their actions

- The ability to communicate effectively

- Investment resources for improvement, including people, dollars, information, and equipment

Documentation nimbleness requires an empowered workforce, which includes skilled, self-directed personnel, clear roles and responsibilities, cutting-edge training, accountable performance, constructive performance evaluation, and adequate resources.

The following exemplify employee empowerment.

- A documentation COE achieved 100 percent participation in continuous measurable improvement teams. Every function, every task, and every staff member was expected to lead or contribute in other ways to at least one process improvement team. It was not enough for employees to do a satisfactory job of performing to the department's statements of responsibility. The COE demanded teams to benchmark and exceed the best by reducing processing time for organization charts, implementing error-free procedures, developing e-mail distribution of bulletins, and creating password-approved online forms. Self-directed teams evolved from these focused work team accomplishments.

- One hundred percent of staff trained in continuous measurable improvement processes. An empowered staff is a knowledgeable, skilled staff. Every member of the COE participated in training that included quality tools, metrics, team dynamics, process mapping, and other critical elements. Some members also were trained in team leadership.

- A self-directed team of documentation writers and editors reached consensus on objectives that flowed down from company goals. The team members refined the company's team performance appraisal and planning process and form and administered it to support performance that met or exceeded objectives and planned course corrections for performance that did not. Team members participated in work assignment decisions. A team empowered meant a team accountable.

Quality managed. The TQM philosophy begins with leadership commitment to initiate and sustain managed improvement. It embraces all of a company's operations and all of its employees. It is not a program *du jour*, a quick fix that an executive introduces (and forgets) after reading about it in an in-flight magazine. A documentation COE breathes TQM; every aspect of the organization is devoted to quality from continuously assessing the needs of software user manual readers to rearranging a group's offices to facilitate team consulting. The following few examples characterize a quality managed documentation function.

- A team installed monitors in a cafeteria so all employees could access online bulletins.

- Monthly metrics indicated that a function responsible for writing and editing company documentation maintained publication of error-free procedures so consistently that it was awarded world-class status for zero defects.

OUTSOURCING AND INSOURCING

Why would an organization want to outsource a documentation function? This section addresses the benefits and the drawbacks of outsourcing, briefly discusses insourcing, and lists considerations for seeking outside documentation assistance.

Outsourcing has become a global megatrend for business. Employee leasing, accounting services, back office management, and many other outsourced functions help companies not only cut operating costs but also reshape the way they do business. Organizations have benefited from the specialization, skills, and quality of outsourced functions. Outsourcing lets companies focus their resources on core business.

Insourcing is a newer term. To some, it means that a contracting firm or consultant manages internal staff, in other words, outsourcing inside. Employees continue to work for a company, but an outsider manages the function. Others interpret insourcing as transferring responsibilities for a function to specialists inside a company. For example, rather than having a quality assurance employee write a quality manual, and an IS employee document intranet uploading procedures, and then someone from accounting write a cashier's desk instructions, a documentation function assumes responsibility for all three activities. Insourcing, according to the second interpretation, shares some characteristics of a COE, particularly specialized staffing and equipment capabilities. Last, insourcing can mean a specialty firm hiring a company's employees but maintaining them in their former function. This interpretation of insourcing shares many of the benefits of outsourcing. (To some it is a special category of outsourcing.) The insourced function, according to the last meaning, improves processes and, usually, reduces expenses. To the extent that insourcing tilts the status quo in the direction of improvement, it shares many of the benefits of outsourcing—and some of the drawbacks.

Benefits

Sandra Golden presented to the Society for Advancement of Management (SAM) the results of a Coopers and Lybrand study on outsourcing HR administration. Golden told the group:

- 70 percent of respondents said they achieved greater efficiency

- 45 percent increased the focus on product and growth

- 42 percent saved costs and administration

- 41 percent lowered overhead investment or debt

- 21 percent eased their regulatory compliance burden

- 18 percent outsourced because they could not find skilled employees

The Outsourcing Institute (1995) offers 10 top reasons for outsourcing, compiled from surveys of more than 1200 companies and ongoing work with its members. Consider their application to documentation functions. Potential drawbacks to outsourcing follow the benefits.

The top 10 reasons for outsourcing, and representative documentation applications, include:

1. *Reduce or control operating costs.* This is the single most important tactical reason for outsourcing. An outside provider's lower cost structure can be a compelling short-term benefit.

- Outsourced documentation functions that apply zero-based methodology, empowered staff, and continuous measured process improvement can reduce operating costs typically from 25 to 60 percent, depending on the organization's existing processes.

2. *Make capital funds available.* Outsourcing can reduce the need to invest capital funds in noncore functions, making capital funds more available for core domains.

- Computers, printers, scanners, and telecommunications equipment and facilities are primary capital expenses reduced or eliminated by documentation outsourcing.

3. *Infuse cash.* Transferring assets from the customer to a provider is an outsourcing option. Equipment, facilities, licensing, and other assets may be sold to the provider, resulting in a cash payment.

- Cash may be available from transferring computers, printers, scanners, and telecommunications and other equipment and licenses for documentation software.

4. *Substitute for resources not available internally.* Outsourcing can be a viable alternative to developing needed capability, either from the ground up, as in a new facility or geographic area added in a business expansion, or because internal resources are inaccessible.

- Implementing quality initiatives, such as ISO 9001, and other documentation requirements may exceed available staffing capacities.

5. *Obtain assistance with a function difficult to manage or out of control.* Outsourcing does not substitute for management responsibility, but it can offer an option for addressing problematic workplace situations.

- Traditionally, documentation functions have had low visibility in their organizations (unless litigation, audits, or disaster recovery activities demanded their involvement). Sometimes in a low visibility environment, management practices and work processes become static. For some, change can be intimidating. Outsourcing can introduce new performance expectations and objectivity.

6. *Improve business focus.* Outside experts can assume operational details while a company focuses on broader business issues. Implementation issues can siphon off management resources and attention.

- Unless documentation is a company's core business (for example, technical writing firms), documentation supports manufacturing, engineering, or other functions. Managing an organization's documentation need not distract core leaders.

7. *Access world-class capabilities.* Outsourcing providers, because of their specialization, can bring extensive global, world-class resources to meet their customers' needs. Some of the capabilities an outsourcing partner can offer include access to new technology, tools, and techniques; better career opportunities for personnel who transition to the outsourcing provider; more structured approaches, procedures, and documentation; and a competitive advantage from expanded skills.

- World-class documentation, like other functions, is a result of highly trained personnel experienced in continuous process improvement and powerful technology, knowledgeable and skilled leadership, ready access to professional publications and conferences, and supportive career development. Outsourcing can deliver access to these capabilities.

8. *Accelerate reengineering benefits.* An outside organization that has already reengineered to world-class standards can allow a company to realize immediately the projected benefits of its own business process reengineering initiative.

- An outsourced documentation function can bring the quality tools, metrics, developed teamwork, and results that reengineering initiatives seek. Outsourcing can reduce a project's cycle time.

9. *Share risks.* Companies that outsource can become more flexible and dynamic. They can adapt better to changing opportunities.

- Major documentation streamlining efforts commonly require increased attention at their initiation, then taper off as processes improve. Outsourcing can better absorb the ups and downs without an organization paying for staffing that may be needed for just part of a year or without paying the hiring, learning curve, and severance costs of an expanding and contracting internal workforce.

10. *Free resources for other purposes.* No organization has unlimited resources. Outsourcing can permit an organization to redirect its resources from noncore business toward gaining a greater return in serving its customers.

- Core business produces revenue. Generally, documentation does not (unless it is a company's core business). Documentation for most companies is a separate administrative function, or it is produced to some extent by several employees, most of whom have primary responsibilities to make a product or provide a service to paying customers.

As just shown, organizations can benefit in many ways from outsourcing their documentation. Because of their access to large warehousing facilities and specialized software and skilled personnel, records storage and management firms can provide a full range of outsourcing services. Records outsourcers include huge national firms and local companies. Firms that offer outsourcing services for policies and procedures have begun to spring up. But what are the drawbacks? What are the reasons organizations might not want to outsource their documentation activities?

Drawbacks

Company documentation, traditionally, has been a private matter. Organizations are concerned that proprietary information may get into the wrong hands. Employees believe that intimate knowledge of the organizational structure and individuals who make things happen in a company are critical to documentation processing. Company jargon, acronyms, and the details that only an insider would know could trip up outsourced staff.

Organizations proud of a long record of layoff-free operations are reluctant to risk damaging employee loyalty. They believe employees engaged in core business are the best choices for generating and processing their documentation. Employees handling documentation see outsourcing as a slap in the face, a lack of confidence in their skills and performance. Customers may be used to and enjoy good rapport with internal personnel; organizations do not want to risk damaging customer relationships.

Further, companies question projected cost savings in light of an outside organization's incentive to create more work by charging fees according to time worked. Employees are concerned that an outsourcing firm's culture may be incompatible with their own.

Make the decision to outsource a documentation function only after carefully considering the organization's goals compared with the benefits and drawbacks of outsourcing. Note that some of the benefits of outsourcing may be achieved without some of the drawbacks by hiring or training an internal documentation specialist or by contracting with an outside specialist. Specialists can train staff and lead improvement efforts. The following considerations may help an organization decide whether to seek outside assistance— outsourcing or insourcing:

- Documentation function costs are perceived to be too high.

- No one knows the cost to produce an average policy or procedure or any other company document.

- Capital equipment and facilities are outdated for competitive documentation processing.

- Facilities or personnel are unavailable or inadequate to meet the company's expansion requirements.

- The documentation function is difficult to manage and processes are out of control. The company is buried in too much documentation. It takes too long to process new documents, revisions, or cancellations. It is difficult to find needed current or archived information quickly. Documentation is obsolete.

- Management is spending too much time putting out fires in the documentation function.

- Documentation staff members are using processes, technology, and tools that are inappropriate for world-class organizations.

- Career development is limited for documentation specialists.

- Reengineering the documentation function is taking too long.

- Core business staff members are being pulled away from serving the customer to writing documentation.

SKILLS

Empowerment without the skills to accomplish a goal is not empowerment at all. It is a recipe for failure. Documentation responsibilities are far-ranging and can include everything from facilitating management focus groups to drafting a procedure to formatting one and from coordinating a policy for review to uploading to a Web-based system. These are technical skills. No one should be given responsibility for accomplishing a goal if he or she does not have the skills to achieve it or plan the training to develop those skills.

For empowered documentation functions, technical skills are just the beginning. An organization can achieve nimbleness only if its members

---

Checklist 10.2: Considerations for Seeking Outside Assistance— Outsourcing or Insourcing Documentation Function

❐ Documentation function costs perceived to be too high

❐ No knowledge of document cost

❐ Outdated capital equipment and facilities

❐ Facilities or personnel cannot meet expansion requirements

❐ Documentation function difficult to manage

   ❐ Too much documentation

   ❐ Takes too long to process documents

   ❐ Difficult to find information quickly

   ❐ Documentation is obsolete

❐ Management spends too much time putting out fires in documentation function

Continued

❐ Documentation staff use non-world-class processes, technology, and tools

❐ Career development limited for documentation specialists

❐ Takes too long to reengineer documentation function

❐ Core business diverted to writing documentation

are skilled in decision making and team or group dynamics, for example, leadership responsibilities and communication, and the most overlooked team skill: active listening.

Functions often take group communication skills for granted. You may have seen the *Abilene Paradox*, the ageless video about mismanaged agreement. A reluctant family drives far in a hot, unair-conditioned car to get ice cream that nobody wants. A faculty tortures itself in a boring go-nowhere meeting that nobody is brave enough to call off. Two people unhappily agree to marry because each thinks the other person will be devastated if he or she doesn't go through with it. A company attempts to produce a product that is unproducible, but everyone thinks everyone else is in favor of it. The point, of course, is that managing group agreement does not always come naturally. It is a learned skill.

Empowered documentation staff members know how to measure quality, whether it applies to accurate and current procedures or speedy cycle time for revising company forms.

Documentation functions planning to move from a traditional arrangement of supervisors dictating and employees following are urged to inventory employees' skills and provide training that addresses both technical *and* participation skills.

SELF-DIRECTED TEAMS

Hitting hard in the late 1980s and into the 1990s, in response to a shrinking, more competitive market, companies everywhere flattened their organizational structures to reduce operating costs. At the same time, and for the same reasons, they demanded increased customer focus, higher quality work, and greater productivity. Also at the same time, employees watched waves of their colleagues—not just marginal performers—being laid off. Hard workers joined the unemployed, leaving survivors who now were expected to perform their own work as well as the tasks of those who left. The result in many firms was a personally threatening and highly stressful work environment, one that immobilized employees like deer in the headlights and dampened risk-taking and innovation.

More recently, companies are challenged by mergers, acquisitions, consolidations, and other restructuring activities. Upstart companies used to communicating face-to-face and working in an entrepreneurial environment, now struggle to adjust to rapid growth and sometimes contraction without the support of a traditional management structure.

A consolidated organization of self-directed teams gives employees a sense of empowerment, control over their work processes, and even some dominion over their own destiny. Increased customer focus paired with better decisions, greater motivation paired with higher productivity and quality, and elimination of non-value-added activities results in lower operating costs, and empowerment translates into less stress—for team members as well as management.

How are self-directed documentation teams developed? What factors are important to the success of their unconventional organizational structure? Specific work situations, management styles, and team maturity dictate the ingredients and their proportions for launching successful self-directed teams. However, the following critical elements—customers, managers and teams, goals and performance, leadership, professional development, processes, metrics, facilities, technology, and recognition—can be considered raw materials for organizations looking to develop self-directed teams.

Customers. It is far from coincidental that focusing on customers comes first in the list of critical elements for self-directed teams. Everything else depends on understanding and knowing internal as well as external customers and other sources of need. Inaugurating self-directed documentation teams is no exception. Teams need to know they have been formed to serve their customers.

Surveying customers (owners and users) helps self-directed teams stay directed. Communicating to customers that team members are front-line decision makers is not just a nicety; it pays off. Successful teams have managers who take the time up front to tell customers directly that team members are responsible for and have the authority to make decisions. Managers can do this best in person, either by presentations or informal meetings.

Managers and teams. Who hasn't known a team whose members were frustrated and impotent because management bypassed the team and cut deals with those outside the team? Especially in an internal documentation function, which often is considered low priority in a company, without proactive management communication most people assume managers make the important decisions. Many treat documentation teams as merely decorative.

However, when management sends a clear message both to the team and to customers that this team means business and does business, its members begin to behave as if they really do have decision-making authority. As a result they become more responsible, focused, innovative, and productive. Managers who personally introduce team members to customers help teams build rapport and smooth the way for team decisions and operational improvements.

Finally, successful self-directed teams position team members in slots highly visible to customers, for example, making high-level presentations. For inexperienced teams, a communications coach can be brought in to help ensure their success.

Checklist 10.3: Elements of Self-Directed Teams

Note: The team performs the actions unless otherwise indicated.

Customers

❐ Surveys customer requirements and other sources of need

❐ Manager communicates that members are front-line decision makers

Managers and Teams

❐ Manager introduces team members and helps to build rapport

❐ Manager refrains from speaking on behalf of team

❐ Manager positions members in high visibility slots

Goals and Performance

❐ Sets team and, jointly, department objectives, estimated completion dates, members responsible for action

❐ Researches and requests resources

Continued

❏ Regularly reviews objectives and status; refines strategies

❏ Reports on objectives and status

Leadership

❏ Determines rotating or fixed leadership

❏ Communicates with management

❏ Defines leadership roles and responsibilities

❏ Conducts team meetings

❏ Assigns subteam leaders for tasks

❏ Requests feedback from team members

❏ Represents department in interdepartmental committees

❏ Shares in evaluating job candidates

Professional Development

❏ Participates in training such as team building, team dynamics, leadership, communication, continuous

Continued

Goals and performance. Empowerment doesn't mean do the job after someone else decides what it shall be and how it shall be done. Empowered team members must participate in shaping the goals that direct their own performance.

Self-directed documentation teams flow down performance objectives from company goals to individuals' responsibilities. Say, for instance, one company goal is achieving 100 percent participation in continuous measured improvement. One of the ways a division implements this goal is speeding current plans for delivering a medical device to its customer at less cost than contracted. The company's administration function adopts the goal and lowers overhead expenses. The documentation function contributes to the savings with its flatter organizational structure by empowering self-directed teams, thereby reducing its operating costs. Documentation staff meet a zero-defects objective and reduce the expenses they would have incurred and passed on if they had to correct errors in the product operating procedures.

Goals, however, are insufficient for performance success. Self-directed teams also have to measure performance to goals and report on it regularly. A closed-loop reporting system works for self-directed teams as it does for corrective action systems. Members are held responsible for actions and documented follow-up is essential for success in meeting defined goals.

Leadership. Team leadership can be rotating or fixed. Effective self-directed teams decide. A documentation team at one company decided first to rotate leadership monthly. After a couple of months, it switched to fixed, choosing a team leader for a six-month term, which team members later extended to a year. The support team, comprised of members responsible for word processing, secretarial, and clerical support, decided on rotating leadership weekly, then changed it to monthly. The forms team chose a leader for the year. Each leader participated with the department manager in a combined weekly team leader meeting, communicating upward, downward, and across teams; solving problems; and making decisions. A representative from each of the documentation work teams participated in the other teams' regular meetings and reported to his or her own team, which was critical in a documentation function, where many hands touch the same piece of work (see Figure 10.1). For example, writers and editors were considering changes to online screens, to which document uploaders needed input.

Using the Joiner Associates *The Team Handbook* (Scholtes, 1988), each team defined the roles and responsibilities of its leaders and assigned tasks to ad hoc subteam leaders. A key to each leader's effectiveness was specifically requesting feedback from members at each meeting. Team leaders also represented their teams regularly in interdepartmental

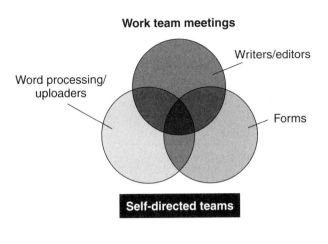

Work team meetings

Word processing/
uploaders

Writers/editors

Forms

Self-directed teams

Figure 10.1 Work team meetings.

committees. Leaders shared in many other traditional management activities, including evaluating candidates for job openings.

Professional development. Declaring an organization a team does not make it so. Just because members have been on umpteen committees in their careers does not mean they will automatically function effectively as a group. Sometimes, people need to learn different ways of looking at teams. Training helps.

Empowered, self-directed documentation teams are trained in key group processes and technical skills, such as team building; team dynamics; leadership; communication; continuous measured improvement; performance evaluation; tools, such as hardware and software; editing; word processing; proofreading; presentations; and process mapping. To be able to satisfy customers' needs, yet maintain a trim organization, empowered teams cross train members. Every function has a backup. The team assigns responsibility to a member to research training resources, such as courses, publications, Web sites, and videotapes. Team leaders learn coaching techniques for optimum performance. And teams recognize the value of extending job boundaries to familiarize employees with new situations and skills they may need to meet planned objectives. In this chapter's section on Training, each of these elements of professional development is discussed further.

Processes. Successful self-directed teams, and traditional groups too, establish ground rules for productive meetings. They use metrics to chart current processes and target performance. They look for ways to eliminate routine but unnecessary activities, then use tools to improve processes. Another critical element related to processes is defining decision making.

Clear ground rules make sense for teams. Take meetings, for example. Team meetings are expensive; even a few minutes of delay costs

---

measurable improvement, performance appraisal, hardware and software, proofreading, presentations, and process mapping

❑ Cross-trains (every function has a backup)

❑ Researches and requests resources

❑ Coaches

❑ Extends job boundaries

Processes

❑ Establishes ground rules

❑ Charts current processes

❑ Identifies value-added and non-value-added activities

❑ Defines new and refines current processes

❑ Defines decision-making processes

❑ Researches and uses tools to improve processes

❑ Benchmarks and benchtrends processes

Continued

❏ Achieves
consensus

Metrics

❏ Researches and
develops metrics
for processes

❏ Maintains
metrics

❏ Publicizes metrics

❏ Refines metrics

Facilities

❏ Researches and
requests room
arrangements to
support team
structure

❏ Requests
ergonomics
consultation

❏ Researches and
requests
modification
of lighting,
furniture, and
equipment
to support
processes

Technology

❏ Researches
and requests
standardized
hardware and
software

❏ Develops and
implements
conversion plans

❏ Researches,
requests, and
maintains library
of technology
publications

Continued

money. An effective and enjoyable technique that most teams agree to encourages members to be on time. At the start of each meeting, an inexpensive piggy bank is placed on the conference table. Late members pay a fine (usually a quarter, but some teams prefer a dollar). When the project is complete, or after a specified time period, the team spends the money on lunch. For this technique to work, the team must reach consensus on adopting it, and then allow no exceptions.

The article in Figure 10.2 emphasizes the benefits of well-managed meetings.

Ground rules for self-directed teams can include "Everyone must participate." That means no team member may merely go along for the ride and let colleagues make important decisions. Another ground rule is "Tell the truth." When a process is not working well, each team member is responsible for attending to it. Ignoring process snags delays solutions or steers a team down an unproductive path. Other ground rules borrowed from seminar participation apply to self-directed team meetings: "Show courtesy to colleagues," "Share your experience," and "Stay on topic."

To implement continuous measured improvement, team members first must examine the current processes to identify those that add value to their product or service and the ones that do not. For example, one company's writing and editing department, with a quality assurance facilitator, traced the cycle time for producing a hard copy procedure. First, the team flowcharted all activities involved in producing the document. Then it estimated the number of hours for each activity, such as word processing or filing the master. If an activity was essential to producing the procedure according to quality, cost, and schedule requirements, the team drew the hours for the activity above the axis. If eliminating the activity did not affect the requirements, the process fell below the axis. The team resisted categorizing an activity that was "nice to have" with the essential ones. The process charting activity opened eyes. Surprised to learn that some of the most time-consuming activities (for example, stapling a cover sheet) contributed nothing to the procedure, team members became receptive to changing the process. Identifying value-added and non-value-added activities proved very useful. If an activity was unneeded, it was discarded. As a result, refining the existing process yielded about a 45 percent reduction in processing procedures.

During the course of charting a process, a self-directed team is empowered to add new processes or activities when critical gaps are discovered and to revise or resequence current ones. How does the team do that?

The scope of this book excludes detailed discussion of the variety of continuous measured improvement techniques, most born in the quality assurance community. You can learn more about these techniques by consulting a general handbook on quality or participating in meetings of ASQ or other organizations that are devoted to quality. An empowered self-directed team, however, is familiar with the most popular techniques and knows where to find more information or engage others to help. The basics are to collect, record, and analyze data; identify important discrepancies; find the root causes of the discrepancies; and fix and prevent the discrepancies.

Another useful tool is benchmarking to discover best processes elsewhere (and benchtrending to anticipate future ones). The documentation team talked with policies and procedures representatives from several companies to learn alternate strategies to accomplish the same objectives.

Self-directed teams early on define decision-making processes: Will it be by consensus or vote? What is the difference? Smart teams understand the power of consensus, which does not necessarily mean agreement. When a group is stuck on a particularly controversial issue, team facilitators wisely ask, "Is there anyone who can't live with it?" They don't ask, "Does everyone agree." They say, "You don't have to love it. You simply have to be able to accept it and work with it." With those words, peer pressure alone often dissolves deadlocks.

Consensus usually brings buy-in and, in the best case, commitment. Where documentation functions merge (for example, in a company restructuring), staff members may disagree on writing style, format, and many other elements with which they have become familiar. Making decisions based on consensus, not votes, helps unify a team.

Metrics. Say *metrics* to beginning teams, and eyes roll and voices sigh. Overburdened employees balk at adding tasks, even if the activity ultimately reduces workload. Depending on requirements, documentation teams keep metrics on customer satisfaction, defect rates, currentness, cycle time, volume, and cost. Metrics need not be elaborate. Simple tallying (such as for proofreading errors) or counting (such as the number of documents or number of pages) usually suffices. Spreadsheet software, such as Microsoft Excel, is easy to use and creates charts for showing data and demonstrating progress.

Clear responsibility for researching, developing, and maintaining metrics is characteristic of successful self-directed teams. Publicizing progress via metrics is important too to encourage teams when self-direction gets difficult. Some organizations post monthly metrics in a well-traveled corridor both to acknowledge team accomplishments and to share ideas with other teams. Metrics are like mirrors. You do not always like what you see, but a clear picture can stimulate action. The best metrics continue to evolve; they do not stagnate. Teams review the appropriateness of the charts regularly and revise them to keep them useful. See chapter 6 for more about documentation metrics.

Recognition

❑ At department staff meetings, acknowledges member kindnesses and accomplishments

❑ Approves responses to employee suggestion program

❑ Dispenses "at-a-persons"

❑ Applies for team awards

❑ Publicizes accomplishments in newsletters

Checklist 10.4: Guidelines for Conducting a Productive Meeting

❑ Decide if the potential results are worth the cost.

❑ Identify the fewest participants needed to accomplish the goal.

❑ Draft an agenda.

❑ State the nature of the meeting.

❑ Establish ground rules.

❑ Encourage participation.

❑ Summarize.

❑ Draft minutes.

What time is it? Time for your next meeting? Maybe you just came out of one. Or maybe you're in one right now and you have no idea what's being discussed. If so, now would be a good time to look up and nod. OK—continue reading.

Chances are you spend a good deal of your day in meetings. Yes, they cost time. But have you ever stopped to figure out how much money they cost?

Think of one of your recent meetings. Jot down the:

- Number of participants

- Hours spent preparing for, attending, and then reporting on the meeting

- Average hourly salary for participants plus 40 percent to 50 percent for labor burden

Multiply these three numbers to find out the approximate cost of the meeting. It's not cheap. Good meetings identify challenges, speed communication, and spawn solutions. Bad meetings waste time and discourage—even alienate—participants. That's why it's a good idea to follow these simple guidelines for conducting a good, productive meeting.

- *Decide if the potential results are worth the cost.* Do this before you schedule the meeting.

- *Identify the fewest participants needed to accomplish the goal.*

- *Draft an agenda.* Include the goal of the meeting, presenters, and allotted start and stop times for each item. Distribute the agenda (use e-mail or meeting management software if possible) before a scheduled meeting to allow participants to prepare for it. Even if the meeting is ad hoc for only a few people, take a few moments to establish an agenda, then stick to it.

- *State the nature of the meeting.* Clearly communicate whether the meeting is scheduled to convey information, generate ideas, or make decisions. Few work events are more discouraging than meetings where you expect to make a decision, only to find out you are on the receiving end of a data dump.

- *Encourage participation.* Call participants out individually if they haven't contributed and ask their opinion. Be prepared for disagreement. If the meeting's goal was easy to achieve, you probably wouldn't need the meeting. Listen.

- *Summarize.* Clearly define decisions and action items. Be sure that everyone understands his or her action items.

- *Draft minutes.* If a meeting is worth holding, it is worth recording. Minutes prevent misunderstandings. Include action items and individuals responsible for them. Spell out a reason for attendees to review the minutes.

Source: Normand L. Frigon, Harry K. Jackson, Jr., and Adrienne S. Escoe, "Meetings—Spawning Ground or Sewer?" *The Escoe/Bliss Insider for World Class Systems and Procedures.* (Summer 1996). Used with permission.

Figure 10.2 Meetings—spawning ground or sewer?

Facilities. Typically, when they are told that rearranging facilities can support team processes, people say they have no funding for it. However, the benefits from team-friendly facilities often outweigh the costs.

Office arrangement can facilitate intrateam communication. One department investigated the effect facilities had on team processes and justified a few fairly inexpensive changes. Department members relocated a door so team members' offices surrounded a small office that housed a central printer, bulletin board, and coffee machine. They did not recreate the Taj Mahal, but did speed informal decision making and improve productivity (see Figure 10.3). The department was able to pay for the remodeling and for ergonomic improvements by eliminating several individual printers and transferring depreciation costs to other departments. A team member volunteered to consult with a representative from the safety and health office and learned to conduct an ergonomics audit of the department. The result was egg crate fixtures that reduced glare on computer screens, loop-and-hook fasteners that provided earthquake protection for expensive hardware, and desks raised for two tall staff members. The potential dollar savings from these three improvements were unknown, but people enjoyed the increased comfort and peace of mind.

Technology. Self-directed teams research and justify standardized hardware and software such as computers, peripherals (printers and scanners), and programs (see chapter 5). To maintain customer service and avoid costly rework, teams develop and implement conversion plans. To promote staff development, team members research, request, and maintain a library of publications focused on documentation technology (see the Training section in this chapter).

Recognition. If you think acknowledging kindnesses to begin each department staff meeting is hokey, think again. Particularly when self-directed teams form from merged or consolidated organizations, every act that allies people works toward speeding process improvement, or at least toward reducing expensive divisiveness. Self-directed teams are authorized to approve recommendations in an employee suggestion program, even minor improvements, as shown by the following situation.

An organization issued an official performance improvement suggestion about a typo, a reversed closing parenthesis mark in a published bulletin. This was "trivial," they said. The self-directed team said, "Thank you for letting us know."

Office remodeling can support self-directed teams and pay for itself, but it is no Taj Mahal.

Figure 10.3 No Taj Mahal.

Why did the team respond that way? For one, any defect, no matter how small, that slips through a documentation system indicates a process gap. If the system is not fixed, the next defect could be a major one; perhaps something that violates a regulatory requirement. Second, by acknowledging all improvement suggestions, team members adopt an attitude of constantly thinking improvement.

Other ways teams recognize performance are applying for company-sponsored team awards, dispensing "at-a-persons," publicizing accomplishments in company and division newsletters, and being compensated partly on the basis of team performance. Xerox Corporation celebrates an annual Teamwork Day, where successful teams go on stage and report their improvements. Events throughout the day are satellite-broadcast to several cities in which the corporation has facilities. Many organizations award prizes to teams that improve processes significantly. Generally, either the team submits its entry or a manager nominates the team. Managers and team leaders set the tone; they encourage team members to relate others' good deeds and share customers' commendations. Teams catch "at-a-person fever." They catch people doing things right (see Figure 10.4).

A documentation streamlining team structured themselves using several guidelines, as follows:

- Identify the biggest obstacles to streamlining policies and procedures, causes, and solutions (fishbone diagram).

- Establish the composition of work teams.

- Hold productive meetings:

  - Give advance notice of each meeting (e-mail, fax, or hard copy), with specific agenda items listed and participants' preparation—for example, to confer with their management or staff for ideas.

  - State what participants should bring to the meeting.

At department staff meetings, self-directed teams acknowledge member kindnesses and accomplishments.

Figure 10.4   Recognition.

- Include participants' immediate managers on the courtesy copies, especially for the list of members attending and those not.

- Assign a scribe to take minutes, including agenda and action items for the next meeting.

- Assign a facilitator (for example, a quality assurance person) to keep the meeting and the leader on track.

- Establish due dates for assignments.

- Designate team membership. Include each functional area, corporate documentation staff, perhaps bargaining-unit representative, and an executive for the kickoff meeting. Perhaps plan for a team photo in the company's newsletter (helps impart value to the project).

- Develop a process for team members' alternates.

- Establish consensus versus voting decision making.

- Define tools for starting and ending on time (for example, piggy bank for latecomers, with luncheon to divide the bounty).

ROLES AND RESPONSIBILITIES

Without clearly defined roles and responsibilities, documentation functions can waste much time participating in ineffective meetings, challenged performance evaluations, and rework.

Teams frequently initiate projects by defining roles of the leader, facilitator, and scribe (minute-taker). Many teams, however, fail to outline the roles and responsibilities of other participants. Focus groups assembled for writing procedures and instructions and teams for documentation system improvement are no exceptions. The most effective groups define clearly at the start of the project, work year, or other interval the expectations held for each member and the consequences of failing to meet them. Time spent defining roles and responsibilities is time well spent. Having roles and responsibilities clearly defined is empowering. *The Team Handbook* (Scholtes 1988) is a useful resource, spelling out ingredients for a team's success, where clear roles and responsibilities are a primary component. A successful team must have:

- Clear goals

- An improvement plan

- Clearly defined roles and responsibilities

- Clear communication

- Behaviors that benefit the whole team

- Well-defined decision processes

- Balanced participation

Checklist 10.5: Ingredients for Team Success

❑ Clear goals

❑ Improvement plan

❑ Clearly defined roles and responsibilities

❑ Clear communication

❑ Behaviors that benefit the whole team

❑ Well-defined decision processes

❑ Balanced participation

❑ Established ground rules

❑ An awareness of group process

❑ Use of a scientific approach

• Established ground rules

• An awareness of group process

• Use of a scientific approach

In just hours, one school district's food services department developed solid work objectives for the year by mixing these ingredients into its leadership council meetings. A county probation department and sheriff's department did the same in a brief workshop. A company documentation department issued *The Team Handbook* (Scholtes, 1988) to each team member and paid particular attention to clarifying participants' roles and responsibilities.

A few years prior to forming self-directed teams, this organization developed performance criteria upon which to evaluate employees. Structured according to performance elements described on the company's performance planning and appraisal form, the criteria were created expressly for writers and editors and word processing staff. At the time, the department had been operating for about a quarter of a century without the benefit of significant quality or process improvement initiatives. This was also a time when personal computers were replacing dedicated word processing equipment and new managers came into the department with fairly revolutionary ideas about quality, performance, and accountability. The performance criteria were keyed to *meets company standards*, which was the third of five assessment options, from *does not meet requirements* to *far exceeds requirements* (see Appendices A and B).

TRAINING

People are like bananas: They are either green and growing or ripe and rotting.

World-class documentation functions cannot afford to rest on old knowledge. Change is everywhere: technology, quality initiatives, and competition. The old paradigm was that staff became trained for a career path—period. That paradigm no longer applies, especially to a successful, empowered workforce.

One company's documentation work teams participated in several kinds of training, including formal classroom, self-training, cross training, coaching and one-on-one training, and extended job boundaries.

Classroom training included the company's cascaded continuous measurable improvement workshop. First, managers were team-trained by their directors or division heads and staff members from the company's training department. Next, each manager team-trained his or her staff members with a member from the company's quality assurance function. The eight-hour workshop for staff covered the basics of continuous measurable improvement. The curriculum also included improvement benefits and processes, metrics, process maps, working environments conducive to initiating improvements, empowerment, team dynamics, benchmarking, and problem solving with quality tools. Every documentation staff member participated in the workshop.

Other classroom training for work team members covered standardized hardware and software—a standard desktop computer platform and standardized software were adopted across the department—including word processing, communications, drawing, publishing, presentations, project scheduling, database, and spreadsheet applications. Support personnel received specialized training in networks and the online system.

Depending on individual objectives, staff members participated in a wide variety of other classes and seminars, including creativity, time management, goal setting, performance evaluation, meetings management, and many others. Team leaders participated in organizational change and team communication classes. Staff members were trained in proofreading.

Self-training consisted of books and videos recommended by managers, team leaders, or colleagues, or they were individuals' selections. The department routed information on journal articles, news clips, and other pertinent information to share with colleagues. At a team member's suggestion, the department established a small technical library and subscribed to leadership, documentation, and software-oriented publications.

To develop and multiply employee skills, at least one person was cross trained in each major process performed within the department. That way, a minimum number of staff members could achieve department objectives. Cross training helped the department continue to serve its customers during staff leaves of absence and the work load peaks and valleys common to documentation functions. For example, a writer and editor was trained in basic network processes to fill in for a vacationing support team member. A forms administrator did editing when several functions updated all of their procedures at one time, swamping the writers and editors. By the end of the first year of consolidation, every process had a trained backup.

It has been said that the function of a coach is to take people from where they are to where they want to be. With good coaching, people tend to reduce their mistakes and unproductive habits of the past and succeed in creating a vision of the future. Through training in coaching, team leaders joined managers in assuming the coach's role, in everything from following team meeting ground rules to performance appraisal and planning discussions.

One-on-one training is an important but often overlooked training method. Empowered organizations not only rely on one-on-one training, but tie it to company objectives and record it. The quality assurance manager of a spring manufacturer seeking ISO 9001 registration is responsible for training a group of employees to draft work instructions for all functions. The one-on-one training sessions are paced to each employee's learning speed and avoid the disruption that group training would bring to the production line. However, because one-on-one training sessions tend to be informal, it is easy to overlook important points. The manager developed a list of considerations to help:

- Describe the big picture.

- Don't assume the trainee knows why he or she is being trained. Give the reasons.

**Checklist 10.6:
One-on-One
Training to Write
Work Instructions**

❐ Describe the
big picture.

❐ Explain reason
for training.

❐ Describe trainee's
responsibilities.

❐ Communicate
that you don't
expect perfect
spelling, perfect
grammar, and so
on. Use word
processing expert
to format and fix.

❐ Provide a
reference
(finished)
document.

❐ Show examples:
what
"deliverable"
should look like.

❐ Give or ask
for reasonable
schedule.

❐ State clearly times
trainer is available
for questions
and help.

- Describe the trainee's responsibilities.

- Make it easy. If you can, communicate that you don't expect perfect spelling, grammar, and so on. Use a word processing expert to format and fix the instructions later.

- Provide a reference (finished) document.

- Show examples of what the employee's "deliverable" should look like.

- Give or ask for a reasonable schedule.

- State clearly when the trainer is available for questions and help.

People learn by doing, which sometimes is the most effective kind of training. In a documentation department, a doubting department secretary, who was responsible for developing and coordinating organization charts for the division, became the leader of a successful cross-functional team chartered to improve chart processing cycle time. Previously, support staff were invisible to major improvement teams. Not only did the staff member learn a lot about team dynamics, but the entire department learned about the importance of including everyone involved in a process.

ACCOUNTABILITY

Accountability for documentation begins with customers and other sources of need. People who are responsible for world-class documentation develop performance goals to meet the needs of legal requirements, external customers, users, subject matter owners, and certification auditors and examiners. Direct supervisors are customers, too. Accountability closes the loop between sources of need and an organization's performance. The best organizations document their need-driven goals, and all functions within the organization document operational objectives that flow from the goals. In multilevel organizations, company goals translate into division goals, then department objectives, team objectives, and finally, individual performance objectives. Each level's performance is measured against its goals or objectives. If performance falls short, the performing organization, team, or individual takes corrective action or justifies nonperformance. At each level, performers answer to customers and other sources of need. Consequences are expected at each level both for meeting goals (for example, commendations, positive performance evaluations, and career growth) and for falling short of them (such as corrective action and progressive discipline).

An empowered documentation department drafts its objectives at the beginning of the evaluation period. A documentation department's employees studied their division's goals, which flowed down from company goals. One of the higher level goals was to make the company an excellent place in which to work. After flowing down to documentation staff, a writer and editor team translated this goal into the practice of "catching employees doing something right" and rewarding them. Team leaders received coupons to a local fast food restaurant to give to team members on the spot for actions that contributed to the well-being of the team. The individual who coordinated the coupons assumed that responsibility, and a time for developing it, at an earlier goal-setting meeting. Quarterly meetings, where performance was reviewed, facilitated accountability for meeting goals. And the individual's annual formal performance appraisal included the goal and his or her performance to it.

Another example started with the company's goal on quality products and services. The documentation department flowed this goal into the division's defect-free procedures manual. The department reviewed defect metrics monthly and watched them reach zero as staff members trained in proofreading techniques. For its accomplishments, the department won an award for world-class documentation. And individual employees were held accountable for their part. Achieving zero defects was an individual objective as well.

EVALUATION

Empowerment requires accountability. And accountability is impossible without performance evaluation.

Evaluation is a powerful tool for focusing a team's energies. It furnishes critical feedback and data for continued measured improvement. A company established a companywide performance and appraisal planning system around five elements—documentation, communication, goal-setting, employee development, and active participation—which documentation consolidation and improvement work teams modified for team use. Each element of the system is described briefly followed by the process the work teams used to customize the system for team performance evaluation.

- *Documentation.* A four-page form for salaried employees describes performance in specified areas of work. The documentation work teams added a fifth page to compile and compute team ratings.

- *Communication.* Discussions centered on the described performance tell employees how well their performance is meeting goals and standards.

Checklist 10.7: Elements of Team Performance Evaluation

❐ Documentation

❐ Communication

❐ Goal-setting

❐ Employee development

❐ Active participation

❐ Flexibility for rating in a team environment

❐ Team participation in appraising performance

❐ Rater weighting modifiable according to maturity of the system

❐ Ratings compatible with company systems

❐ Familiarity of form

- *Goal-setting.* Team leaders, supervisors, and employees collaborate to establish reachable work objectives for the next evaluation period.

- *Employee development.* Team leaders, supervisors, and employees identify competencies to strengthen or develop, and resources such as training courses to help them achieve the competencies.

- *Active participation.* Active involvement throughout the performance appraisal and planning process produces the most valid information and employees' commitment to achieving agreed-upon goals.

Soon after the work teams were organized, it became clear that the company's standard performance appraisal and planning form was inadequate for evaluating performance in a self-directed team environment. Individual evaluations, with their implications for comparisons among individual performers, it was thought, could result in individual competitiveness and work against team objectives. For example, when individuals are rewarded for their own accomplishments, and not for the team's, they may be tempted not to communicate or share ideas and solutions.

The work teams sponsored a small subteam to benchmark with other local companies known for progressive administrative processes. The subteam members also consulted with other company divisions to find other groups that may have been developing team performance evaluations. They benchmarked with a bank, insurance company, several defense electronics firms, transportation company, automobile manufacturers, Air Force base, harbor, document businesses, and three internal divisions.

At the time, the team found that only three of the benchmarked sources had a form to evaluate team performance. Work team leaders reviewed form samples, reached consensus on content and format, voted on a rating scale and weighting (when consensus could not be reached), and created a team performance evaluation form modified from the company's standard form. Advantages of the modified form were flexibility, team participation, modifiable rater weighting, compatibility with companywide compensation and employee relations systems, and familiarity.

- *Flexibility for rating in a team environment.* The new form could be modified to accept performance ratings from an employee's supervisor, team leader, manager, or peer. Each work team decided who it wanted to rate team members. If one team decided to have its team leader and peers rate performance, then the performance of each member of that team was rated by the same raters. (Company personnel systems at the time required the function's supervisor of record to sign the form.) Because the form was computerized, it could be revised easily for each team. Ratings from internal customers were later added to the process.

- *Team participation in appraising performance.* Work teams participated fully by describing performance elements and rating them for each team member. They submitted a form for each team peer to the manager, who compiled comments and ratings. Several members asked to remain anonymous in their peer rating.

- *Rater weighting could be modified according to the maturity of the team.* At the time the new form was introduced, the documentation work teams were in various stages of maturity—from the "green" support team that had been established for a short time to the self-directed writer and editor team that had been working together for many months. The newest team weighted the manager's, team leader's, and peers' rating nearly equally, whereas the writer and editor team assigned 15 percent to the manager's rating. The closer the team members were to self-direction, the more they trusted their own judgment in rating their peers.

- *Resulting letter ratings were compatible with compensation and employee relations systems.* Although the route to determining letter ratings was nonstandard for the company, each employee's overall performance rating fit within the company's compensation and employee relations systems, thus empowering the teams to improve the documentation function processes.

- *Familiarity.* The new form departed slightly from the company standard. *Team, team member,* and *team leader* were incorporated into the evaluation form and process. Because the new form was similar to the company's standard form, the only training needed was in entering and computing weighted ratings and peer evaluation narratives.

The team performance planning and appraisal form was a hybrid between the company's performance reporting requirements for individual employees and a company form, yet to be created, expressly for evaluating teams. But it was the best way the teams at the time could evaluate their own performance without compromising the company's compensation and employee relations systems.

Appraisal and planning discussions were held between each employee, his or her work team leader, and the department manager.

How did empowerment work for the documentation function? In months, not years, four discrete documentation departments, each representing a division of several thousand employees, merged. The new function consolidated the procedures manuals, forms, and approval authority systems of each division. Staff members agreed upon a common writing style. They reduced documentation cycle time, volume, and expenses and achieved zero defects. They made documentation accessible to employees through an online system. Team members learned to work collaboratively, strengthen leadership and communication skills, give presentations to senior managers, and expand their professional skills, such as familiarity with cutting-edge documentation technology. Other indicators of successful empowerment were increased staff creativity (evidenced by the skyrocketing number and quality of company-issued performance improvement and cost improvement certificates) and a flattened management structure. Chapter 6 presents improvement points of focus and metrics for a documentation COE.

Part IV

Information Tools

Appendix A

Performance Criteria for Policies and Procedures Writers and Editors

The following describes the minimum performance criteria for *meets company standards*. This document is not all-inclusive, but is provided to summarize and baseline performance standards.

QUALITY

Delivering a product or service that meets the needs of customers and the goals of the organization. Providing a product or service that satisfies customers. One's work reflects dependability, consistency, accuracy, thoroughness, and pride in workmanship—exemplifying that one has given one's best effort to the task. Finished products (such as directive documents, internal memos, and research analyses) are accurate.

PERFORMANCE TO SCHEDULE

Meets targeted deadlines. Exercises good time management so (1) individual doesn't have to readjust schedule, and (2) individual doesn't experience last-minute time crunch, which can result in the inability to take on other tasks and assignments. Balances workload so individual can manage long-term projects (such as restructuring a manual or designing a system), as well as routine tasks, paper flow, and the preparation of directive material (such as editing documents, preparing coordinations, and interfacing with division representatives). Understands the nature of the profession and that an individual works to complete the job to quality standards even it if requires working hours in excess of the standard work week.

COST-EFFECTIVENESS

Compares costs prior to recommending purchases. Collects and uses data to determine the most cost-effective means of acquiring materials and services. Identifies key factors in work efficiency, then looks for ways to improve efficiency without sacrificing quality or good customer service practices. Recommends expenditures acknowledging short- as well as long-term impact on the department.

TECHNICAL CONTRIBUTION

Contributes innovative and practical solutions to business challenges. Keeps informed of and communicates information about tools of the trade, such as editing, analysis, and search software; e-mail; and training materials. Seeks out technical solutions from best practices in other organizations, such as departments, divisions, and groups.

DECISION MAKING

Makes decisions that are based upon relevant facts, are well thought out, and reflect good judgment, including:

- The best way to accomplish a task

- Asking for assistance from other personnel when given or having assumed an overwhelming task or assignment

- Assisting customers in person or over the telephone with problems such as setting priorities for reviewing directive documents

Has working knowledge of problem-solving processes and the ability to generate options. Demonstrates resourcefulness by calling upon managers, colleagues, or other sources for assistance. Researches, analyzes, and recommends alternatives for resolving difficult situations. Handles customer requests directly whenever possible. Determines when a coordination, editing, publication, or administrative procedure requires modification to meet customer or organization needs (that is, goes outside established routines).

KNOWLEDGE

Demonstrates knowledge in each of the following areas:

- Management principles and practices

- Operating systems, procedures, forms, and office equipment

- Online systems application

- Business English, particularly writing, editing, and proofreading

- Ability to identify and locate subject matter expertise

Draws upon past professional experience as well as education to contribute to the department's products and services. Uses knowledge to select the best means of meeting a business objective, project, or assignment. Takes responsibility for developing or modifying systems applications, designing reporting media, and preparing and publishing brochures, manuals, bulletins, and other documents. May be assigned and is expected to take responsibility for surveillance, maintenance, and coordination of management or operations control system.

PERSONAL PRODUCTIVITY

Demonstrates concern for and supports the department's role by participating fully in department-sponsored programs and services, such as demonstrations, presentations, improvement teams, and corporate functions. Sets challenging goals that build upon one's current level of competency. Goals reflect job-related issues, the process of work, and the end result. Individual is punctual. Attendance is consistent and reliable to ensure person (1) is dependable and available, and (2) is at work during the times department customers expect staff to be at work. Demonstrates ability to prioritize work assignments and reduce non-value-added time. Demonstrates ability to take initiative on new projects. Continually evaluates projects for improvement. Needs minimal direction and supervisory follow-through.

COMMUNICATION

Demonstrates knowledge of effective oral and written communication techniques for varied situations. Individual shows flexibility and professional business manners in adjusting communication approach to people he or she encounters. Uses tact and courtesy in communicating with customers, colleagues, and managers. Participates in staff meetings and other forums that are a vehicle for communicating information regarding the progress and direction of the department. Escalates problems and issues in a timely manner (that is, no surprises when a project or task promises to miss a deadline). Communicates to other staff and to supervisors to keep them apprised of current issues. Exercises professional and sound judgment in the use of written communication. Using past professional experience and education, demonstrates ability to communicate in a coherent, professional manner to employees at all levels, including frequent contacts with division and corporate staff managers. Demonstrates competency in written communication by less need for clarification following the publication of documents. Is effective in interpretive and persuasive contacts with supervisors and managers regarding analysis, development, and communication, and assists management, when requested, in the preparation of formal analyses and presentations.

ETHICS

Demonstrates honesty in all aspects of the job. Upholds the Company's ethics policies. Recognizes one's own abilities and is honest about one's capabilities and limitations—"truth in advertising." Exercises discretion in the work environment.

Appendix B

Performance Criteria for Policies and Procedures Word Processing and Secretarial Staff

The following criteria define the work standards for *meets company standards*. This is not an all-inclusive document, but is provided to summarize and baseline performance standards. The performance criteria are cumulative, that is, criteria listed for the secretary position also apply to the word processing senior and specialist positions, whenever separate criteria are assigned to those positions.

QUALITY

Delivering a product or service that meets the needs of the customer and the goals of the organization. Providing a product or service that satisfies customers. One's work reflects dependability, consistency, accuracy, thoroughness, and pride in workmanship—exemplifying that one has given one's best effort to the task. Finished products (such as word processing, copying, preparing distributions, filing, and so on) are accurate. Proofreads own copy for accuracy, format, and consistency and makes corrections as needed.

PERFORMANCE TO SCHEDULE

Secretary. Meets due dates and requirements of assigned tasks. When setting own due dates, meets the committed dates. Provides realistic estimate of time to complete an assignment.

Word Processing Senior. Demonstrates skills in planning ahead and managing time to meet the schedule while working for multiple staff and projects. Responds well to priority changes while accomplishing tasks for multiple staff and projects.

Word Processing Specialist. Maintains staff schedules, that is, keeps track of attendance, meetings, and other staff events.

COST-EFFECTIVENESS

Secretary. Compares costs prior to purchasing supplies. Collects and uses data to determine the most cost-effective means of acquiring materials and services.

Word Processing Senior. Accurately tracks expenses and statistical data. Maintains accurate and reasonable inventory of office supplies.

Word Processing Specialist. Identifies key factors in work efficiency, then looks for ways to improve efficiency without sacrificing quality or good customer service practices.

DECISION MAKING

Secretary. Makes decisions that are within the scope of one's responsibilities including:

- The best way to accomplish a task

- Asking for assistance from other word processing or secretarial personnel on an overwhelming task or assignment

- Assisting customers in person or over the telephone on problems, such as requesting manuals or directing customers to the person or organization that can help them

Word Processing Senior. Researches, analyzes, and recommends alternatives for resolving difficult situations.

Word Processing Specialist. Determines the types of documents and information needed to maintain a project. Determines when an office procedure requires modification to meet customer or staff needs (that is, goes outside established policies). Handles customer requests directly whenever possible, to reduce cycle time.

KNOWLEDGE

Secretary. Knows Company policies and procedures related to office transactions, for example, timecards, personal car mileage, HR services, and MRTs [material transfers]. Competent in operating office equipment such as computers, fax machines, copiers, and multiple line telephones. Competent in using various computer software used in the department. Knows process of using support services, for example, Marketing Publications, Reproduction Services, Photo Lab, and Mail Services. Knows how to establish and maintain filing systems for quick retrieval of records and references.

Word Processing Senior. Maintains accurate inventory for department demonstrations and presentations, for example, handouts and viewgraphs.

Word Processing Specialist. Knows the administrative procedures for all department-sponsored projects. Has solid working knowledge of related functions, for example, Distribution Center and Product Operations Procedures [which later merged with the department]. This knowledge is reflected in accurate referrals and information.

PERSONAL PRODUCTIVITY

Secretary. Proactively shares job-related information with colleagues and supervisors in a timely manner. Establishes good rapport with customers to increase job efficiency. Assists other support personnel. Individual is punctual. Has consistent and reliable attendance to ensure person (1) is dependable and available, so that work assignments do not have to be reassigned to other support personnel, (2) is at work during the times customers expect staff to be at work, and (3) provides department telephone coverage. Participates in job-related problem solving, such as workload appraisal and scheduling and responsibility for copying. Follows through on commitments. Proactively follows up with customers to determine quality of service provided by support staff.

Word Processing Senior and Specialist. Establishes work flow processes or files, when such processes or information will improve efficiency for future needs. Maintains readily accessible files and documentation on procedural and administrative tasks. Provides logistical support to ensure that a project runs smoothly even if a writer and editor isn't available to help make decisions. Contributes ideas that will maintain the professional image of the department. Gathers information to support reports, budgets, and presentations.

COMMUNICATION

Secretary. Communicates in a clear, articulate, and courteous manner. Exercises good use of English (oral and written). Can diffuse angry customers to (1) resolve the issue or (2) refer the customer to a writer and editor or supervisor. Escalates problems or issues in a timely manner, for example, conflicts with work priorities. Proactively provides job information to colleagues and supervisors (for example, changes in mail delivery, new administrative procedures, and messages) in a timely manner. Follows up to ensure understanding. When customers call or drop in with questions, the individual responds courteously, accurately, and reflects a united department. That is, one does not respond with "I don't know anything about it." Records messages accurately and legibly and places them in message slots immediately. Hand delivers urgent messages immediately. Records assignments in writing to ensure accuracy. Takes and composes meeting minutes.

Word Processing Senior and Specialist. Initiates communication with all individuals needed to complete a quality job (for example, with other word processing staff, writers and editors and administrators, supervisors, and managers). Composes and edits routine correspondence (within the area of job responsibility) necessary to ensure smooth running of a project or administrative process.

ETHICS

Is honest in all aspects of the job. Maintains confidential information. Honors and handles Company Private and Sensitive information according to established procedures. Adheres to Company standards. Because secretary and word processing personnel are often privy to sensitive information (such as phone messages, interoffice memos, and verbal conversations), exercises discretion and good judgment in handling such information.

Appendix C

Resources

The entries listed in this chapter are a sample of organizations, including their publications, and software useful for developing and managing documentation. Some, such as Internet Web sites (see section, Software), are excellent starting points for seeking additional resources. This information is provided for readers' convenience; an entry's inclusion is not an endorsement nor is an omission an indication of criticism. Expect changes in listed telephone numbers, especially area codes, e-mail addresses, and Web sites. All information in this chapter was drawn from organizations' promotional literature, Web sites, or correspondence originating from those sources.

ORGANIZATIONS

American Society for Quality (ASQ)
PO Box 3005
Milwaukee, WI 53201-3005
Tel 800-248-1946; 414-272-8575 (outside North America)
Fax 414-272-1734
E-mail asq@asq.org
Web site www.asq.org

National association for quality professionals and all others interested in quality information and technology. Divisions focus on 21 distinct industries and markets. Local sections. Provides training in quality audits, ISO 9000, SPC, TQM, and other initiatives. Certifies quality engineers and other quality professionals. More than 130,000 members.

ASQ Quality Press Publications Catalog
American Society for Quality (ASQ)
Customer Service
PO Box 3066
Milwaukee, WI 53201-3066
Tel 800-248-1946; 414-272-8575 (outside North America)
Fax 414-272-1734
E-mail cs@asq.org

Nearly 100 pages of books, software, videotapes, CDs, audiotapes, and quality standards. Quality initiatives, such as ISO 9000, are well represented as are all other current quality topics.

ASQ journals: *Quality Progress, Journal of Quality Technology, Quality Engineering, Technometric,* and *Quality Management Journal.*

Association for Information and Image Management (AIIM)

1100 Wayne Avenue, Suite 1100
Silver Spring, MD 20910-5603
Tel 301-587-8202
Fax 301-587-2711
E-mail aiim@aiim.org
Web site www.aiim.org

Association for information management professionals and providers of digital document technologies. Membership of more than 9000 is represented in 150 countries, with about 50 chapters. Actively involved in promoting interoperability and multivendor integration.

AIIM InfoShop
Association for Information and Image Management (AIIM)

More than 370 books, CDs, video and audio programs, slide shows, and disks on technology, professional development, education tools, and industry standards.
AIIM magazine: *INFORM*

Association for Records Managers and Administrators (ARMA) International

4200 Somerset Drive, Suite 215
Prairie Village, KS 66208
Tel 800-422-2762; 913-341-3808 (outside North America)
Fax 913-341-3742
E-mail hq@arma.org
Web site www.arma.org

Organization for records and information managers. Promotes programs of research, education, training, and networking. More than 10,000 members in 39 countries.

Technical Publications Catalog
Association for Records Managers and Administrators (ARMA) International

More than 30 pages of books and videotapes on records and information management.
ARMA international journal: *Records Management Quarterly*

Society for Technical Communication (STC)
901 N. Stuart Street, Suite 904
Arlington, VA 22203-1822
Tel 703-522-4114
Fax 703-522-2075
E-mail stc@stc.org
Web site www.stc.org

Worldwide association serving the technical communication profession, including writers, editors, graphic artists and technical illustrators, translators, independent consultants and contractors, photographers, and audiovisual specialists. Serves 19,000 members in 144 chapters.
STC journal: *Technical Communication Journal*
STC magazine: *Intercom*

SOFTWARE

Many software packages listed in this section are widely available at electronics, office supply, and software retailers; through software mail order catalogs; and through the Internet. Some of the software, especially office suites, is stocked by department stores and larger discount variety stores. Suppliers of specialized software, such as for records management, demonstrate their products at exhibitions, for example, at ARMA International's annual conferences (see Organizations section). ASQ's *Quality Progress* publishes an annual directory of quality software (usually in April), including packages related to documentation.

Document Control

ApproveIt Silanis Technology: 888-745-2647; info@silanis.com; www.silanis.com

DOC9000 JK Technologies: 800-792-4693; www.jkt9000.com

DocControl Manager Documentum: 925-600-5256; www.documentum.com

Document Control 2.0 The Harrington Group: 800-476-9000;
www.harrington-group.com

Document Control System Quality Systems International: 781-862-9002;
www.qualitysys.com

DC PRO Document Control Pister Group: 905-886-9470; www.pister.com

EtQ Solutions EtQ: 800-354-4476; www.etq.com

Intelex Intelex Technologies: 800-387-4019; www.intelex.com

ISOlutions Insite Technology Group: 800-446-8665; www.insite-inc.com

ISOQuest Global Quality Institute: 905-452-9788; www.globalquality.com

MASTERControl Document Control Systems: 800-825-9117; www.mastercontrol.com

Powerway Document Management Solution Powerway: 800-964-9004; www.powerway.com

QualTrax QualTrax: 540-382-4234; www.qualtrax.com

Real World Document and Records Manager 3C Technologies: 800-327-6583; www.3ctech.com

TMS Quality Systems Integrators: 800-458-0539; www.qsi-inc.com

Trove Ringwood Software: 800-949-6753; www.ringwood.com

Document and Information Management

DOCS Open Hummingbird: 877-359-4866; www.hummingbird.com

DocuShare Xerox: docushare.xerox.com

extemporé Select Technologies: 208-375-7100; select@micron.net; www.selectec.com

PowerDOCS Hummingbird: 877-359-4866; www.hummingbird.com

RetrievalWare Convera: 703-761-3700; www.convera.com

Verity Portal|One Verity: 408-541-1500; info@verity.com; www.verity.com

Worldview Interleaf: 617-290-0710; i-direct@interleaf.com; www.interleaf.com

Employee Performance

Employee Appraiser SuccessFactors: 888-850-3566; info@successfactors.com; www.successfactors.com

Performance Impact KnowledgePoint: 800-727-1133; kp@knowledgepoint.com; www.knowledgepoint.com

PerformanceManager SuccessFactors: 888-850-3566; info@successfactors.com; www.successfactors.com

The Complete Employee Handbook Made Easy ISBE Employers of America: 800-728-3187; employer@employerhelp.org; www.biztrain.com

Flowcharts, Process Maps, and Organization Charts

ABC FlowCharter Micrografx: 800-671-0144; sales@micrografx.com; www.micrografx.com

AllCLEAR: www.proquis.com

ComponentOne Chart ComponentOne: 800-858-2739; sales@componentone.com; www.componentone.com

ETQ 9000 Maps EtQ: 800-354-4476; www.etq.com/maps.htm

Flow Charting PDQ Patton & Patton Software: 800-525-0082; www.patton-patton.com

IGrafx FlowCharter 2000 Professional Micrografx: 800-744-1210; www.micrografx.com

Instruction Writer Powerway: 800-525-0082; www.powerway.com

MEGA Process MEGA International: 800-920-6342; info@us.mega.com; www.mega.com

MEGA Suite MEGA International: 800-920-6342; www.mega.com

Microsoft Visio Microsoft: 800-426-9400; www.microsoft.com

Org Plus IMSI: 800-548-1798; www.imsisoft.com

RFFlow RFF Electronics: 970-663-5767; www.rff.com

Scitor Process Scitor: 800-549-9876; info@scitor.com; www.scitor.com

TeamFlow CFM: 800-647-1708; www.teamflow.com

TopDown Flowcharter Kaetron Software: 800-938-8900; sales@kaetron.com; www.kaetron.com

WinFlow Mainstay: 805-484-9400; www.mstay.com

Forms

Adobe Capture Adobe: 800-833-6687; www.adobe.com

FIXPro Ironwood Computer Systems: 800-661-2978; www.fixpro.com

InternetForm UWI.com: 888-517-2675; www.uwi.com

OmniForm Caere: 800-535-7226; www.caere.com

Premier Forms Processor Pro Mitek Systems: 888-363-6767; sales@miteksys.com; www.miteksys.com

QuickModules Mitek Systems: 888-363-6767; sales@miteksys.com; www.miteksys.com

Teleform Cardiff Software: 800-659-8755; www.cardiffsw.com

Imaging

Eyes & Hands for Forms ReadSoft: 858-546-4858; info-us@readsoft.com; www.readsoft.com

FormAgent Ceresoft: 301-445-8413; formagent@ceresoft.com; www.ceresoft.com

LaserFiche Compulink Management Center: 800-985-8533; www.laserfiche.com/arma

Transform dakota imaging: 800-833-3137; sales@dakotaimaging.com; www.dakotaimaging.com

Versatile Enterprise Zasio Enterprises: 800-513-1000; www.zasio.com

Layout and Publishing

Adobe FrameMaker Adobe: 800-833-6687; www.adobe.com

Adobe PageMaker Adobe: 800-833-6687; www.adobe.com

Microsoft Publisher Microsoft: 800-426-9400; www.microsoft.com

QuarkXPress Quark: 800-676-4575; www.quark.com

Office Suites

(Suite packages typically include word processing, spreadsheet, database, and presentation; some also include scheduling and contact management.)

Corel WordPerfect Suite Corel: 800-772-6735; www.corel.com

Lotus SmartSuite Lotus Development: 800-343-5414; www.lotus.com

Microsoft Office Microsoft: 800-426-9400; www.microsoft.com

Online Help

ForeHelp HALLoGRAM: 303-340-3404; sales@hallogram.com; www.hallogram.com

RoboHelp eHelp: 800-358-9370; robohelp@ehelp.com; www.ehelp.com

True Help ComponentOne: 800-858-2739; sales@componentone.com; www.componentone.com

Policies and Procedures

Descriptions Now KnowledgePoint: 800-727-1133; kp@knowledgepoint.com; www.knowledgepoint.com

Instruction Writer 9000 Powerway: 800-964-9004; www.powerway.com

Policies Now KnowledgePoint: 800-727-1133; kp@knowledgepoint.com;
  www.knowledgepoint.com

Policy Writer 9000 Powerway: 800-964-9004; www.powerway.com

Procedure Writer 9000 Powerway: 800-964-9004; www.powerway.com

Portable Document Format (PDF)

(Used for converting documents to share on networks and intranet applications)

Adobe Acrobat Adobe: 800-833-6687; www.adobe.com

Records Management

ACCUTRAC Accutrac Software: 800-578-9361; info@accutrac.com; www.accutrac.com

ADVANTAGE Information Technology Group: 800-978-3268; www.technologygroup.net

Cuadra STAR Cuadra Associates: 310-478-0066; sales@cuadra.com;
  www.cuadra.com

extemporé Select Technologies: 208-375-7100; select@micron.net;
  www.selectec.com

FileTracker TAB: 901-794-3878; tab@tabofmemphis.com; www.tabofmemphis.com

GAIN 2000 Triadd Software: 800-877-9564; webmaster@triaddsoftware.com;
  www.triaddsoftware.com

ImageTrax Document Control Solutions: 714-738-6131; www.docsolutions.com

OmniRIM Systems Auditing: 800-667-0332; www.omnirim.com

RecFind GMB Support: 616-392-7034; chrisk@gmb.com; www.gmb.com

RMS FileSurf MDY Advanced Technologies: 888-639-6200; info@mdy.com;
  www.mdyadvtech.com

SIMPLE Records Manager Records Center Software: 800-432-8160;
  info@recordsmanager.com; www.recordsmanager.com

Smeadlink Smead: 800-216-3832; tony.gouletas@smead.com; www.smead.com

Total Recall DHS Associates: 800-377-8406; dhyman@dhsassociates.com;
  www.dhsassociates.com

TRIM Captura TOWER Software: 800-255-9914; www.ustrim.com

Versatile Zasio Enterprises: 800-513-1000; admin@zasio.com; www.zasio.com

Web Page Development

Adobe PageMill Adobe: 800-833-6687; www.adobe.com

Chameleon HostLink NetManage: 408-973-7171; info@netmanage.com; www.netmanage.com

Dreamweaver Macromedia: 800-457-1774; www.macromedia.com

HoTMetaL Pro SoftQuad Software: 800-387-2777; mail@softquad.com; www.hotmetalpro.com

Microsoft FrontPage Microsoft: 800-426-9400; www.microsoft.com

NetObjects Fusion: 888-892-0702; sales@netobjects.com; www.netobjects.com

Netscape Composer Netscape: 650-254-1900; www.netscape.com

WebPublisher click2learn: 800-448-6543; www.click2learn.com

Web Site Searching

Web site addresses, called URLs (Uniform Resource Locators), change frequently. If, during a search, a URL listed in this chapter no longer can be found, go to one of the Web sites listed in this section and type in the product or company name, or select a category listed there. You may be able to find the Web site through this alternate route.

AltaVista www.altavista.com

Ask Jeeves www.ask.com

Electric Library www.infonautics.com

excite www.excite.com

Google www.google.com

GoTo www.goto.com

Hotbot www.hotbot.lycos.com

LookSmart www.looksmart.com

Lycos www.lycos.com

Internet Explorer www.microsoft.com

Netscape www.netscape.com

Yahoo www.yahoo.com

References

Abilene Paradox. CRM Films, 1991. Screenplay by Kirby Timmons, adapted from the article "The Abilene Paradox: The Mismanagement of Agreement," in *Organizational Dynamics*, by Jerry B. Harvey. New York: AMACOM, 1974.

American Society for Quality Control, International Organization for Standardization, and American National Standards Institute. *Environmental Management Systems—Specification with Guidance for Use* (ANSI/ISO/ASQC Q14001-1996). Milwaukee: ASQC Quality Press, 1996.

American Society for Quality. *Quality Management Systems—Requirements* (ANSI/ISO/ASQ Q9001-2000). Milwaukee: ASQ Quality Press, 2000.

Brumm, Eugenia K. *Managing Records for ISO 9000 Compliance*. Milwaukee: ASQC Quality Press, 1995.

Escoe, Adrienne. *Nimble Documentation®: The Practical Guide for World-Class Organizations*. Milwaukee: ASQ Quality Press, 1998.

The Forum Corporation. *cmi Leadership:* Cascaded Training. 1992.

Frigon, Norman L., Harry K. Jackson, Jr., and Adrienne S. Escoe. "Meetings—Spawning Ground or Sewer." *Escoe/Bliss Insider for World Class Systems and Procedures* (Summer, 1996): 2.

Hackos, JoAnn, and Ann Rockley. *Single Sourcing White Paper*. Denver, CO and Markham, Ontario: SingleSource Associates, 1999.

Hudiburg, John J. *Winning with Quality: The FPL Story*. White Plains, N.Y.: Quality Resources, 1991.

Huyink, David S. "From ISO 9000 to Total Quality Management: How ISO 9000 Makes TQM Easier." In *Proceedings of ASQC's 50th Annual Quality Congress*. Milwaukee: ASQC Quality Press, 1996.

International Communications. *Accent on Internationalization: Guidelines for Internationalizing Software and Documentation*. Los Angeles, 1999.

"ISO 9000 for Quality's Sake." *Journal of Business Strategy* (September/October, 1996): 7.

Jackson, Harry K., Jr. Personal communication. 31 January 2001.

Jacobson, David C., Michael R. Lowenbaum, and John C. Koski. "Peril of the E-Mail Trail." *The National Law Journal*, (16 January, 1995): C1.

Kerr, John. "But Is It Better than Baldrige?" In *An Insider's Guide to ISO 9000.* Newport Beach, CA: IMPAC Integrated Systems, n.d. Reprinted in *Escoe/Bliss Insider for World Class Systems and Procedures* (Summer 1996): 4.

Krell, Susan K. "Revision of Personnel Manuals: An Exercise in Futility?" *The Personnel Law Update* (November 1995): 4.

Microsoft. *The Microsoft Manual of Style.* Redmond, WA, 1998.

National Institute of Standards and Technology. *Malcolm Baldrige National Quality Award 2001 Criteria for Performance Excellence.* Gaithersburg, MD: National Institute of Standards and Technology, 2001.

The Outsourcing Institute. "Redefining the Corporation of the Future." *Fortune* (16 October 1995) (Advertising supplement.)

Propson, David. G. "Everything You Wanted to Know about Digital Signatures, But Were Afraid to Ask." *Small Business Computing.* (January 2001): 88.

Quality Excellence for Suppliers of Telecommunications Forum. *TL 9000 Management System Requirements Handbook, Release 3.0* (31 March 2001).

Quality Excellence for Suppliers of Telecommunications Forum. *TL 9000 Management System Measurements Handbook, Release 3.0* (31 March 2001).

The Rummler-Brache Group. *Cross-Functional Process Flow.* 1987.

Scholtes, Peter R. *The Team Handbook.* Madison, WI: Joiner Associates, 1988.

Schriver, Karen A. *Dynamics in Document Design.* New York: John Wiley, 1997.

Skupsky, Donald S. *Records Retention Procedures.* Englewood, CO: Information Requirements Clearinghouse, 1995.

"Speaking of Quality," *On Q* (November 1996): 6.

Streetman, Kibbee. "Who Holds the Keys to Encrypted Electronic Documents?" *Technologies for Managing Information* 1, no. 4 (May 1996): 2–5.

The University of Chicago Press. *The Chicago Manual of Style.* 14th ed. Chicago: The University of Chicago Press, 1993.

The University of the State of New York/The State Education Department. "Managing Records in E-Mail Systems." In *State Government Records Management Information Series.* Albany, NY, 1997.

Urgo, Raymond E. *Comparison Test: Non-Structured/Non-Modular Version.* Participant materials presented at the Orange Empire Section, American Society for Quality Control. Los Angeles: Urgo & Associates, 1995.

Williams, Robin and John Tollett. *The Non-Designer's Web Book.* Berkeley, CA: Peachpit Press, 1998.

Index

A

Abilene Paradox, 180
Access features, of electronic document management systems, 88–89
Accessibility, 3, 4, 172
Accountability, 192–93
Accuracy, 101–6
Action paragraphs, 41
Active listening, 179–80
Active voice, 60–59
Activities, of improvement teams, 18–26, 46
Addition screens, 90
Administrative COEs, 171
AIIM (Association for Information and Image Management), 208
Alignment, in Web design, 70, *71*
American Society for Quality (ASQ), 129, 207–8
Announcement documents, 35, 51–52
ANSI/ISO/ASQ Q9001-2000, 4, 8, 11, 15, 34, 38, 47, 52, 56, 77, 86, 88, 92, 99–101, 117, 146, 149. *See also* ISO 9001
   auditing requirements, 11
   benefits of, 118–19
   clauses, 121, 122–27 (table)
   documentation requirements, 16, 119–29, 153
   record keeping requirements, 16
   records retention requirements, 154
   registration to, 118–19, 129
      gap analysis and, 130
   sections of, 119
   and Six Sigma improvements, 133
   and TL 9000, 150–51

versus total quality management, 134
Any key, 9–10
Applicability section, 53
Applicable documents section, 53
Approval authority
   charts of, 35, 164, 165–68 (tables)
   and digital signatures, 164, 169–70
   format element for, 56
   forms transmission and, 164
   ISO 14001 and, 146
   litmus test for, 163
   online systems and, 56, 92–93, 164
   by password, 161
   safety programs and, 141
   systems, 6, 35, 136, 163–70
Archiving, 159. *See also* backups
ARMA (Association for Records Managers and Administrators International), 208
ASQ (American Society for Quality), 129, 207–8
Association for Information and Image Management (AIIM), 208
Association for Records Managers and Administrators International (ARMA), 208
At-a-person recognition, 188
Audio format, 47–48
Auditors, as sources of need, 11
Audits, ergonomic, 187
Audit trails, 92, 160
Auto makers, and QS-9000, 150
Automated formatting, 77
Automation, 81–82, 161, 164, 169. *See also* electronic systems

B

Backups, 92, 159–60
Baldrige Award. *See* Malcolm Baldrige National Quality Award
Benchmarking, 185, 194
Benchtrending, 183, 185
Bernoulli drives, 160
Bold type, 57, 59
Boxes, for emphasis, 59
Browser-safe colors, 76
Bulletins, 35
Bullets, 55
Business focus, 177

C

California Codes of Regulations, 141
Canceled documents, 37. *See also* obsolete documents; revisions
Cancellation screens, 90
Candidates for jobs, 183
Cascade training, 26
Cash, and outsourcing, 176
CDs (compact disks), 25, 47, 87, 89, 93
Changes, in documents. *See* revisions
Charts of approvals, 35, 164, 165–68 (tables)
Chicago Manual of Style, 61
Chronologies, of improvement, 22–23, 27–30
Chrysler Corporation, 150
Clarity, need for, 3
Classroom training, 190
Clauses
    of ISO 9001, 120, 122–27 (table)
    of ISO 14001, 146, 147–48 (table), 149
Clinton, Bill, 169
CMI (continuous measurable improvement) workshop, 190–91
Coaching, 183, 190–91
COEs (centers of excellence), 171–72. *See also* documentation COEs; self-directed teams; teamwork
Color, in Web design, 76
Colors, browser-safe, 76
Common areas, terminals in, 89
Communication
    documents as vehicles for, 38
    performance criteria for, 201, 205
    performance evaluation and, 192–93
    publicity campaign for, 19–21, *22*
    self-directed teams and, 181
    skills in, 179–80
    with sources of need, 11

Communications network, 89
Compact disks (CDs), 25, 47, 87, 89, 93
Computer platforms, xv
Conciseness, 3, 59
Consensus, 185
Consultants, 19, 93
Context-specific searching, 90–91
Continuous measurable improvement (CMI) workshop, 190–91
Contracts, 11
    disclaimers and, 139
    litmus test and, 15
Contrast, in Web design, 72, *73*
Conversational style, 58
Conversion costs, 92, 111, 113
Coordination, of documents, 92–93
Coordination time, 108
Cost-effectiveness, performance criteria for, 200, 204
Costs
    COEs and, 173
    of conversions, 92, 111, 112
    of cumbersome documentation, 14–15
    of defects, 101
    of documentation, 63, *113*
    imaging and, 97
    model of, 23, 24, 26, 111–13
    outsourcing and, 176, 179
    of records maintenance, 157
    of rework, 101–3
    of safety program documentation, 145
    of storage, 91–92
    of upgrades, 92
Creators, perspective of, 6–7. *See also* writers; writing
Cross references, in indexes, 38, 141. *See also* synonyms
Cross training, 183, 190
Cross-functional processes, 46
Cross-functional teams, 136
Currentness, 106–7
    of employee handbooks, 139
    metrics for, 23–24, 107, 145
    need for, 3
Customers
    COEs and, 172–73
    feedback from, 11, 101, 138, 140
        in usability testing, 64
    focus on, 180–81
    outsourcing and, 178
    responsiveness to, 172–73
    self-directed teams and, 180–81
    as sources of need, 11, 13
    surveys of, 181

TQM and, 134–35
trust from, 103
Customer satisfaction, measurement of, 100–101
Cycle time, 24, 108, *109*

D

Data, 23–24, 34
Databases, 23–26. *See also* electronic systems;
    online systems
Data protection, 159–60
Dates
    effective, 52
    format of, 52
    issued, 37
    printing of, 91
    published, 52
    viewing of, 90
Deadlines, 199, 203
Decision making
    performance criteria for, 200, 204
    self-directed teams and, 181, 183, 185
    skills for, 179–80
    in streamlining activities, 22–23
Decision points, *if–then,* 43, 46
Defects, 101, 103, 145, 188. *See also* zero defects
Definitions, placement of, 23, 56
Deleted documents. *See* canceled documents;
    obsolete documents
Desktop publishing, 81
Digital signatures, 161, 164, 169–70
    versus electronic signatures, 169
Directive documents, sacredness of, 14
Disasters, recovery from, 159–60
    e-mail provisions, 95
Disclaimers, for employee handbooks, 91, 139
Display features. *See* viewing features
Distributed input system, 87
Distribution schedules, 37
Document
    format, 22
    hierarchy, 22
    management program, 34
    numbers, 52, 90, 91. *See also* numbering schemes
    owners, 50
    relatives, 153–54. *See also* approval authority;
        forms; records
    structure, 22–23, 34
    titles, 51. *See also* titles
Document and information management software
    (listings), 210
Document control software (listings), 209–10

Documentation
    compared to records, 121
    meanings of, 7
    roles of, 117–18
    usability testing of, 64–65
    Web-based, 48
Documentation COEs, 25. *See also* insourcing;
    outsourcing
    benefits of, xiii, 11
    characteristics of, 172–75
    skills required for, 179–80
    and total quality management (TQM), 134–35, 175
Document-group titles, 51. *See also* titles
Dog puppies, 59, *61*
Drafts, 108. *See also* reviewing
Dreamweaver, Macromedia, 76
Dynamics of Document Design, 64

E

E-commerce, 130
Editing, group, 106
Editorial guidelines, 24, 26, 59, 61, 85
Editors, policies and procedures, performance criteria
    for, 199
Education. *See* training
Effective date, 52
Electronic approval systems, 8
Electronic document management systems, 81–86. *See
    also* online documentation systems
    in case study, 19, 21, 24–26
    checklist for, 87–89
    for forms, 161, 164, 169
    standardization and, 83–85, 88, 187, 191
    for storage and retrieval, 85–97
Electronic hits on employee handbooks, 138
    on intranets, 24
    as a metric, 24, 101
Electronic imaging, 97
Electronic signatures, 164, 169–70
    versus digital signatures, 169
Elements, format, 49–57
E-mail, xv
    etiquette, 96
    managing, 95
    policy, in electronic document management systems,
        94–96
    printing to, 91
    public key management and, 164
    for revision notification, 90, 93
    subject lines in, 51–52
    WYSIWYG, difficulties in, 90

Emphasis, in style, 57, 59
Employee handbooks, 138–40
    disclaimer in, 139
    litmus test applied to, 138–39
Employee participation
    in performance appraisal, 194
    in TQM, 135
Employee performance, software (listings), 210
Employee suggestion programs, 187
Employees
    in COEs, 174–75
    empowerment of. *See* empowerment
    insourcing and, 175, 179
    outsourcing and, 175–79
    performance evaluation, 190
    skills required for, 179–80
    S&P. *See* systems and procedures personnel
    suggestions from, 187–88
Empowerment, 174–75
    and accountability, 193
    self-directed teams and, 180–81, 182
    skills and, 179–80
Enabling directive document, 34
Encryption keys, 164, 169–70
Environmental management systems, 145–49
EPS file format, 77
Ergonomic audits, 187
Error control, 103, 107. *See also* zero defects
Ethics, performance criteria for, 202, 206
European Union (EU), 118
Evaluation
    checklist on, 193
    of performance, 190, 193–95
        software (listings), 210
Evidence
    Baldrige Award and, 131
    for including documents, 15, 17
Examiners, as sources of need, 11
Exclusion versus inclusion of documents, 15
Expiration date, 35
External customers, as sources of need, 11–13

F

Facilities, for self-directed teams, 186–87
FDA (Food and Drug Administration), 16, 118
Federal laws, 10, 16, 138
Feedback
    from customers, 11, 101, 138, 140
    self-directed teams and, 181, 182
Fields, in forms, 6, 71, 160–61, 162
Fingerprinting, 170

Fixed leadership, 182
Flattened organizations, 180
Flesch Readability Formula, 67–68
Flowcharts
    format of, 45–46
    software, 46
        (listings), 211
Focus groups, 13, 50, 64, 140, 173, 189
FOG Readability Formula, 69–70
Fonts, for emphasis, 56
Food and Drug Administration (FDA), 16, 118
Ford Motor Company, 150
Format, document, 22, 34
    advantages and disadvantages in, 38–49
    alternatives of, 38–49
    of dates, 52
    definition of, 34
    in document management program, 34
    elements of, 49–57
    of numbers, 52–53
Formatting, automated, 77
Forms
    approval authority for, 163–64
    automated, 161, 169
    automated transmission of, 164, 169
    automation levels for, 161
    checklist for, 162
    in document hierarchy, 34–35
    electronic library of, 161
    fields in, 160–61, 162
    inventory of, 173
    ISO 14001 and, 146
    litmus test for, 161–72
    online, 71
    in other documents, 55
    as records, 161
    section for, 55
    software (listings), 211
    standardization of, 160–61
    streamlining of, 161–63
Frames, in Web design, 75
Funds. *See* costs

G

Gap analysis, 129
General Motors, 150
General section, 53
Goals
    of improvement teams, 18
    performance evaluation and, 193–95
    self-directed teams and, 182
Golden, Sandra, 176

Graphical user interface (GUI), 85
Graphics. *See also* flowcharts; process maps
    for emphasis, 59
    PDF for, 90
    in presentation slides, 79
    and readability, 66
    in user manuals, 140
    in Web design, 72, 74, 75–76
Ground rules, for self-directed teams, 184
Group dynamics, 180. *See also* teams
Group editing, 106
GUI (graphical user interface), 85

H

Hackos, JoAnn, 82
Handbooks, employee. *See* employee handbooks
Hardware, standardization of, 84, 88, 187, 191
Harm, and litmus test, 16–17
Headers, and format, 39, 51, 57
Help line databases, 101, 140
Help software, Web, 48, 140
Hertz, Harry, 130
Hidden processes, 111, 112
Hierarchy, document, 22–23, 33–38
    definition of, 33
    ISO 9001 and, 120–21
History files, 160, 161. *See also* audit trails
Hits, electronic. *See* electronic hits
HTML (hypertext markup language), 24, 48, 145
Hudiburg, John J., 134
Hughes Aircraft Company, disclaimer used by, 144
Humor, 77, 96
Huyink, David S., 134
Hyperlinks, 48, 56, 72, 74

I

Iceberg model, of cost, 111–12
If-then decision points, 43, 46
Imaging, 97
    software (listings), 212
Improvement chronologies, 22–23, 27–30
Improvement investing, 99–98
Improvement teams
    accomplishments of, 24
    activities of, 18–26, 46
    goals of, 18
Inclusion versus exclusion of documents, 15
Indentations, in text, 39, 59
Independent Small Business Employers of America, 139
Indexes, 37–38. *See also* search engines
    for employee handbooks, 139

legal research, 154–55
    for safety program documentation, 145
    updating of, 112
    in user manuals, 140–41
Information management, 82–83
Input features, of electronic document management
    systems, 87
Insourcing, 175, 179. *See also* documentation COEs
Instruction manuals. *See* user manuals
Integration of document relatives, 153–54. *See also*
    approval authority; forms; records
Interaction, in storage and retrieval systems, 87
Interested parties, as sources of need in ISO 14001,
    147, 149
International legal requirements, 16
International Organization for Standardization, 118
Internationalization, of documentation, 77
Internet, xv, 48, 70, 72, 77, 82, 89
    economy, 130
Intranets, xv, 5, 22, 24–26, 37, 48, 65, 70, 72, 74, 76,
    82–84, 89–91, 93, 96, 101, 111, 145
    access via, 24–25, 88
    for approval authority, 164
    definitions on, 56
    and online documentation systems, 85–86
Inventory
    of forms, 173
    of records, 157
Investing, in improvement, 99–100
ISO 9001, 150
    compared to Baldrige Award, 130–31, 134
    on continuum of initiatives, 119, *120*
    documentation requirements of, 119–29
    gap analysis and, 129
    numbering schemes tied to, 52
    obstacles to registration in, 117
    page hits metric, 24, 25
    registration to, 117
    Web sites for, 129
    zero-based approach for, 121, 129
ISO 9001, clauses of, 120, 122–27 (table), 146
    records retention requirements, 122–27 (table), 154
    registration to, 119
ISO 14000, 146
ISO 14001, 145–49
    clauses of, 146, 147–48 (table), 149
    goals of, 146
    and interested parties, *147,* 149
    litmus test for, 149
    and Nimble Documentation,® 145
    prudent business operations and, 16
    requirements for records retention, 153
    and TL 9000 documentation requirements, 151

Issue date, 52
Italic type, 59, 90

J

Job boundaries, extended, 183
Job candidates, 183
Job descriptions, 34, 35
Jumping, in online systems, 88
Justification, of type, 56–57, 79

K

Kerr, John, 130
Knowledge management, 82–83
Knowledge, performance criteria for, 200, 204
Krell, Susan K., 139

L

Language relationships, in searching, 90–91
Laws. *See* legal requirements
Layoffs, 180
Layout software (listings), 212
Leadership
    self-directed teams and, 182–83
    skills in, 180
    TQM and, 135
Legal group file, 154, 155
Legal requirements. *See also* audit trails
    employee handbooks and, 138
    litmus test and, 16
    responsiveness to, 172
    for safety programs, 141
    as sources of need, 10–11, 13, 149, 172
Legal Requirements for Business Records, 155
Legal research index, 154–55
Legibility, versus readability, 57, 65
Length
    of policies, 35
    of quality system manuals, 34, 120
    of sentences, 59
Liability
    disclaimers and, 139
    document volume and, 110, 112
    and e-mail policy, 94
    obsolete documentation and, 139
    and records retention, 154
Links, in online systems, 88
Listening, active, 179–80
Litigation. *See* legal requirements; liability
Litmus test, xvii, 14–17. *See also* zero-based approach
    for approval authority, 163

Baldrige Award and, 16, 131
    checklist for, 15
    for employee handbooks, 138–39
    for format elements, 50
    for forms, 161–62
    for ISO 14001, 149
    for lean documentation, xv, xvii, 7, 14–17
    for prudent business operations, 16
    for safety program documentation, 141
    TQM and, 135
    in usability testing, 65
    for user manuals, 140
    volume metrics and, 110
    and Web navigation tools, 74
Local ordinances, 11, 16, 138
Logistics, for storage and retrieval systems, 92–93
Logos, 51

M

Macromedia Dreamweaver, 76
Macros, 84–85
Malcolm Baldrige National Quality Award, 4, 8, 11,
    117–18
    compared to ISO 9001, 130–31, 134
    on continuum of initiatives, 119, *120*
    criteria categories of, 131–32
    documentation requirements, 131–32
    four-stage process of, 130
    litmus test and, 16, 131
    purposes of, 130
    zero-based approach to, 131
Malcolm Baldrige National Quality Improvement Act
    of 1987, 130
Management, commitment from, 134
Management Sciences Institute, 132
Management support, for self-directed teams, 181
Manuals, user, 140–41. *See also* employee handbooks
Margins, 59
Masters, of document revisions, 160
Matrix, of documents, 160
Measurement
    COEs and, 174
    of currentness, 107
    of customer satisfaction, 100–101
    of cycle time, 108, *109*
    of improvement investing, 100
    as a tool, 100
    of volume, 110
    zero defects and, 101–106
Media mailers, 16–17
Meetings
    announcements of, 51–52

checklist for, 185
    productive, 183–84, *186,* 188–89
Meets company standards, 190, 199, 203
Memoranda, 35, 51–52
Menus, online, 37
Meta data, 75, 82, 86, 145
Metrics, 23–24, 25. *See also* costs
    COEs and, 175
    for currentness, 23–24, 107, 145
    for customer satisfaction, 101
    for cycle time, 108
    for defect-free writing, 101–106, 145
    to fulfill Baldrige Award criteria, 131
    for proofreading, 101, 103
    for safety program documentation, 145
    for self-directed teams, 185
    TQM and, 135
    for training, 145
    for volume, 24, 110, 145
Microsoft Excel, 185
Microsoft FrontPage, 76
Microsoft Internet Explorer, 74, 86
Microsoft Manual of Style for Technical Publications, 61
Microsoft PowerPoint, 79, 152
Microsoft Word, 57, 84
Military specifications, 118
Modular format, 42, 43–44, 140
Modular instructions, 6
Monitoring of usage, 88
Motion studies, 173
Motorola Corporation, 132
Multiple functions
    of forms, 162
    process maps for, 46
Multiple platforms, 88
Multiple users, 89
Municipal ordinances. *See* local ordinances

N

Names, 51, 162. *See also* titles
Narrative format, 45
NASA (National Aeronautics and Space Administration), 118
Navigation, in Web design, 72–74
Need
    case study of, 18–26
    finding out about, 11–13
    litmus test of, 14–17
    perspectives and, 6–7
    sources of, 7, 10–11, 149
Netscape Composer, 76

Netscape Navigator, 74, 86
Nimble Documentation®
    benefits of, xiii, xvi, xvii, 9
    characteristics of, 5–7, 58, 137
    framework for, 7
    and ISO 14001 requirements, 145
Nimble writing style, checklist for, 58
Non-Designer's Web Book, The, 70
Numbering schemes
    for dates, 52
    document, 52
    for document components, 53–55
    for document groups, 37
    for electronic systems, 90
    for format alternatives, 41, 43
    for format elements, 52–53
    for forms, 163
    ISO 9001 clauses and, 120–21
    in modular format, 42
    for pages, 53
    in plain vanilla text, 39–41
    in play script, 41–43
    printing and, 91
    for revisions, 52
    viewing and, 90

O

Objectives, and self-directed teams, 182
Obsolete documents, 37, 55, 139
Office arrangements, 186–87
Office suite software, (listings), 212
Off-site storage, 160
OnQ magazine, 94
One-on-one training, 191–92
Online documentation systems. *See* also electronic document management systems
    approval authority and, 56, 92–93, 164
    backups for, 92, 159–60
    cost of conversion to, 92, 111, 112
    definitions stored in, 56
    design and implementation of, 24–25
    document numbering in, 55
    error control in, 103, 107
    for forms library, 161
    formats and, 48, 53
    indexing capabilities of, 38
    publicity campaign for, 19, 21, *22*
    related documents and, 53
    search engines in, 38, 53, 86
    for storage and retrieval, 85–97
    uploading to, 106–108
    Web-based, 86, 138

Online help, 76–77, 140
    software (listings), 212
Online procedures, 48
Operating procedures. *See* procedures
Operating systems, xv
Organization charts, 92, 173
    software (listings), 211
Organization name, 51
Organization, of documents. *See* hierarchy; structure
Organizational structure, 180–81
Organizations, listings of, 207–9
Out-of-control functions, 177
Outsourcing, 145, 175–79
    benefits of, 176–78
    checklist for, 179–80
    drawbacks of, 178–79
    and insourcing, 175, 179
    resources and, 177, 178
    of systems support, 93
Outsourcing Institute, 176

P

Page numbers, 53
Paperless systems, 161
Paragraphs, 41
    numbering of, 53–55
Passive voice, 58–59, *60*
Passwords, 88, 161, 164
PDF (portable document format), for graphics, 48, 90, 145
    software, 213
Performance
    accountability and, 192–93
    criteria for, 190, 199–206
    evaluation of, 190, 193–95
        software (listings), 210
    self-directed teams and, 182
Personal productivity, 201, 205
Personnel. *See* Employees
Perspectives, writer's and user's, 6–7
Piloting, of user instructions, 10, 145
Plain vanilla text, 39–40, 43, 145
Platforms, multiple, 88
Play script format, 41, 43, 140
Point-and-click systems, 85
Policies
    in employee handbooks, 138–39
    length of, 35
    quantity of, 35
    section for, 53
    software (listings), 212–13
    streamlined, case study of, 35–36

Policy manual, 34
Portable document format (PDF), for graphics, 48, 90, 145
    software, 213
PowerPoint, Microsoft , 79, 152
Presentation, of documents. *See* format; style
Presentation slides, 78–79, *80*
Printing features, of storage and retrieval systems, 91
Privacy, of e-mail messages, 94–95
Private key management, 164, *169*
Procedures, 33–34, 35
    formats for, 38–49
    for forms, 55
    ISO 9001 and, 119, 120, 121
    in modular format, *42,* 43–44
    online, 48
    in play script, 41–43
    section for, 41, 53
    software (listings), 212–13
    streamlined, case study of, 18–26
    Web-based, 48
Process maps, 46, 47
    software (listings), 211
Processes
    charting of, 184
    cross-functional, 46
    hidden, 111, 112
    improvement of, 183–85
    self-directed teams and, 183–85
    standardization of, 85
Production COEs, 171
Productivity, personal, 201, 205
Products, standardization of, 85
Professional development, 183. *See also* training
Project management activities, 19, 21
Promotional campaign, for online documentation system, 19, 21, *22*
Proofreading, 101–6
Protected documents, 87
Proximity, in Web design, 71, 75
Prudent business operations, 18, 153
Public key management, 164, *169*
Publicity campaign, 19, 21, *22*
Published date, 52
Publishing software, (listings), 212
Purchase orders, 16
Purpose statements, 50

Q

QS-9000, 86, 118, 133
    documentation requirements, 150, 151
Quality circles, 173

Quality Excellence for Suppliers of
  Telecommunications (QuEST) Forum, 150
Quality, performance criteria for, 199, 203
Quality initiatives, 117–18, 119. *See also* ISO 9001;
  Malcolm Baldrige National Quality Award
Quality policies, 33
Quality policy statement, 120
Quality Progress, 129
Quality system documentation, 86
Quality system manual, 34, 35, 119–20
Questionnaires, for need analysis, 11
  in usability testing, 64
Questions, in litmus test, 15–17

R

Readability, 57, 65–70
  formulas, 66–70
  versus legibility, 57, 65
Readers. *See also* users
  importance of, to writers, 13
  observation of, in usability testing, 64
  perspective of, 6–7
Read-only documents, 87
Reagan, Ronald, 130
Reciprocal storage, 160
Recognition programs, 187–88
Records
  ANSI/ISO/ASQ Q9001-2000 and, 121
  audit trails for, 160
  compared to documentation, 121
  data protection and, 159–60
  in document hierarchy, 34–35
  forms as, 161
  integrated files and reports for, 154, 159
  ISO 14001 and, 149
  related, section for, 56
  retention program, 153–60
    checklist for, 159
    e-mail issues, 95
    seven-step method for, 157, 159
    Skupsky method for, 156–59
  titles of, 154
Records management, software (listings), 213
Records Retention Procedures, 154, 157
Redundancies, 59, 141
Reengineering, 174, 177
Regional laws, 138. *See also* local ordinances;
  state laws
Regulations, 141, 145. *See also* legal requirements
  in employee handbooks, 138
  records and, 157
Related documents section, 53

Relatives, document, 153–54. *See also* approval
  authority; forms; records
Relevant documents section, 53
Remote access, 88–89
Remote storage, 160
Repetition, in Web design, 72
Resistance, by managers, 14
Resources. *See also* costs
  consumption of, 63
  investment of, 99–98
  listings of, 207–14
  and outsourcing, 177, 178
  for self-directed teams, 201
  for training, 183
Responsibilities
  section for, 53
  in teamwork, 189–90
Responsiveness
  of COEs, 172–73
  of documentation, 172
  of world-class organizations, xv
Restricted documents, 87
Restricted printing, 91
Retention program, for records, 153–60
Retinal scanning, 170
Retrieval systems. *See* storage and retrieval systems
Reviewing
  cycle time for, 108, *109*
  electronic systems for, 93
  perspective in, 6
  priorities for, 112
  of safety program documentation, 145
Revisions
  costs of, 111
  dates of, 163
  on electronic systems, 90, 92–93
  of forms, 55
  indexes and, 38
  letter or number for, 52, 90
  masters of, 160
  passive notification of, 90
  related documents and, 53
  tables of contents and, 37–38
Revision screens, 90
Rework, cost of, 101–3
Risks, 177, 180
RoboHelp, 48, 57, 140
Rockley, Ann, 82
Room arrangements, 186–87
Root causes, 185
Rotating leadership, 182
Rotating storage, 160
Rubber stamps

approval authority as, 163
phrases as, 58

S

S&P personnel. *See* systems and procedures personnel
Safety programs, 141–45
Scanning, 97
Schedules
distribution, 37
of improvement, 22–23, 27–30
performance to, criteria for satisfying, 199, 203
records retention, 154–55, 156 (table), 159
Schriver, Karen, 64
Scope section, 41, 53
Screen captures, 140
Screen numbers, 90
Screen-to-print mismatches, 90
Search engines, 38, 48, 86, 90–91. *See also* indexes
context-dependent, 38, 86
software (listings), 214
Searching features, of electronic document
management systems, 90–91
Secretarial staff, performance criteria for, 203–6
Sections, 53
Security, 87, 160
Self-directed teams, 180–89. *See also* teamwork
checklist for, 181–85
critical elements of, 181–89
ground rules for, 184
meetings of, 183–84, 188–89
performance evaluation of, 193–95
structure of, 188–89
technology and, 187
Self-training, 191
Sentences, 58–59
Servers, 91–92
Sigma, definition, 133
Signatories. *See* approval authority
Signature authority. *See* approval authority
Signatures, digital, 161
electronic, 164, 169–70
Simplification, 173
Simultaneous users, 87
Single sourcing, 82–83
benefits, 133
Six Sigma, 8, 78, 101
definition, 132–33
documentation for, 133–34
Size. *See* Length
Skills, required for employees, 179–80
Skupsky, Donald S., 154–55, 157, 159

Slang, 77
Slides, presentation, 78–79, *80*
SMOG Readability Formula, 68–69
Society for Technical Communication (STC), 77, 209
Software
help line databases and, 101
listings of, 209–14
standardization of, 84, 88, 187, 191
Sources of need, 7, 10–11, 149
Space, for emphasis, 59
Spache, George, 66
Spache Readability Formula, 66
Special characters, viewing of, 90
Specialists, outside, 178–79. *See also* consultants;
outsourcing
Spellchecking, 103
readability measures in, 67
Spreadsheet software, 185
Standard operating procedures. *See* procedures
Standardization
checklist for, 85
in electronic systems, 83–85, 88, 187, 191
of forms, 160–61
for graphics viewing, 89–90
impact of, 85
of writing guides, 85
Standards. *See also* ANSI/ISO/ASQ Q9001-2000;
ISO 9001; ISO 14001; QS-9000
for encryption keys, 169
litmus test and, 16
for performance, 190, 199–206
for writing, 25, 26
State laws, 11, 16, 138
Storage, 91–92, 160
remote, 160
Storage and retrieval systems, 85–97. *See also*
electronic systems; online systems
cost of conversion to, 92, 111, 112
features of, 87–93
imaging for, 97
logistics for, 92–93
systems support for, 93
Strategic business goals, 135
Streamlining, of documentation, 14, 16–17, 18
case study of, 18–26
reasons for, 18
via COEs, 173
Structure, document 22–23, 34
Style, 34
guides to, 26, 59–61
departmental, 26
Style sheets, 57

Style, writing, 57
  nimble, 58
Subject lines, 51–52
Subject matter owners, as sources of need, 11, 13
Suggestion programs, employee, 187
Suppliers, 150
Surveys, of customers, 64, 181
Synonyms, 38, 140–41, 145
Systems and procedures (S&P) personnel. *See also*
    employees
  electronic systems and, 84, 101
  evaluation and, 194–95
  sources of need and, 10, 11
  zero-based approach by, 24
  zero defects and, 101
Systems support, for electronic document management
    systems, 93

T

Tables of contents, 37–38
Tape systems, for backup, 160
Team Handbook, The, 182, 189, 190
Team performance evaluation form, 194–95
Teams
  checklist for performance evaluation, 193
  in COEs, 174, 175, 180
  cross-functional, 136
  for ISO 9000 registration, 119
  as sources of need, 11
Teamwork. *See also* self-directed teams
  accountability and, 192–93
  elements for success of, 189–90
  roles and responsibilities for, 189–90
  in TQM, 134, 135
  training for, 190–92
Technical contributions, of performance, 200
Technical skills, 179
Technology. *See* electronic document management
    systems; hardware; online documentation
    systems; software
Terminals, in common areas, 89
Text
  emphasized, 59
  quality of, 101–3
Thud test, 3, *4, 5*
Tickler software, 87
Tiers, of documents, 120–21
TIFF file format, 77
Time
  coordination, 108
  cycle, 108, *109*

  studies, 173
Timetables. *See* schedules
Titles
  clarity of, 50
  as format elements, 51–52
  of forms, 162
  of records, and retention, 154
  TL 9000 requirements, 150–51
Tollett, John, 70
Total quality managed documentation checklist, 135
Total quality management (TQM), 8, 118
  COEs and, 134–35, 175
  commitment to, from top management, 134
  versus ISO 9001, 134
  litmus test and, 135
  as a philosophy, 134
  success factors for, 134–35
TQM. *See* total quality management
Training, 190–92
  ANSI/ISO/ASQ Q9001-2000 and, 129
  cascade, 26
  COEs and, 174, 179
  for electronic access, 24–25
  metrics for, 145
  one-on-one, 191–92
  outsourcing and, 178–79
  for proofreading, 102, 103
  safety, 141
  for storage and retrieval systems, 87, 92–93
  for teamwork, 183
  in TQM, 134, 136
Trouble calls, 101, 140
True Help, 48, 140
Typefaces, 56, 79

U

Underscoring, 59, 90
Undoing, instructions for, 140
Updates. *See* revisions
Upgrades, cost of, 92
Uploading, to online systems, 106, 108
Urgo, Raymond, 43
Usability testing, 64–65
  of forms, 163
  study, 140
Usage monitoring, 88
User manuals, 140–41
Users. *See also* readers
  observation of, in usability testing, 64
  perspective of, 6–7
  as sources of need, 11, 13

V

Value-added activities, identifying, 184
Versions, 52, 86. *See also* revisions
Video format, 47
Videotex, 85
Viewing features, in electronic document management systems, 89–90
Voice data entry, 161
Voice, of sentences, 58–59
Voice recognition, 161
Volume, as a metric, 24, 110, 145

W

Web design, 70–77
Web page development, software (listings), 214
Web site searching, software (listings), 214
Web sites, xv, 17, 48, 51
    design, 70–77
Web, the. *See* World Wide Web
Web-based online documentation systems, 86, 138
White space, 59
Williams, Robin, 70
Word, Microsoft, 57, 84
WordPerfect, 84
Word processing
    for forms, 161
    index features in, 38
    limitations of, 81
    macros and style sheets in, 57
    readability measures in, 57, 67
    search capabilities of, 91
    specialists, 102
    spellcheckers in, 103
    staff, performance criteria for, 203–6
Workforce. *See* employees
Work instructions
    in document hierarchy, 34, 35
    ISO 9001 and, 120–21
Workload, and improvement investing, 100
World Wide Web, 17, 48, 82
    help software, 48, 57
World-class organizations, responsiveness of, xvii, 5

Writers
    importance of readers to, 13
    policies and procedures, performance criteria for, 199–202
    perspective of, 6–7
Writing
    defect-free, 101–3, 106, 145
    for the reader, 13–14, 63, 173
    skills, 86
    standards for, 25, 26
    style, 34, 57–61
        nimble, 58
    "you" attitude in, 173
Writing style guide, 59–61
WYSIWYG, 90

X

Xerox Corporation, 188

Y

"You" attitude, in writing, 173

Z

Zero defects, 24, 101–6
Zero-based approach, xv, 7. *See also* litmus test
    to ANSI/ISO/ASQ Q9001-2000, 121, 129
    to Baldrige Award, 131
    case study of, 9–26
    checklist for, 18–19
    to forms, 161
    integration with COE characteristics, 18
    to ISO 14001, 149
    litmus test and, 7, 14–17
    meaning of, 7, 14
    to purpose statements, 50
    to records retention, 157, 159
    to safety program documentation, 141
    in streamlining effort, 18
Zero-based documentation, producing, *20*
Zip drives, 160